A SOARING SEASON

A SOARING SEASON

The Incredible, Inspiring Story of the
2003–04 Saint Joseph's Hawks

AARON BRACY

BROOKLINE
books

Havertown, Pennsylvania

Brookline Books is an imprint of Casemate Publishers

Published in the United States of America and Great Britain in 2025 by
BROOKLINE BOOKS
1950 Lawrence Road, Havertown, PA 19083
and
47 Church Street, Barnsley, S70 2AS, UK

Hardback Edition: ISBN 978-1-955041-43-0
Digital Edition: ISBN 978-1-955041-44-7

A CIP record for this book is available from the British Library

Printed and bound in the United States of America by Integrated Books International

Typeset in India by Lapiz Digital Services, Chennai.

For a complete list of Brookline Books titles, please contact:

CASEMATE PUBLISHERS (US)
Telephone (610) 853-9131
Fax (610) 853-9146
Email: casemate@casematepublishers.com
www.casematepublishers.com

CASEMATE PUBLISHERS (UK)
Telephone (0)1226 734350
Email: casemate@casemateuk.com
www.casemateuk.com

Cover images courtesy of Greg Carroccio/Sideline Photos

A Soaring Season is dedicated to my mom, Susan; my wife, Jeanne; and my three children, Gabe, Julia, and Evelyn for all of their love, support, and encouragement.

Contents

Foreword

To be continued ...

Those were the final words of the 2002–03 Saint Joseph's Hawks highlight film. The screen cut to black as sophomore Pat Carroll launched a potential game-winning three-pointer. An uphill affair against Auburn in the NCAA tournament's first round hung in the balance.

Moments earlier, two pressure free throws from Jameer Nelson—who else?—had forced overtime with less than a second to play. The Hawks needed every one of their junior point guard's 32 points to claw back from a 13-point halftime deficit. Running mate Delonte West gimped through 32 minutes on a stress fracture in his right leg, limiting the St. Joe's attack and putting even more responsibility on Nelson's remarkable shoulders.

In many ways, the Hawks weren't supposed to be in this position. Four 1,000-point scorers had graduated after a disappointing 2001–02 campaign, one that dissolved from a top 10 ranking in November to a second-round National Invitation Tournament (NIT) exit in March. Yet it was from those ashes that a perfect season would be born.

For long stretches, the 2002–03 prequel was every bit as good as the 2003–04 feature. The Hawks ran Boston College out of the building on opening night, 85-58, with Carroll a perfect five for five from the arc as one of Phil Martelli's four new starters. Nelson was also magnificent, stuffing the stat sheet with 22 points, eight assists, and only one turnover. As he walked out of Conte Forum with young son Jameer Jr. in hand, there was a sense that Nelson—no longer in the shadow of his former, older teammates—was taking the entire program by the hand.

It was one statement victory among many. The Hawks were 7-0 at Christmas and No. 1 in the all-important Rating Percentage Index (RPI). They would lose the first game after Christmas, at Pacific, but split a West Coast trip with an overtime victory at Gonzaga on New Year's Eve, becoming the last nonconference team to win at the original Kennel. Naturally, Nelson hit the game-winner.

The Hawks were picked fourth in the six-team Atlantic 10 East in preseason voting, but instead won eight of their first 10 conference games. They also eviscerated all of their Philadelphia Big 5 opponents, winning four times by an impressive average of

16.8 points per game. Included was a Palestra rout of Jay Wright's second Villanova team, a contest in which SJU led at one point by the video game score of 40-9.

West suffered his injury soon after. The splendid sophomore missed three of the final eight games, and played on one leg when able to suit up. Denied a full-strength Robin, Nelson took his Batman act up a notch. Having already poured in 30 against Villanova, Nelson went for 33 in an overtime loss to No. 11 Xavier and a career-high 39 at No. 22 Dayton in an Atlantic 10 semifinal loss.

Hawk fans could only wonder "what if" as they awaited the 2003 NCAA bracket. What if Nelson could keep it up? What if a week off was enough for West to recover? What if Martelli could get on another postseason roll? The always approachable, always quotable coach had already guided SJU to an NIT championship game, the NCAA Sweet 16, an Atlantic 10 tournament title, and a near-miss against No. 1 Stanford in Nelson's 2001 March Madness debut.

Longtime supporters knew just how good this team had been to reach a pre-injury record of 18-4. The 2002–03 Hawks were sixth in the country in team defense and held a staggering eight opponents under the 50-point mark. They were first in the country in effective field goal percentage defense and, sneakily, also first in defending two-pointers thanks to underrated shot-blockers Dwayne Jones, John Bryant, Alexandre Sazonov, Dave Mallon, and Chris Cologer. Throw in 40.2 percent three-point shooting and peak SJU seemed built for March.

But it was not to be. At least not yet. West was little more than a decoy against Auburn. Carroll, who couldn't miss when the season began, was zero for five, drawing nothing but air on the final three-point attempt after connecting on a school-record 45.2 percent of his previous 168. Nelson had done all he could, scoring more than half the Hawks' points in 45 exhausting minutes. St. Joe's would exit the frigid St. Pete Times Forum, otherwise home to Tampa's pro hockey team, with a chilling 65-63 defeat.

As the traveling party regrouped at its Florida hotel, surrounded by family, friends, and alumni at an unexpected pool party, hope was confronted by despair. Again, "what if?" What if Nelson made the perfectly reasonable decision to forgo his senior year? What if Martelli was lured away to a big-money school? What if a new university president, set to take office that summer, didn't care much about basketball?

Mostly, what if this pure, wonderful team—which had pressured and shared the ball like none on Hawk Hill since the halcyon days of Dr. Jack—had just played together for the last time? A great friend and colleague, Aaron Bracy, picks up the story from here.

To be continued …

Joe Lunardi
ESPN bracketologist

A Soaring Season

Jameer Nelson caught the inbounds pass from Pat Carroll underneath Saint Joseph's basket in stride and ready to sprint up the court. There were precious 6.9 seconds showing on the game clock at the Meadowlands in East Rutherford, New Jersey.

Nelson's No. 1-seeded Saint Joseph's Hawks trailed the second-seeded Oklahoma State Cowboys by just two points in the waning moments of the second half in the NCAA tournament's Elite Eight on March 27, 2004. A three-pointer would improbably send St. Joe's, the little Catholic school that hugs tightly to Philadelphia's western boundary line, into the 2004 NCAA Division I men's basketball Final Four. A two-point basket would force overtime and give life to the most unlikely and most captivating story in college basketball in the 2003–04 season.

Nelson shot a quick glance toward the Hawks bench. His coach, Phil Martelli, would be recognized as the John Wooden Coach of the Year after the season for his Houdini-like guidance of this once-in-a-lifetime magical team, but there wasn't much coaching needed now. Martelli never thought for even a second to call timeout, not with the ball in the hands of Nelson, the undersized senior point guard whose oversized, sensational game dwarfed his listed height of 5 feet, 11 inches tall.

Carroll's pass, like the go-ahead three-point shot he had just drained from the top of the key exactly 23 seconds earlier, was perfect. Nelson caught it at head level and burst toward half-court with one left dribble, then another left dribble, and then one with his right hand.

Now, 5.0 seconds showed on the clock.

Martelli was standing tall and looking calm and confident, hands behind his back as per usual, hiding any other internal emotions so his team would play the way he looked. He had reason to be at ease now with the ball in Nelson's hands because, as the coach had proclaimed over and over that season to anyone and everyone—reporters interviewing the quotable coach; viewers tuning into to his wacky, half-hour television show; people who wrote, called, or emailed and always got a response—Nelson was the best player in America.

To Martelli's left were St. Joe's three assistant coaches, Mark Bass, Matt Brady, and Monté Ross, in that order. Each rose from his seat as Nelson dribbled upcourt.

Bass, a former St. Joe's guard who hit the biggest shot of his life in the same arena eight seasons prior, knew from personal experience that a game-winning three-pointer was possible for the Hawks. And he had rebounded countless shots, and countless swishes, for Nelson in practice for the last four years. Bass and everyone knew that all the hard work had prepared Nelson to hit this shot.

Brady, St. Joe's shooting guru, had spent hours refining Nelson's shooting mechanics, altering his release point, and getting him to square his shoulders consistently. And the Hawks point guard had taken the advice and worked and worked and worked some more on perfecting his shot. Nelson already had hit several game-winners that season, and Brady and everyone knew he had honed his shooting form to do it again.

Ross had fallen in love with Nelson the first time he saw him as a sophomore at Chester High School, the hoops powerhouse hard by the Delaware River 15 miles southwest of St. Joe's, enamored by watching Nelson have the greatest impact on the court with the fewest points. It was Nelson's floor game, not his scoring, that most impressed Ross. But Ross and everyone knew Nelson could score whenever he needed.

And now, more than ever, the Hawks needed a score.

Nelson had options if he wanted to set up a teammate with yet another perfectly placed assist as he had done 170 times in the 2003–04 season and a school-record 713 times in his historic, four-year career.

Out on the left was Delonte West, the athletically gifted junior wing who had willed himself from a lightly recruited college prospect into a surefire, first-round NBA draft pick with a work ethic and competitive drive that never had been seen before or since on Hawk Hill.

To his right, there was Tyrone Barley, the senior defensive wizard whose everyday guarding of Nelson in practice would help Nelson become the 2004 Naismith Player of the Year and, like West, a 2004 NBA first-round draft pick. Barley, thinking he might be the starting point guard with Nelson considering early entry into the pros following a spectacular junior season, had worked tirelessly on his game in the offseason, developing a dependable three-point shot so he could be more than just every offensive player's worst nightmare. Now, Barley had a jump shot that made him a problem for opponents on both ends of the floor.

Trailing the play was Carroll, the sweet-stroking junior lefty whose confidence was sky-high and who made long-range shots look like mere layups with a stroke as pure as the driven snow.

Closer to the basket was sophomore Dwayne Jones, the Hawks' muscular big man whose voice was quiet but whose blocked shots and dunks had echoed loudly in gyms and arenas all season.

Not on the court as options for Nelson were sophomore Chet Stachitas, the former youth soccer star who transformed himself from a prolific high school scorer with an archaic set shot into a jump-shooting three-point threat and important substitute who relished doing all of the little things well; junior John Bryant, like Jones, another tough, interior big man who banged bodies all season long to free Nelson, West, and Carroll with screen after screen after screen; and sophomore Dave Mallon, a backup big who battled injuries and desperately wanted to be part of this incredible run despite playing in pain, taking to heart Nelson's words, that if Nelson could do it, so could Mallon.

To the left of Stachitas, Bryant, and Mallon and prone on the floor at the edge of the bench was senior Robert Hartshorn, the former St. Joe's cheerleader who grew up playing youth basketball with Nelson in their hometown of Chester, Pennsylvania, and now was his biggest backer, always in his ear with positive reinforcement, like Bundini was for Ali.

For Hartshorn, though, it was *Nelson* who was the greatest. And he wasn't alone in that thinking.

Nelson's No. 14 jersey hung proudly over the chests of many in East Rutherford among the crowd of 19,779, most of whom were Hawks fans—or became Hawks fans because of the pull of this remarkable underdog story. Heck, the school itself enrolled only 3,850 undergraduates but somehow still managed to fill buildings all season, home and away, like the Meadowlands, and set record ticket sales along the way.

St. Joe's games at Alumni Memorial Fieldhouse, their cozy on-campus home, had become the toughest ticket in Philly. The Fieldhouse really was just a gym, not an arena, not even as modern as many high school gyms. When it wasn't in use for games or practices, students played pickup five-on-five right there on the Hawks' home floor. And Martelli and company sometimes stood and watched, patiently waiting for their turn to practice on their own court.

An overhang from the Fieldhouse court led to Martelli's office, which, with its thick cinder-block walls and cramped quarters, felt more like a closet. Its low ceiling forced tall players, like Jones and Bryant and Mallon, to duck upon entry and quickly find a seat to avoid injury from banging their heads on the ceiling or craning their necks or bending their backs in an uncomfortably necessary manner. It was cluttered, like most everything else at the Fieldhouse, where everything was in tight quarters and had to be shared, including the weight room, where professors, students, and even the general public might be doing workouts next to the likes of Nelson or West or Carroll and using the same equipment.

For sure, Saint Joseph's facilities were outdated, undersized, and underfunded. Not much about the Hawks' home felt big-time, not much except their team. It was this low-budget, mom-and-pop men's basketball program that somehow had risen to the No. 1 ranking in the country, becoming the envy of the blue bloods of the sport, including the ones at traditional powerhouses like Kentucky, Duke, and North Carolina.

You wondered how they did so much with so little. Maybe some of the success could be attributed to the school's never-quit mantra, *The Hawk Will Never Die*, and its mascot, The Hawk, which featured a student on full scholarship inside of a full-body, feathered costume who flapped the wings from the moment the beaked head of the costume went on until it came off. That was nearly three hours of flapping, thousands of one- or two-arm raises, against Oklahoma State.

All of this led to a mystique and charm about St. Joe's that made people feel good, as if one didn't need to be the biggest to beat the biggest or have the best to be the best.

And, yes, these Hawks were the very best.

They were unanimously ranked No. 1 in the country after unbelievably finishing 27-0 in the regular season, packing nearly double the capacity of 3,200 into the Fieldhouse for their perfection-clinching final home victory. The Philadelphia fire marshal did indeed come to the Fieldhouse—to watch, that is, so he and his son also could be part of history, probably so captivated by what he saw on the court that the people sitting in the aisles and standing shoulder to shoulder blocking the exits during that regular-season finale went unnoticed. The school wanted to retire Nelson's jersey on that Senior Night in his last game at the Fieldhouse, but he deferred, saying there was still more work to be done.

Like right now, with just 5.0 seconds left in regulation against Oklahoma State.

Nelson broke past midcourt, dribbled hard to his left once and then again. Now, a mere 3.9 seconds showed on the clock with Nelson at the three-point line. Carroll was to Nelson's right and a bit behind him, ready and willing to shoot. Barley was farther to the right, West way to the left, Jones in the middle. All had scored key buckets that season and could again.

Really, though, there was never a doubt that this would be Nelson's shot.

Oklahoma State's Daniel Bobik had the unenviable task of guarding Nelson. At 6-foot-6, Bobik had seven inches on Nelson. It mattered little, though, who was guarding Nelson that season. If you were quick, Nelson was quicker. If you were strong, Nelson was stronger. If you were tall, Nelson could beat you off the dribble, blow by you for a layup, or find an open teammate. Or maybe, step back for a pull-up jumper. There really wasn't any stopping Nelson. Many tried, but no one could do it.

Bobik braced himself for Nelson's speed and retreated but, paying due respect to his outside game, also stayed close enough to contest a jump shot. Nelson thought about trying a game-winning three-pointer but instead drove hard toward the foul line, forcing Bobik to his heels.

This situation was nothing new to Nelson. He hit a 38-footer with nine seconds left to win it at Old Dominion in the third game of the season, saving the undefeated regular-season run practically before it even started. Five games later, in Oakland, California, Nelson pulled up from the right wing and drained an 18-footer with five ticks left to send the Hawks past the Cal Golden Bears. Any time the Hawks needed a big play, whether it was a shot, a pass, a defensive stop—whatever it was—Nelson was always ready, willing, and able to make it.

Now, 2.8 seconds showed on the clock.

Bobik had to know he was in deep trouble. Seeing that Nelson was not going to continue his forward motion toward the basket, Bobik moved from his heels to his toes. It was too late.

Nelson, settling on a game-tying two-point attempt, stopped on a dime, drove his right foot hard into the hardwood, sprang off of both feet high into the air, fading just so slightly backward, and cupped his right wrist on the ball ready to launch. Bobik lunged with his left hand and forced every single inch of his 6-foot-6 frame toward the ball. But he couldn't reach it.

Nelson had broken free from yet another defender yet again.

It was Nelson's time to make a little more magic. He released a high-arcing shot. It was from 18 feet away. Everything went quiet. Everyone stopped. Everyone held their breaths. And looked up at the basket.

CHAPTER I

How the Hawks Landed Jameer Nelson

Monté Ross settled into the hard, wooden high school bleachers. The Saint Joseph's assistant coach was on the lookout for a point guard. The Hawks were coming off a stellar season in 1996–97, capturing the Atlantic 10 Conference tournament title and making it all the way to the NCAA Sweet 16, where they lost to eventual NCAA runner-up Kentucky. St. Joe's point guard that season, the fabulous Rashid Bey, would be a senior in 1997–98, and Ross was searching for a replacement:

So, Ross scoured area high school gyms during the 1997–98 season and one night was eager to see a prospect who was playing against Chester High School. Arriving early, Ross chatted with Chester coach Fred Pickett in the stands.

"He said to me, 'Who are you here to watch?'" Ross remembered more than 25 years later. "I told him it was a point guard from the other team. And he told me, 'I have a point guard who is pretty good. He's only a sophomore, but just take a look at him and tell me what you think.'"

No one had recruited Jameer Nelson before that night.

Nelson was always a superb athlete who starred in Chester's youth sports league, known as Chester Biddy, excelling in baseball, basketball, and football. While strong and skilled, Nelson was never tall. The Clippers were then and today the best public school basketball program in Delaware County, a hotbed of hoops that is rich with high school talent. But Nelson, perhaps because of his height, perhaps because of Chester's seemingly endless talent pool, wasn't regarded as a program-changer when he entered high school. In fact, he only got a chance to start as a sophomore because one player was hurt and another decided to play football.[1]

Ross was smitten with Nelson from the opening whistle.

"Jameer might have scored three points in the game, but he controlled the whole game," Ross said. "Defensively, he was a menace. He was all over the court. They were always pressuring the ball, but he was the leader of that. Offensively, he had good players around him, and he was just distributing the ball. And he was just making sure they were in the right places at the right time. You could see the leadership even back then, him leading good players and putting them in the right spot. It was something that he's had for a long time."

Nelson didn't put up huge offensive statistics as a sophomore, but he guided the Clippers to a 23-7 record.[2] Ross and the St. Joe's coaching staff were watching closely and loved what they saw.

"He was a guy who was going to control everything from that position," Ross said. "He was a guy who was vocal on the court. He was tough as nails. Back then, you needed your point guard to lead. That's not to say he couldn't score because junior and senior year, he was doing a lot of scoring. But at the same time, it showed us that he did what was needed. Sophomore year, he was just distributing because he had good players around him. When those players left, he started scoring the basketball and being a factor that way."

With Pickett's encouragement to develop more offense, Nelson improved his jump shooting between his sophomore and junior seasons while playing for coach Earl Pearsall for the AAU Gym-Rats out of Voorhees, New Jersey.[3] As a result, his game really blossomed as a high school junior in the 1998–99 season.

All of the offseason work came together for Nelson in the semifinals of the Pennsylvania Interscholastic Athletic Association (PIAA) District 1 Class AAAA tournament against Hatboro-Horsham at Temple University on March 2, 1999. Nelson drained a buzzer-beating, 16-foot fadeaway jumper to lift the Clippers to a 67-65 overtime victory. Defending Nelson on the play was a Hatters sophomore by the name of Pat Carroll—the same Carroll who later teamed with Nelson for three years at St. Joe's.

"I didn't know much about Jameer before the game," Carroll said. "By the end, I could easily tell that he had that 'it' factor. He was different."

The victory earned Chester a spot in the PIAA District 1 Class AAAA final at Villanova University on March 5, 1999. In attendance that night among the packed crowd of 6,500 were Hawks coach Phil Martelli and *Philadelphia Daily News* college basketball writer Dick Jerardi. Jerardi, whose children attended schools in the Pennsbury School District, was there as a fan after Pennsbury High had upset perennial District 1 power Norristown in the other semifinal at Temple.

Martelli, Ross, and the Hawks had remained hot on the recruiting trail for Nelson, continually enamored with his game, his leadership, and his character. Their affection for Nelson would only increase following the game against Pennsbury. The Falcons were deep and talented, led by eventual Notre Dame recruit Torrian Jones. But Nelson and Chester were too much, beating Pennsbury 59-47. The Clippers turned a 37-36 deficit into a comfortable 55-38 advantage with a game-changing 19-1 second-half run that was keyed by Nelson.

"What struck you with him was his basketball IQ," said well-respected high school coach Frank Sciolla, who was at the helm of Pennsbury that night. "It was so developed for an eleventh-grader. It was one of the highest I'd ever competed against. We had a really hard time getting into our offense. And Jameer refused to turn the ball over. When they went on their run, he took control."

Nelson finished with 13 points—all of which came after halftime.[4]

"Jameer did not score in the first half of that game, and despite the fact that he didn't score in the first half he completely controlled the game," Sciolla said.

Jerardi, who had seen every great college basketball player locally and nationally since taking over the city's college basketball beat in 1987, knew immediately that Nelson was special.

"I didn't know who he was," Jerardi said. "I knew nothing about him. I knew Chester. They were always really good. They went up and down the court five times. I said to my guys, 'See those four guys? We're good with them. See that guy (Nelson)? No chance. I don't know who he is, but they ain't going to guard him.'"

Martelli, of course, knew who Nelson was. Like Ross and Jerardi, the Hawks' head coach had recognized Nelson's special talent immediately. Martelli knew right away that Nelson was going to be a difference-maker for his program. Nelson's performance against Pennsbury only confirmed this, and Martelli called St. Joe's athletic director Don DiJulia at halftime from Villanova to gush over Nelson's dominance that occurred without even a single point.

"He understood that he could dominate a game without scoring," Sciolla said. "We used him as an example for years, I mean for a decade we would bring him up to our players or when I would speak at camps or clinics, about the imprint you can have on the game without feeling the need to shoot it every time."

Martelli didn't just want Nelson. He knew that he could build a championship team around him. He had to have him.

But there were two major hurdles facing the Hawks' pursuit: Bruiser Flint and John Chaney.

***

James "Bruiser" Flint was a lot like Nelson. At 5-foot-9, Flint also was an undersized point guard—even shorter than Nelson. Like Nelson, Flint was tough and fearless in the mold of classic Philly guards. As a junior in 1985–86, Flint helped Saint Joseph's to a 26-6 record and a second-round appearance in the NCAA tournament. A natural leader like Nelson, Flint quickly got into coaching after leaving St. Joe's. Before helping UMass reach the Final Four in 1996 as John Calipari's lead assistant, Flint was on the staff of legendary Coppin State coach Ron "Fang" Mitchell in the late '80s. Flint helped recruit a talented Chester guard named Larry Yarbray to Coppin State, where Yarbray would go on to set the school's all-time record with 622 career assists.

Yarbray, who tragically died in a bicycle accident in 2022 at 51 years old, later went on to coach after Coppin State, including as an assistant on Pickett's staff at Chester during Nelson's time there. With affection for his former coach, Yarbray gave Flint, who had taken over as head coach at UMass in 1996, an early heads-up about Nelson.

"[Yarbray] called me and said, 'I got one for you,'" Flint said. "He said, 'Now, he's not going to put up gaudy numbers. But Bru, this is the type of stuff you used to talk to me about when you coached me at Coppin. This kid is unbelievable. Come watch him play.'"

Flint did just that and was impressed.

"Unbelievable balance," Flint said. "He never turned the ball over and always found the right guy. He wasn't a great shooter as a high school player, but he became one in college. But you talk about controlling the action, even in AAU where things can get crazy from time to time, he really controlled the action. But what I really liked about him was the stuff I talked to Larry about. Be on balance. If you're on balance, you won't turn the ball over too much. I thought Jameer really played that way, and I thought he played that way throughout his entire career. He wasn't going to jump over top of you and those things like that, but when you went to watch him, he made the right pass, did all those types of things like that.

"Unbelievable strength, unbelievable lower body strength, I think that's really important for a guard. And that was the thing that attracted me to him."

Flint arranged for Nelson to visit UMass, along with Yarbray and Pickett. The visit went well enough. Yarbray and Pickett were in Flint's corner, and Nelson liked what he saw and heard.

"I really thought that could have been a real good spot for me," Nelson said.

But then the trio headed for home during a weekday rush hour, driving from Amherst, Massachusetts, through New York City and back to Chester.

"A lot of traffic, man," Nelson said. "A five-hour drive took us eight hours, and I was like, 'Man, I don't know if I can do this.'"

For years, Flint regretted not making other travel arrangements for Nelson.

"They hit traffic in New York," Flint recalled. "Jameer always said, 'That was it for me.' Like, 'That was way too far.' I said, 'I should have had you stay over and then go back the next day.' He said, 'Yeah, that might have been better. Once we took seven or eight hours to get back from UMass to Chester, that was it for me. Bru, I liked y'all, I really liked y'all. Plus, Larry and Fred were really big on you guys. But that trip back, that was it right there.'"

"I was done after that," Flint said.

So, Flint and UMass were out.

But traffic was not a major problem getting from Chester to Temple University's Philadelphia campus, where the legendary Chaney had built a powerhouse program that yearly made the NCAA tournament and was among the most feared and respected programs in the country.

Nelson was yet another top local player who had his eyes set on playing for Chaney and Temple. "Honestly, I thought Temple would be the spot for me," Nelson said.

Somehow, Martelli, Ross, and the Hawks would have to convince Nelson otherwise. Somehow, they would have to out-recruit John Chaney.

***

There are not many living legends in sports. In 1999, Chaney inarguably was one of them. He grew up playing high school basketball in the Philadelphia Public League at Benjamin Franklin High, then starred at Bethune-Cookman, where he once scored 57 points in a contest, before a professional stint in the Eastern Basketball League. His calling, though, was as a coach. After a successful stop at Division II Cheyney State, where he won a national championship in 1978, Chaney was hired at Temple in 1982. He missed the NCAA tournament that first season but would reach the Big Dance in 17 of the following 18 seasons. The Owls made five appearances in the NCAA Elite Eight during his tenure, and his 1987 and '88 teams each won 32 games.

Chaney, who was inducted into the Naismith Hall of Fame in 2001 and passed away on January 29, 2021, cast an intimidating figure on the sidelines, with his loosened tie, scratchy voice, and imploring body gestures. If you didn't like to be hollered at, you couldn't play for Chaney. But behind the sometimes loud, angry voice, was a man who had a deep, true love for his players, Temple University, Philadelphia, and the game of basketball. He loved people—as long as you didn't turn the ball over or foul a three-point shooter. Chaney's matchup zone confused most opponents' offenses, especially during the NCAA tournament with limited time to prep. His teams were known to battle on the court for every second. Chaney demanded nothing less, probably in part because he was battling every second off the court, whether challenging the NCAA's admission policies, providing life-changing opportunities for his players, or participating in a cause in support of Temple or Philadelphia.

Recruiting against Chaney was like trying to score against his matchup zone. You could try, but you weren't likely to succeed.

Martelli knew this all too well. The schools' gyms were separated by five miles; they played in the same conference; and participated in the historic Philadelphia Big 5, which pits La Salle, Penn, Saint Joseph's, Temple, Villanova, and, beginning in 2023–24, Drexel in intra-city games. Chaney's teams had beaten Saint Joseph's so many times on the court that Martelli had become obsessed with Temple, knowing that any success in the Big 5 or the Atlantic 10 Conference would go through Chaney. Martelli studied the matchup zone and studied it and studied it some more, finally devising a formula that he thought might work. As any scientist or baker would attest, formulas are great when the ingredients are present. In this case, the main ingredient was Jameer Nelson.

Martelli and St. Joe's, as the first school to recruit Nelson, got a head start on Chaney. And the Hawks staff continued to run way out ahead in the race for Nelson. After the Pennsbury game at Villanova, Martelli was in the stands for a second-round state playoff matchup against McCaskey High School when Nelson had 24 points, 11 rebounds, and eight assists in a 79-63 Clippers win.[5] The Hawks staff stayed close to Nelson after the season, too. When he competed in a prestigious Las Vegas recruiting showcase in the summer following his junior season, either Ross or Martelli, or both, were practically members of Nelson's entourage.

"I got out there to make sure that I saw every dribble that he took in every game," Ross said. "Whenever they landed, I probably landed the same time, if not before, because I didn't want to miss a game."

It was a good thing, too, because Nelson was starting to get noticed after outplaying higher-profile recruits in Las Vegas and other showcases, like the elite ABCD camp in New Jersey.

"Everybody was enthralled," Ross said of Nelson's play versus big-time recruits. "I'm not going to say he destroyed them or anything like that, but he clearly was not, not as good as them. He was as good as them every time he played against those guys. I'm like, 'Wow.' They were being recruited highly. Jameer was just Jameer. He was just doing his thing.

"You could never take him out of what he wanted to do. He had the strength. He had the foot speed. He had the quickness. He had it all in terms of being an elite point guard. What separated him was his mental (game). He was so smart and so in tune to getting everybody else involved, even at a situation like that when those camps can be selfish. He was always making the right play. So, you always knew that was in his DNA."

While Ross and Martelli were charting Nelson's every move, Chaney wasn't in Las Vegas. This was nothing new. He never went to Las Vegas. In fact, Chaney rarely watched underclassmen play, leaving that to his excellent staff.

"His famous line when you asked him to a see a tenth- or eleventh-grader was, 'I'll be dead by then,'" said Dan Leibovitz, one of Chaney's assistant coaches from 1996–2006. "Coach was a guy who was going to coach the season. And when the season was over, he was going to turn the page on recruiting."

Everyone on the Owls staff was well aware of Martelli's persistence.

"I say this as a compliment, 'He recruited him like an assistant coach,'" Leibovitz said of Martelli's pursuit of Nelson. "Phil beat Coach Chaney in a no-contest in terms of effort that summer."

Again, this was nothing new for Chaney. Now, though, it was time for him to make his move. There was no doubt that Chaney recognized Nelson's potential and wanted him in the Owls program.

"Coach could innately evaluate all of the qualities of a great point guard," Leibovitz said. "He could talk for two hours straight just describing what it is to be a true point guard. And he recognized that Jameer was a true point guard. I remember him saying, and often, that a great point guard can get himself in and out of trouble, invite a double-team, and then attack the double-team, get to the paint crowded with big guys and have the poise to step through or get out.

"Jameer got wherever he wanted on the floor, under control, powerful, confident, good on the defensive side. He recognized exactly what Jameer Nelson was."

Besides Martelli, Chaney had two other problems on hand with recruiting Nelson: the matchup zone and Lynn Greer.

***

Like Nelson, Lynn Greer was a point guard from Chester. And special, too. They met in the Chester Biddy league, the nine-year-old Nelson looking up to the 12-year-old Greer.

"We were really close," Greer said.

Their families were close, too, and Nelson thought so highly of Greer that he proudly wore the number 14 just like Greer had done before him.

"I looked up to Lynn, I really did," Nelson said. "That was his number. He was one of those guys when he played, I sat up and watched. I can say I'm happy to carry on the number 14 and wear it with pride. Not too many people wear that number, and we obviously have a special bond on and off the floor as competitors and friends, but also with the number."

While Nelson was proudly sporting the number 14 on his jersey as a sophomore at Chester in the fall of 1997, Greer was doing so on North Broad Street as a freshman guard for coach John Chaney.

A lefty, Greer could get to the basket with startling speed and athleticism, and then step back and drain a jumper with range as far away from the rim as you want with such beauty and ease. It was no surprise that as one of the best players in the Philadelphia area, Greer ended up on Chaney's roster. He was just another in a long line of great area guards who played for Chaney, with Nelson expected by many to continue the trend.

And Chaney's success recruiting guards was part of the challenge, at first, for Greer. He had Rasheed Brokenborough from Philadelphia's University City High and Pepe Sanchez from Argentina in front of him on the depth chart. Greer started just one of 30 games as a freshman, redshirted as a sophomore after breaking an orbital bone in the sixth contest, and then came off the bench for 25 of 33 games as a redshirt sophomore.

In the 2000–01 season, his junior year, the ball *finally* would be Greer's. That also would be Nelson's freshman season of college. So, when Leibovitz and the Owls staff looked to Greer to help recruit his close friend Nelson, who played the same exact position, it was understandable that Greer wasn't exactly overly enthusiastic.

"We were asking Lynn because of the relationship, 'Would you put in a good word and help us with Jameer? Where do you think it sits?'" Leibovitz said. "Lynn is such an all-time great person. What I sensed from Lynn is, 'I love Jameer, and Jameer is great. I also don't want to ....' Lynn knew how good [Nelson] was. Not that Lynn was going to sit behind him, but he waited to be the point guard at Temple. So, he didn't want to be pushed off the ball while Jameer had the ball."

And Chaney was sending the same message to Nelson, that it was Greer's ball for now, and it would be Nelson's in two years.

"Coach Chaney, with all due respect, told me, 'You're probably going to have to sit behind Lynn Greer for a year or two,'" Nelson said. "Respectfully so, Lynn was a hell of a player. So, I can't argue with that."

But that didn't sound great to Nelson. "I didn't want to sit," he said.

In most any other program in the country, it would not have been an issue to have two breathtaking, ballhandling guards like Greer and Nelson playing side by side. Both could score. Greer was a great shooter; Nelson would become one. Both could do just about everything on the floor. Except both were short for Division I guards, with Greer listed at 6-foot-2 and Nelson at 5-foot-11. Again, this would not be an issue at most programs given their talent. But Chaney's matchup zone was predicated on guards with size and length, players who could contest a three-point shot with long reach without leaving their feet, who could use their long arms to disrupt passing lanes that somehow made the zone feel like opponents were playing five against six.

Chaney's matchup zone simply would not be effective with Greer and Nelson on the court together for long stretches. Everyone knew this.

"Not that I wasn't up for the competition, but we're two small guards," Nelson said. "We can't play together."

For Nelson, the decision started to come into focus. Sure, there were a few big-time programs that came calling late. By then, Martelli, Ross, and the Hawks staff's relationship with Nelson, his family, and, seemingly, the entire city of Chester was deep. The Nelson camp also had the ultimate respect for Chaney and Temple. But St. Joe's early and persistent recruitment, the opportunity to start right away and not have to battle his good friend Greer for playing time, and the proximity to Chester and not having to fight New York City traffic to and from UMass ultimately led Nelson to pick the Hawks in August 1999 before starting his senior year of high school.

"St. Joe's showed me a lot of attention and love," Nelson said. "As I've gotten older, I realize I'm big on relationships, and I started to develop a genuine relationship with the coaching staff. All of those guys [coaches] were involved in the recruiting process. It was cool to have that type of support."

And Nelson knew he was going to have an opportunity to immediately showcase his skills on Hawk Hill.

"St. Joe's basically told me, 'We're going to give you the ball, we're going to let you play, we're going to let you do your thing,'" he said. "That's all I wanted. It wasn't about stardom. It wasn't about coming into a situation to put up certain numbers. I just wanted to play basketball. It just made sense for me to go to a different place [than Temple] knowing I was going to be able to play minutes right away."

Greer would go on to start 68 of 68 games as a junior and senior and had an amazing, four-year career, still ranking second in Owls history with 2,099 career points. Nelson would look to have similar success at St. Joe's. Ross and Martelli were ecstatic to get the news that he was coming—even if it meant skipping a wedding to meet with Nelson.

Ross got a phone call from Pearsall on an August morning in 1999.

"He said, 'Are you going to be at the gym this morning?'" Ross remembered. "I said, 'You know what, I have a wedding to go to, so I won't be there.' I said, 'What's up?' He said, 'Jameer is coming up, and I think he wants to commit.' I said, 'OK, well scratch that, I'm not going to that wedding. I'll be at the gym.'

"So, I hang up with Earl, call Phil and tell him, 'I think Jameer is going to commit to us.' They're coming up to the office this morning. He was like, 'OK, we'll be there.' Now, Phil was supposed to go the same wedding I was going to. Neither one of us went to that wedding. We went to the gym. [Nelson] comes in and commits right away."

Martelli knew he had a program-changer, knew the Hawks could have success with Nelson leading the way. But the head coach's reaction when Nelson committed surprised even Ross.

"Phil said, 'Yes! We're going to the Final Four. Thank you,'" Ross said. "I said to myself, 'I think Jameer is good, but we're going to the Final Four?' I was like, 'What?' But that was Phil's first reaction. Those were the first words out of his mouth when Jameer said he wanted to come."

The St. Joe's head coach had been saying to everyone close to him how special Nelson was. Now that there was no need to hide this from competing coaches, Martelli started to tell everyone else.

"There was no national recruiting service saying that this guy is going to be something special," said Ray Parrillo, who covered the Hawks for the *Philadelphia Inquirer*. "Phil seemed to know it and realized how special it was to get Jameer. I had never seen Jameer play. I was talking to Phil and I remember Phil clearly saying to me, 'Wait until you see how good of a coach I'm going to be for the next four years.'"

The Hawks' head coach had his man. The big-time programs passed over Nelson because of his height. For whatever reasons, Martelli also was overlooked for many years. As time passed and Martelli neared 41 years old still an assistant coach, there were questions whether he would ever get the chance to have the only job he had ever wanted since eighth grade.

CHAPTER 2

Phil Martelli's Dream Job

For many people, finding their life's work takes a lifetime. For Phil Martelli, however, his career path was crystal clear. He knew exactly what he wanted to do even before entering high school.

Martelli had fallen in love with basketball at a young age, honing his game at Finnegan Playground. Unlike many young ballers on those courts, or Philadelphia's countless other neighborhood blacktops, Martelli never dreamt of pulling an NBA jersey over his chest; rather, he wanted to wear a shirt and tie like Jack Ramsay or Jack McKinney.

Ramsay coached Saint Joseph's from 1953 through 1966, and McKinney followed for the next eight seasons. Whenever Martelli took the short, four-mile trolley ride from his childhood home in Southwest Philadelphia to the Palestra, Philadelphia's storied basketball gym on the campus of the University of Pennsylvania, or later a little longer trip after moving to suburban Lansdowne at 12 years old, Martelli was fascinated by Ramsay and McKinney as much as by the players on the floor. In eighth grade, Martelli told his friend Stevie Stefano that one day he would coach the Hawks.[6]

As a player, Martelli started in high school at point guard at St. Joseph's Prep. Years later, he would draw laughs by recounting how he was part of a great backcourt at the Prep that averaged 30 points per game. Mo Howard, who went on to a stellar career at the University of Maryland and a brief stint in the NBA, scored 28 points—and Martelli contributed the other two. But Martelli *was* a good enough player to earn a scholarship to Division II Widener University in, *where else*, Chester, Pennsylvania, helping to lead Widener to the NCAA tournament in 1975 and '76. He was the school's all-time assists leader when he graduated. There was no doubt what Martelli wanted to do after Widener, and he quickly landed a job as the junior varsity coach at Cardinal O'Hara High School in Springfield, Pennsylvania. After returning to Widener as an assistant coach the following season, he got his first opportunity to be a head coach, at Bishop Kenrick High School in Norristown, Pennsylvania.

At Kenrick, where he was assisted by another ambitious young coach by the name of Geno Auriemma, who would go on to a legendary career as UConn's women's basketball coach, Martelli compiled 112 wins in seven years and made the Philadelphia Catholic League playoffs in each of his final six seasons. It was an invaluable experience.

"He was a really, really smart 'X' and 'O' guy," said Dick "Hoops" Weiss, the longtime college basketball writer for the *Philadelphia Daily News* and *New York Daily News*. "A lot of that comes from the Philadelphia Catholic League. If you can win there, you can win in any high school league in the country."

Martelli's success at Kenrick led to a potentially life-changing opportunity. In 1985, head coach Jim Boyle hired Martelli to be an assistant on his staff at Saint Joseph's University. Martelli's dream was alive and well. He was on the Hawks bench now, just a few seats away from where he told Stefano in eighth grade that he would be. But moving those few seats into the head coach's chair would prove anything but easy.

***

Martelli's first season at Hawk Hill went well. With Bruiser Flint at point guard on a team that starred Mo Martin, who averaged 17.8 points and would go on to a brief NBA career, the Hawks finished 26-6 overall, 16-2 in the Atlantic 10, and reached the second round of the NCAA tournament. But Boyle's teams barely finished above .500 in the next two seasons, going a combined 31-27, and dipped to 8-21 in 1988–89. Boyle announced his resignation late in December the following season to take effect at the end of 1989–90, which culminated with a dreadful 7-21 mark.

Maybe now Martelli would get a shot to fulfill his childhood dream. But he was an afterthought to succeed Boyle. On March 7, 1990, Martelli's name was nowhere to be found in a *Philadelphia Inquirer* article that listed potential candidates.[7] The job ultimately went to John Griffin, a former St. Joe's player and assistant coach who also had a successful tenure as head coach at Siena. Griffin left a lucrative Wall Street job to return to Saint Joseph's. In his 1,215-word story on the hiring in the *Philadelphia Daily News*, Dick Jerardi did mention in paragraph 29 of 33 that Martelli would be returning as an assistant coach.

So, why wasn't Martelli a serious candidate?

There were several reasons. It is fair to say that the fact that Martelli wasn't likely to appear on the cover of *GQ* magazine probably played a factor. Phil Martelli wasn't interested much in fashion. He was a basketball coach. And a Philadelphian. He looked like one, talked like one, and coached like one. Sometimes though, like with Nelson's height, one's appearance can misdirect others from one's true qualities and abilities.

Also, Martelli was always affable, humorous, and quick with one-liners. Later, that would make him a media darling, a reporter's dream, and someone who filled up a notebook or a story with quotes that were void of clichés and coachspeak. His detractors, however, would point to his outgoing personality and label him as someone who talked a good game more than he coached one. Similarly, perhaps his gregarious nature and any connected perception, whether true or not, that he couldn't be taken seriously, might have hindered him for consideration to be a head coach.

More than anything else, Martelli had one major thing going against him in his quest to become the Hawks' front man: His degree said "Widener University."

***

On April 4, 1990, Griffin became the 13th head men's basketball coach in Saint Joseph's history. Like Griffin, Boyle (who coached from 1981 to 1990) was a St. Joe's graduate. So was Jim Lynam (1978–81) before Boyle, Harry Booth (1974–78) before Lynam, McKinney (1966–74) before Booth, Ramsay (1955–66) before McKinney, and John McMenamin (1953–55) before Ramsay. The last time a non–St. Joe's graduate led the program was in 1952, when Penn grad Bill Ferguson finished his 25th year at the helm. The Hawks had only one other coach without a St. Joe's degree, Edward Bennis, like Ferguson a Penn grad, who coached just one season in 1910–11.

Even if Martelli had all of the intangibles of a hotshot assistant and was the most serious person in the room, it probably wouldn't have mattered because of his degree. As a consolation, while not the job he *really* wanted, Martelli was still on the Hawks bench, now working for the fiery Griffin. Hurt in part by injuries, Griffin never had the success he anticipated when he returned to Saint Joseph's, and he resigned in the summer following the 1995 season to return to private business after a combined 75-69 record over five seasons that were void of an NCAA appearance.[8]

Griffin officially resigned on July 11, 1995. Martelli was 40 years old, a month away from turning 41. He had been an assistant coach at St. Joe's for 10 years. His only head coaching experience was leading 16- and 17-year-olds at Bishop Kenrick. Late in Griffin's tenure, Martelli was a leading candidate for the head coaching job at Loyola University Maryland. He didn't get it. Devastated, he returned home, only to be uplifted by a handmade card from his three children, Phil Jr., Jimmy, and Elizabeth, telling him how much they loved him. Maybe that would be the closest Martelli would ever come to a head coaching job. But then Griffin resigned.

Would Martelli get a chance to succeed him?

He wasn't a Hawks graduate. He didn't have a head coach's résumé. He didn't quite have the look.

Maybe Martelli never would be a college head coach, at St. Joe's or anywhere. Or maybe, this time, he wouldn't be overlooked. At the very least, unlike after Boyle resigned, Martelli would be a legitimate candidate to become the Hawks coach.

"I knew he was a major part of the program," St. Joe's athletic director Don DiJulia said. "I asked John Griffin if he thought Phil was ready to be a head coach, and John didn't hesitate and said, 'Yes.' OK, fine. He's in the bucket. He's capable. He's internal. He knew the university, knew his love and passion for the university. And he was well-connected in the area from his playing days and coaching days."

Martelli interviewed well enough to become a finalist. Besides his undergraduate institution, there were two additional things working against Martelli: a four-person selection committee and, just as with his later recruitment of Nelson, James "Bruiser" Flint.

***

Unlike Martelli, Flint *could have been* a candidate for a *GQ* magazine cover. Handsome, fit, intense, successful—Flint had it all. He was the prototype for a young, hotshot assistant. He helped head coach John Calipari build a national powerhouse at UMass, unheard of for an Atlantic 10 school. The Minutemen had just wrapped up their fourth straight NCAA tournament appearance, averaging a remarkable 27.8 wins per season over that stretch. The next year, in 1995–96 behind star forward Marcus Camby, UMass would reach the Final Four.

It wasn't a question of whether Flint would become a head coach, it was a matter of when and where. And what better place than his alma mater, where he would continue the tradition of St. Joe's graduates as head coach dating all the way back to when McMenamin took over for Ferguson in 1953. It also likely could not have helped Martelli that Flint publicly expressed his interest in the Hawks job.[9] Like Martelli, Flint interviewed with the four-person committee. And they were impressed. Very impressed.

"At the end of the day, you want someone with high character, with belief in the institution and the mission, and someone you project being able to work across the departments at the university to rally people to support what you need to do," DiJulia said.

The committee felt that both Martelli and Flint possessed the desired traits, but neither coach had a consensus from the four members.

"The bottom line was the group was split," DiJulia said. "It wasn't unanimous in terms of saying, 'This is easy.' It wasn't easy."

Then and today, DiJulia is one of the most respected administrators in college athletics. He officially retired as the Hawks athletic director in 2018 but was still serving the school in a consulting role in 2024. He was a member of the famed

1964–65 Hawks team, began his first of two stints as the school's AD in 1976, and returned home to Hawk Hill in 1988 for his second term as AD after eight years as commissioner for the East Coast Conference (1981–84) and Metro Atlantic Athletic Conference (1984–88).

DiJulia loves the school, loves the alumni, loves Flint, and loves the unique tradition that hiring him would have continued. He also had gotten to know Martelli the previous seven years and just felt, even minus the coveted degree and in spite of the strength of Flint's candidacy, that Martelli was the right choice at that time.

When the deadlocked committee returned for another day of deliberations, DiJulia explained why Martelli was their man. And his voice carried weight.

"After we talked why Phil was at the top of the list on my point, then everyone clearly bought in," DiJulia said.

Martelli had been an anxious wreck for a week and left his office the morning of the committee's final meeting to drive to a destination, not knowing exactly where he was going. He ended up at Valley Forge National Historic Park, found a bench under a tree, unfurled his *Philadelphia Daily News*, opened a bag of soft pretzels, turned up his cell phone ringer, and tried not to think about how his whole life was about to change for better or worse.

DiJulia finally called Martelli. Father Nicholas Rashford, St. Joe's president, delivered the life-altering news Phil Martelli had been dreaming about since eighth grade: He was selected as the 14th head coach in Saint Joseph's history. It became official on July 20, 1995.

Martelli had achieved his dream. "Tears, for sure," he said of his reaction.

After wiping away the tears, it was time to get to work. Martelli had prepared for this moment for nearly 30 years and wouldn't waste even a minute making the most of the coveted opportunity.

"I started to process and it was, 'What's the next steps?'" he said. "I was already in that planning mode of who do I contact, how do I contact them. What about the players? It was always my want to have a plan in mind, and that's what kicked in."

He had learned an important lesson about time management his first time as a head coach, and he wouldn't make the mistake of not being prepared again.

***

After struggling in his first season at Kenrick, Martelli consulted with legendary Immaculata women's basketball coach Cathy Rush. He had met Rush by working at her summer camp, thanks in part to a good word from Weiss. The camp turned out to be much more than a job, as one of Rush's former players, Judy Marra, also was working the camp. Weiss asked Marra to keep an eye on Martelli.

"Phil was looking for a summer job," Weiss said. "I think he was going to work at the Lansdowne Ice House. I went to Cathy and said, 'Are you looking to hire?'

And I told her about Phil. I went to Judy and said, 'You have to take care of this guy. He's a friend of mine.'"

Marra did just that—at the camp and, beginning on November 20, 1976, later as Martelli's wife. The couple celebrated their 48th wedding anniversary in 2024.

"They were a perfect fit," Weiss said. "I was so happy for both of them."

And Martelli was happy to get some advice from Rush, who told him he needed to develop a plan, for practice and for his program.[10] Always organized, helped by being the oldest of eight children to Phillip Edgar Martelli and Mary Jane McCormick Martelli, he began to structure his high school practices to the minute and brought that level of detail to his job as head coach at St. Joe's.

Martelli would write out his practice notes longhand and deliver them to longtime secretary Clare Ariano to be typed.

"Every day I would type up the practice schedule, 3:30 to 3:35 dribbling, 3:35 such and such another drill," Ariano said. "And they went by that. Every single day there was a typed practice schedule."

He studied opponents with precision, sometimes staying up half the night at home watching film, for scouting reports that left players confident and ready. Chet Stachitas, a key sophomore reserve on the 2003–04 team, had to miss a practice during his junior season after his grandmother passed away. He returned in time for the game but was out of place without key knowledge of the opposition.

"I never felt so lost playing a basketball game, and it was that evident how well prepared the coaches got us," Stachitas said. "I was on an island because I missed the practice before the game. Looking back, man, we were the most prepared team that I've ever been on."

Players, like Stachitas, responded well to Martelli's preparation, organization, and leadership. In those first couple of years, the switch from Griffin to Martelli also created a new atmosphere for Griffin's recruits, a shift from hating to lose to loving to win. It all worked right away for Martelli. He led the Hawks to a 19-13 overall mark and 9-7 league record in his first season in 1995–96, ending with a loss in the NIT final to Alabama at Madison Square Garden. The next season was even better, 26-7 overall, 13-3 in the league, an Atlantic 10 tournament title, and a trip to the NCAA Sweet 16, where the Hawks lost to eventual national runner-up Kentucky. Before that game against the Wildcats, Martelli drew national attention by joking that Wildcats coach Rick Pitino recruited McDonald's All-Americans while his Hawks recruits ate at McDonald's.

Quickly, Martelli had become a media darling. He also showed that he could coach.

"He's the best," national college basketball reporter Andy Katz said. "I just always felt like he didn't give you coachspeak. He was real. I always learned something, too, when I talked to him. I liked talking to Phil just about basketball and educating myself. And he's also a great person, family man, everything about him."

While his personal star, and that of the St. Joe's program, was rising, Martelli didn't change who he was.

If you wrote him, he would write you back. "He answered everyone," Ariano said. "Everyone."

Like Brian O'Connell, a Hawks fan who attended every home game with his father, Bill. "Pretty much after every game, I'd email him," O'Connell said. "And he'd always find time to respond."

The responses always came either via a handwritten note or a reply typed by Ariano.

"Everything was on paper," Ariano said. "If you sent a note or a card, he would write his reply on that. He never had a computer. I would print up every email he got every morning, and I would have them on his desk. He would answer every email. He would write it and then hand those back to me. And I would type it back."

Similarly, any media obligations were on paper, with Ariano typing a weekly schedule and handing it to Martelli on Friday for the following week. "That's how we worked," Ariano said. "And it worked."

Responding to reporters' requests never was a chore for Martelli.

"He just is so open to people," said Marie Wozniak, who left Seton Hall to take over as the school's sports information director in August 2003 after longtime SID Larry Dougherty accepted a similar position at Temple. "He literally would not say no. He would find a way to talk to whoever wanted to talk to him. I had never really experienced that before. If you called for an interview, it would be like, 'OK, let me see what time I can get it done.' It wouldn't be like, 'OK, let me see if he can do it.'"

Whether it was a reporter, an autograph seeker, or a request to speak at an event, Martelli was accommodating.

"People wanted him," Ariano said. "He is such a great speaker. He always had demand to begin with. When [in 2003–04] people started to call the office and say, 'If I bring a basketball, can I get it signed by the team?' We never said no to anyone. We said, 'Yeah, sure.'"

Martelli was winning on the court and winning over the media off it. He also was drawing rave reviews inside the university from staff and players.

"I can't say enough about him, not so much as a coach, as a human being," Ariano said. "And I mean that. Yeah."

"He kind of let the individual professionals do their job," said longtime St. Joe's athletic trainer Bill Lukasiewicz. "Not that he wouldn't question on occasion, but he was great to work with."

Martelli was not without flaws. There was an edge about him that occasionally was seen, both on the sidelines and off. Also, his eager promotion of Saint Joseph's, as a way to help draw attention to the school and the basketball program, sometimes was viewed as boasting by critics, many of whom were opposing coaches and rival fans.

Overall, though, Martelli always has been regarded as a good, decent man.

"He's somebody I respect immensely who has always struck me as genuine and sincere and someone who always tries to make things better," said Glen Macnow, a longtime sports radio personality in Philadelphia.

Macnow brushed aside any knock against Martelli for his media persona as stumping for St. Joe's, which included regular appearances and even random call-ins on sports radio station WIP, where Macnow held down various shifts for 31 years before retiring in July 2024. Martelli was doing what many Philadelphians did by calling the radio station to discuss the Eagles, Phillies, 76ers, and Flyers, though getting listeners to know about the Hawks was his main motivator.

"I think his motive for doing it was to get attention to a relatively small program in the city where there are so many teams and sports vying for attention," Macnow said. "If he can get people to know St. Joe's, good for him. We have the Eagles, the Phillies, the Sixers, the Flyers, Villanova, and yet Phil Martelli was a guy who was always there and getting attention for his program. I never think it got in the way of him doing his job."

Jerry Carino, a longtime college basketball writer for the *Asbury Park Press*, has seen other, smaller programs in the northern New Jersey/New York City metropolitan area follow Martelli's example.

"He was everywhere [in 2003–04]," Carino said. "His mission was, 'This is my one shot to promote the school on a national scale.' It's like free advertising. That's a model that FDU, St. Peter's, and even Princeton followed the last couple of years."

Martelli's medium in Philadelphia often was WIP radio.

"He was just the kind of guy who was in the car and either was invited as a guest or was listening to the station and decided he wanted to join in," Macnow said. "And God bless him for that. It made my job easier."

When he wasn't a guest on Macnow or other hosts' shows, Martelli sometimes was helping out at charity events. "He was never a guy who just showed up when you asked him," Macnow said. "He was always a guy who did more."

As an example, Macnow might ask Martelli to sign a basketball for charity, but the coach would instead volunteer to go to lunch with the highest bidder. Helping others is something Martelli had done on the Hawks campus for many years, long before being named head coach, embodying the mantra of the university that was founded by the Jesuits, whose mission is to help others and seek God in all things.

"He taught all of the guys who he had recruited to the program that it was never about you as an individual," said Chuck Sack, a former basketball student manager and The Hawk mascot while Martelli was an assistant who would go on to be the school's student advisor for academics. "There was always something greater for you to think about, how you are impacting your team or your community, always bringing that Ignatian idea and being somebody for somebody else. [Martelli said,] 'What your gifts and talents do, impact others. So, use them well.'"

Martelli's players took notice.

"He cared about each and every person in that building, each and every person on that campus," Jameer Nelson said. "It was something that I didn't know could be a thing. He cared about every manager, everybody. So, it made it easy for me to lead, to learn how to lead. That's what he wanted me to do, and he gave me the keys to do that. He empowered me and a lot of people."

Robert Hartshorn, a former cheerleader who walked on to the Hawks and played very limited minutes, maintains a strong relationship with his former coach to this day.

"You see him for what he is immediately; he's a family man," Hartshorn said. "It's not like once the court lights go out, it's over. He has been there ever since we have been together. He has been a part of everything major that has happened to me. He was at my wedding. He reintroduced me to my dad. That's what makes him a great coach. What coach do you know who has a lifelong bond relationship with the sixteenth guy on their bench?

"I told him when he's an old man and he can't do anything for himself, you know I'm the guy who's going to be at the retirement home feeding you applesauce."

Everything was going just as planned for Martelli, just as he had envisioned it in eighth grade. He was winning, had earned the respect of the media and his players, and was well-liked by his staff. DiJulia and the committee's decision was looking even better than anyone could have imagined.

But then the winning stopped.

***

Martelli followed up that Sweet 16 run in 1997 with a thud, losing 13 of 16 Atlantic 10 contests and finishing 11-17 overall in 1997–98. The next year wasn't much better, going 12-18 overall and 5-11 in the league. The following season, 1999–2000, was more of the same, with the Hawks finishing 13-16 and 7-9.

Over those three seasons, Martelli won just 41.4 percent (36-51 record) of his games, including an even-worse 31.3 percent (15-33) in the Atlantic 10. Suddenly, what looked like a slam dunk hiring now didn't seem as strong.

"Concern was beginning to rise," DiJulia said. "Are we going to be able to get back to being a winning program? So, that was in there."

Martelli knew this. He also knew he had Nelson coming to help in 2000–01. But the Hawks, clearly, would need much more than just Nelson to turn things around. Nelson needed a backcourt mate, and Martelli discovered one who wasn't being recruited heavily at a summer showcase event in New Jersey. Martelli saw something that summer day. He saw just the right fit for Nelson and another important player to help kickstart the Hawks program.

CHAPTER 3

Delonte West's Competitive Drive

Delonte West drove hard to the basket with his usual fearlessness. He was undercut and crashed forcefully into the basket support on the temporary courts set up at The College of New Jersey (TCNJ) for a college prospect showcase. Those in attendance that summer day in 2000 groaned at the impact. Phil Martelli was there. He heard the groans and then marveled at what he saw next: West bounced right up and sprinted back on defense.

Martelli didn't come to TCNJ to scout Delonte West. After what he saw on that one play, however, he left wanting no one else. Martelli had gotten a small glimpse of the competitive drive that West would go on to display for three years at St. Joe's and eight years in the NBA. In all of his experiences, at any level, anywhere, Martelli still has never seen anyone match West's competitiveness.

"It's way beyond anything," Martelli said. "Delonte was driven to be great, driven to win. Delonte's fire, I was blessed to have been exposed to it."

His Hawks teammates felt this in every practice and every workout.

"If he didn't win, he was pissed off, and he wanted to play again," said Dwayne Jones, who roomed with West, a 6-foot-4 guard, at St. Joe's and later with the NBA's Cleveland Cavaliers. "And we were going to keep going until he won. He was ultracompetitive."

"There wasn't a more competitive person that I've ever met," said Dave Mallon, a sophomore reserve on the 2003–04 Hawks. "Losing was never an option with him."

Mallon remembers an example of this during his freshman year while playing a casual game of pickup on a Saturday. Only, it wasn't casual for West after the team West and Mallon were on lost. Mallon headed toward the water cooler after the defeat, only to be abruptly stopped by West.

"He said, 'No water breaks. We're staying,'" Mallon recalled. "And I remember thinking, 'I want some water right now.' He was like, 'Yo, get back here. We're running it back.' You get around somebody who thinks that way all the time, and it starts to become part of your approach as well. I don't accept not winning and not being competitive and not giving 100 percent every time."

West not only led by example, he pushed his teammates to reach his elite level of competitiveness.

"There would be days when he'd bring you in the weight room and say, 'You gotta get in here, you gotta get stronger, you're going to work out with me,'" Mallon said. "He would see where someone needed some effort or some work and he would push them. And he would show you, 'This is how hard I'm going to work. Now you need to work this hard.'"

Glenn Farello saw this mentality up close for three years as West's coach at Eleanor Roosevelt High School in Greenbelt, Maryland. He remembers a game during West's junior year in which Roosevelt played a rival it had blown out by 40 points earlier in the season. Not wanting his team to be overconfident, Farello pointed out to West that one of the opposing players scored six first-quarter points against him in the first matchup. West made sure that didn't happen again.

"I'm trying to figure out how to motivate them," Farello said. "I told Delonte, 'Are you going to play defense today? Last game this kid scored six points on you in the first quarter, made him feel good about himself, probably told everybody about it.' The kid goes on to score two points for the whole game. Delonte had 18 in the first quarter."

West didn't reserve this type of ruthless competitiveness just for opponents. Earlier in that season at Roosevelt, West was working back from injury and had to log a certain number of practices to become eligible. So, Farello gave him an extra session with the JV team, and West did not take it easy on his teammates.

"His stat line was 45 points, 20 rebounds, 20 steals. No lie, those were the exact stats," Farello said. "I'm like, 'Delonte, what are you doing? You're just coming back.' He's like, 'Coach, there's someone on that floor that thinks they belong on the same floor as me, and I want to make sure that I left no doubt that they know they have no business being on the floor with me.'"

***

West transferred to Eleanor Roosevelt as a sophomore in the fall of 1998. By then, he had attended at least five other schools and bounced around from Washington, DC, to the Maryland towns of Largo, Suitland, Clinton, Oxon Hill, Hyattsville, and, finally, Greenbelt, his family at times living in the basement with cousins or a room in an apartment with an aunt. While his childhood was transient, West always took solace and comfort playing basketball, sometimes shooting through a crate attached to a telephone pole.[11]

Farello quickly recognized West's talent and intangibles. "He had this chip on his shoulder," Farello said. "He was so driven."

The coach started out by playing West on the JV team, elevating him to varsity after a few contests. In West's first varsity game, Roosevelt was uncharacteristically routed by 20 points. West's reaction afterward signaled to Farello that there was something special about his new transfer.

"I'm losing my mind on everybody afterwards in the locker room," Farello said. "And Delonte raised his hand. I'm like, 'Oh my gosh, this kid is going to say something.' He stands up and says, 'Coach, I want to apologize to you and all my teammates for the way I played tonight. I promise it will never happen again.' His first varsity game, I'll never forget it: six points, four rebounds, two steals. He had a good start. I was stunned. I looked at him and thought to myself, 'Here's this sophomore, there's something here with this kid.'"

West kept his promise and did whatever he could to improve in order to help not just himself but his team. When Farello explained that West needed to work on his midrange shooting game so that opponents couldn't sit in a zone to deny his breathtaking ability to drive to the basket, West did just that in a way that even the coach couldn't have imagined.

"Two weeks go by and he scores 24 points, and 20 of them were on pull-up, midrange jump shots," Farello said. "I'm like, 'Delonte, this is exactly what I talked about. That was great.' He said, 'Coach, that's all I've done for eight hours a day for the last two weeks ever since you told me I needed to add that to my game.'"

West continued to get better, but big-time college coaches weren't taking much notice. This was in part because some coaches weren't exactly sure what West was positionally, as he wasn't an elite ball handler to be a point guard or an elite shooter to be a shooting guard. What he was, as the world would later find out, was a *basketball player* with an unquenchable desire to improve. In addition to questions about his position, his recruiting was hurt by being overshadowed at Roosevelt by Delonte Holland (DePaul) and Eddie Basden (UNC Charlotte), both of whom went on to play Division I. Besides St. Joe's, West was drawing lower-level Division I interest from Towson, Manhattan, and Siena.

"Delonte was undervalued," Farello said. "Not by any of us locally. We all saw it."

If not for Farello's rule that none of his players could commit on a recruiting visit, West would've ended up at Siena.

"He called me from Siena and was like, 'Coach, I want to commit,'" Farello said. "'Coach, man, the Pepsi Arena, I've never seen such an awesome arena.' I said, 'Well, you're not. You're not going to Siena because of the arena. I'm not letting that happen.'"

Michael Malone, the current coach of the NBA's Denver Nuggets, was an assistant at Manhattan. He recognized West's talents and really wanted him, Farello said. After Martelli saw him in New Jersey, the Hawks also were in strong pursuit of West. Playing against Nelson during his visit to St. Joe's in September 2000 helped convince West to sign with the Hawks.

"Delonte respected Jameer so much and said, 'I want to play with him,'" Farello said.

West also later recounted how the fact that St. Joe's games were on television more than Towson, Manhattan, and Siena helped tip the scale in the Hawks' favor.[12]

With his commitment behind him, West continued to dedicate himself to improving his game and finished his senior season at Roosevelt by averaging 20.3 points, 6.5 rebounds, 5.0 assists, and 4.0 steals. For his success, he was named Metro Player of the Year by the *Washington Post* in the talent-rich DMV (Delaware, Maryland, Virginia) region that has produced some of the game's best players.

It was a notable honor, but West wasn't settling for newspaper accolades.

"I was like, 'That was a nice article, what did you think?'" Farello asked West about the accompanying feature story that came with player of the year. "He said, 'Coach, I didn't like it at all. It was like an obituary, like I'm done. I'm not done yet. I'm just getting started.'"

West couldn't have been more prescient. At St. Joe's, the very best of Delonte West would be on display. But it wouldn't happen right away.

***

A Jesuit education emphasizes developing the whole person, caring for the mind, body, and spirit. At first, West struggled in all three areas after arriving at Hawk Hill.

On the court as a freshman, he was frustrated with his role as a backup and averaged 5.9 points and 3.0 rebounds in 17 minutes while starting just two of 31 contests. West tried 17 attempts from three-point range that season and missed 15 of them, just an 11.8 percent success rate. Off the court, he wasn't faring any better academically, and there were some emotional hurdles that, tragically, would become a more pronounced problem later in life.

Enter Matt Brady and Alicia (DiMarco) Lange.

Lange was Saint Joseph's coordinator of academic services for student-athletes and worked with Chuck Sack to help all Hawks athletes. Lange, who holds master's degrees from the University of Virginia in counselor's education and sports psychology, took a special interest in West. She provided him with just the right combination of empathy and tough love. Academically, Lange discovered that West was misplaced as a business major.

"Delonte always had a marble composition book, and it looked a mess," Lange said. "I remember Chuck and I saying, 'You don't take your notes in that. What is that?' Like, 'This is why you're having a problem.' He's like, 'No, it's my book.' We were like, 'What do you mean, your book?' And he opened it up and the sketches and the poetry. 'Delonte, you're an artist.' And he's like, 'I don't know, am I?' I looked at Chuck and was like, 'He's in the wrong major.'"

Lange immediately switched West's major to fine arts, and he excelled. She recalled him painting a replica of a Georgia O'Keeffe work that hung on her office wall to perfection, getting an "A" on the assignment. Later, Neil Hartman, a sports TV reporter for Comcast SportsNet, spent a day at West's apartment to chronicle his stunning charcoal sketch of Martelli that the coach framed and that is one of four pieces from West that Martelli still has in his house today.

"With Delonte's artistic skills, if he was in today's world with NIL [Name, Image, and Likeness], he would've made a couple hundred thousand dollars," Martelli said. "People would've rallied to his stuff."

The new major was a perfect fit for West.

"He really did blossom in that [major]," Lange said. "He could've had things in galleries. His talent was crazy. He could draw, he could paint, he could've written music. And if you watched him, he was creative on the court. Like, the court and basketball were his instruments [for art] as well. And he loved it. That was his safe place, the court."

The switch to art helped West academically. And while all of his emotional hurdles didn't just disappear, being happier academically and having the support of Lange and others put West in a headspace to succeed.

"Delonte is not able to evolve as a student-athlete if it wasn't for the impact of Alicia," Farello said. "Her work with Delonte and willingness to work with me to help him where he needed to be [were key]. She loved him. I give her so much credit and have so much appreciation for what she did for him to help him. And she held him accountable. She was one of the people Delonte really respected. He doesn't stay or make it through if it wasn't for people like Alicia. They really did a good job of getting Delonte into the type of environment he could thrive. He needed that. That was fun to see."

West also needed some help with his game. And Brady was just the person for it.

***

Brady had been on Martelli's staff from Day One and was the Hawks' shooting guru. He had helped point guard Rashid Bey transform into a very good shooter from 1994 to 1998 and had helped to refine already good shooters, like Terrell Myers and Mark Bass. Right away, Brady saw problems with West's mechanics and invited him to make some changes in September before his freshman season.

"And in his quiet and very humble way, he said, 'Coach, I think I'm good. I think I got it,'" Brady said. "I had him entertain the idea, he immediately kind of rebuffed that opportunity, and I was fine with that. I've done this so many times with other guys. They've got to be willing to change."

After shooting just 11.8 percent from three-point range, missing 15 of 17 shots, in his rookie season, West knocked on Brady's office door.

"'Coach, I see what you mean, I have to get better,'" Brady recalled of the conversation. "That's a humbling thing for such a terrific talent and coming off such a significant senior year. That he had the maturity to seek me out and say, 'Coach, I'm ready. What do we have to do?' We really got right to it."

Brady had noticed that West's release point on his jumper was high over his head. He dropped West's release point by two inches and created a 90-degree angle at his elbow, thus resulting in a more powerful, consistent stroke.

"In sports, you don't really do anything with your arms extended away from your body," Brady said. "If you're a hitter, you want the ball down the middle of the plate. You don't want to reach all the way out across the plate because you lose power. Same with a golf swing. Same with a tennis swing."

They began by shooting from 15 feet away from the basket with West's feet planted to the ground. Then, they added a jump shot from that distance. Slowly, they worked back farther and farther away from the basket.

"Delonte took right to it," Brady said. "Inside of a couple of days, if not the first day, the ball was going in at a really high level. Once a teacher and student get together and they see immediate success, the buy-in is clearly going to be there for both of us. Once the buy-in is there, it becomes, 'How much time are they willing to put into it?'"

Putting the work in was West's strength. Much like after Farello suggested improving his midrange game, West practiced jumper after jumper after jumper from long range.

"He just took it and ran with it," Brady said. "He worked on it so hard, so diligently. He would be in the gym late when nobody else was in the gym because he was very determined to maximize his own ability."

Unlike in high school with the midrange jumper, West wasn't satisfied with devoting *just* eight hours per day to his long-range shot.

"I know there were times when Delonte was getting kicked out of the gym because it was two, three in the morning," Jones said. "Security is like, 'Delonte, you can't be in here.'"

So, West would head to the locker room for a few hours of rest.

"He would sleep in the locker room so he could get up extra shots," Jones said.

West's relentless devotion to his craft, along with being in a more peaceful place academically and emotionally, led to a breakout sophomore season. He started 22 of 26 games in 2002–03 and earned first-team Atlantic 10 and Big 5 honors, being named the Most Improved Player in both, after averaging 17.3 points, 4.3 rebounds, and 3.2 assists. Incredibly, he increased his three-point percentage by more than 25 percent, hitting 37.4 percent (55 of 147) from beyond the arc as a sophomore. His sophomore statistics might have been even better had he not suffered a stress fracture in his right fibula down the stretch that forced him to miss three of the final eight games and play like a shell of himself in the five others.

West had gone from a barely recruited Division I player to one of the best in the Atlantic 10. With West's emergence, combined with Nelson's dominance, St. Joe's now had arguably one of the best backcourts in the country heading into the 2003–04 season. And Martelli had recruited just the right complements around Nelson and West for the Hawks to excel.

CHAPTER 4

Supporting Cast Relishes Their Roles

With Jameer Nelson, Saint Joseph's had a bona fide star and a legitimate contender for the country's top player entering the 2003–04 season. Beside him, Delonte West gave the Hawks a 1-2 backcourt punch that would be the envy of every Division I head coach.

But Nelson and West couldn't do it all by themselves. Luckily for them, they were surrounded by the perfect supporting cast. Individually, none of their running mates would be mentioned as an All-American candidate. Put all of the Hawks together, however, and you had a practically unstoppable force. Not only did Nelson and West's teammates accept their roles, they relished them. And each player's contribution was crucial to the entire team's success.

"Everybody knew their role," Nelson said. "We had a team full of selfless guys. Nobody cared who scored, nobody cared who got the assists. It was collaborative, man. I always tell people we didn't have the most athletic team, but we had the overall best group of guys that you can put on the floor."

Nelson's impact on the team was felt long before he ever took the floor at St. Joe's. Both Pat Carroll and Dwayne Jones came to Hawk Hill largely because of him.

***

Carroll, a 6-foot-5 guard, had competed against Nelson in high school at Hatboro-Horsham. He was not highly recruited like his brother, Matt, who was two years older and would go on to play at Notre Dame. But Pat Carroll was an excellent shooter from long range and a winner, having helped the Hatters to 105 victories while lettering in all four seasons. Phil Martelli saw a lot of Pat Carroll as a high school freshman when he was recruiting Matt. That also played an important factor when Pat Carroll chose St. Joe's over Duquesne.

"My family developed a great relationship with Martelli when he recruited Matt," Pat Carroll said. "He put in a lot of time. Over those years, he built trust and was genuine with not just me but my whole family. I knew he was the coach I wanted to play for in college. He helped make that decision an easy one for me."

Also, there was the Nelson factor.

Carroll experienced Nelson's greatness firsthand when Nelson hit a game-winning shot in overtime over Carroll's outstretched arms in the PIAA District 1 Class AAAA semifinals in 1999. Nelson's Chester teams also won the other two matchups against Hatboro-Horsham while Carroll was there. Carroll knew how good the Hawks' future point guard was and got even more of a taste of it up close following his junior season when teaming with Nelson at the Donofrio Classic, the postseason All-Star game in Conshohocken, Pennsylvania, which has featured practically all of the Philadelphia area's top talent over the years.

"Jameer and I always had a mutual respect competing against each other in high school, but having the opportunity to play together in the Donofrio opened my eyes to the type of teammate and person he was," Carroll said. "Complete respect. The ultimate teammate."

Along with Martelli, Nelson lured Carroll to Hawk Hill.

"It was a no-brainer to team up with him in college," Carroll said. "And, besides, he beat me three times in high school. It was about damn time I got to team up with him at SJU!"

Martelli recognized that Nelson's recruiting of Carroll, without having to say any words, worked as well as the coach's well-received pitch.

"[Carroll's] family would say to him, 'That kid is going to make you really special,'" Martelli said.

And they were right. After playing a bit part as a freshman, Carroll emerged as a sophomore in 2002–03 when he started 30 games and made 76 of 169 three-pointers, hitting on an Atlantic 10-leading 45 percent from beyond the arc, while averaging 11.5 points in 25.3 minutes per contest. Besides Nelson's playmaking and Martelli's coaching, Carroll also was helped that season by the constant encouragement of Phil Martelli Jr., a little-used senior reserve guard who, like his father, would go on to become a Division I head coach.

Martelli Jr. rebounded every Carroll three-point shot during warm-ups with a pass back and a message: You're the best shooter in the nation.

"I used to tell him that every single time," Martelli Jr. said. "I believed that. I thought Pat was incredible."

Carroll also started to believe the message, something that was reiterated by the head coach and assistants Mark Bass, Matt Brady, and Monté Ross.

"They built the confidence in me, and I think that's something special that Coach Martelli, Phil Jr., and the three assistants did," Carroll said. "They made me believe that I was the best shooter in the nation. Whether I was or not, it didn't matter."

In fact, Carroll was close to the best three-point shooter in the country as a sophomore, ranking seventh. And, as a junior in 2003–04, he was primed to continue right where he left off.

***

Unlike Carroll, Jones was not going to impress anyone with his shooting. In fact, the 6-foot-11 center didn't attempt a single three-pointer in his three-year Hawks career. Around the rim, though, Jones was an intimidating presence on offense and defense.

Like Nelson, Jones was from Chester. They also played together on the AAU circuit. Unlike Nelson, Jones didn't attend Chester High School, instead going to Chester's American Christian Academy, where he put up ridiculously good stats as a senior of 25.8 points, 17.8 rebounds, and 6.4 blocks per contest. When Jones heard that Nelson and another AAU teammate, Jeff Miller, had committed to the Hawks, he figured he'd follow in their footsteps.

"Having two good friends, teammates that I was comfortable with, definitely played a big part in me choosing St. Joe's," he said.

Had he known what would happen when he arrived on campus, though, Jones might have picked another school. He was buried on the depth chart, and the Hawks staff, seeing the opportunity for Jones to bulk up even more, convinced him to redshirt for what would have been his freshman season in 2001–02. For Jones, it was difficult and disappointing to sit idly during games and watch, and it took several calls home for encouragement to stick it out.

"It was just going from playing all of the time and being 'the man' in high school the past three years before that, and coming here and being told to wait a year was definitely rough for me," Jones, known by his nickname of "DJ," said. "I remember that first year I was kind of upset. I remember talking to my dad and trying to figure it out."

In today's era of college basketball, with the NCAA transfer portal and Name, Image, and Likeness (NIL) deals, it's unlikely Jones would have returned for his redshirt freshman season. Back then, his dad counseled him to hang in there.

"Taking a step back and putting my ego aside and realizing I'm 18 years old and there wasn't going to be much playing time," he said. "So, I appreciate Coach Martelli and his staff thinking about me long-term and realizing I would be better off waiting a year."

Jones used that redshirt season to practice, learn the speed of the college game, and continue to add to his already muscular frame. As the season went on, and particularly looking back, he realized how valuable it was.

"It helped me to sit back," he said. "I got to practice every day and compete against a lot of good guys. I was able to add muscle and strength. And being able to sit there and analyze the game, going into next summer [I knew] what I need to work on: getting stronger, being more physical, focus on finishing around the rim and, defensively, the timing and speed of the game. I think I was able to use [the redshirt year] to my advantage."

He took all that he learned and applied it on the court in a fantastic debut season as a redshirt freshman in 2002–03, leading the Hawks in rebounding (6.3 per game) and the A-10 in blocks (2.0 per contest).

"DJ blocked and rebounded everything," Dave Mallon said.

Mallon wouldn't have the statistical impact of Jones, but his role also helped define what made the Hawks great. It wasn't exactly the role he wanted, but it was the role he had—and he was going to play it to perfection.

***

Like Jones, Mallon was tall, at 6-foot-10. But their games were different. Though not physically imposing like Jones, Mallon could bang inside. However, he also could play away from the basket and knock down a jump shot, including a three-pointer. He showed that at East Aurora (NY) High School, where he put up big numbers as a senior, accumulating 21 points, 11 rebounds, and 7.3 blocks per game. Martelli thought so highly of Mallon that he started him in 29 of 30 contests as a freshman in 2002–03. But Mallon wasn't asked to score. Mostly, he was setting screens to free Nelson, West, and Carroll.

In part due to injuries, Mallon's role would diminish even more heading into 2003–04, as he would mostly be coming off the bench. Of course, Mallon would've loved to have been a more prominent option, but he embraced helping the team however he could.

"I think Jameer said it, 'It's amazing how many games you can win when you don't care who scores the ball,'" Mallon said. "And that was that [2003–04] team. Everybody's ego was in check and was out the door. Jameer was always steady, Eddie out there. The rest of us were like, 'Who's cooking? Who's got it going? How are we going to beat this team? What can we contribute?' Nobody cared about stat stuffing. The only thing that mattered in the end was, 'Did we score more than them?' Everybody took pride in that."

Mallon never complained to Martelli about his role. And the coach never heard from family members of Mallon, or any other player. That was also what helped set up the Hawks for success.

"It just fit," Martelli said of Mallon's new reserve role as a sophomore. "And never, never, like, 'Ah, I'm leaving.' And his parents, that's the great, untold thing about that team, the parental support, the family support, was just extraordinary. There was no Little League parenting. Dave is a beautiful, beautiful example of: It was always about the greater good. There was no individual thing, even with all the things that came at Jameer and everything that came at me. It was always going to be about the whole group. Not any one."

Mallon pressed forward, battling through bumps and bruises to help in any way he could. He was inspired by Nelson's example.

"Jameer had an attitude that if I can do it, you can do it," Mallon said. "If I can shoot five thousand jumpers after practice, you can. If I can go get six rebounds, you can go get six rebounds. He had this way of carrying himself but also bringing his teammates with him. He never acted better, or on a pedestal, or anything. His thing was, 'I give it my all, I need you to give your all. It's not fair to me if you're not going to give equal to what I'm giving.' He gave everything. The way that he carried himself with that and that attitude is really what kept us going along.

"You knew to trust him. You believe everything he said. You believe every move he makes. And he made mistakes, too. He'd say, 'I need to see you on that.' He was a coach on the court. He held you to his own standard. As a young player, you need that. And you need a voice like that."

Even today, successfully established in business as an insurance broker, Mallon never sells himself short, in part because of Nelson.

"Whatever he can do, there's no reason for you not to do it," Mallon said of Nelson's message. "And to learn from that. That has carried into different aspects of my life. When I see people at work doing something, I say, 'That's brilliant.' Well, they had to learn from somewhere. If they can do it, why can't I do it? It was a cool lesson that has carried on. Like, don't cut yourself short. You can do just as much as anyone else."

With Nelson as his guide, Mallon was going to do everything he could to help the Hawks in 2003–04. Even if that meant reversing roles with John Bryant.

***

At 6-foot-7, Bryant was a frontcourt player like Mallon and Jones. Unlike them, Bryant put up comparably modest numbers as a senior at Woodbridge High School in Virginia, averaging 9.9 points and 7.8 rebounds. None of the Division I schools in his home state recruited him, and there was little interest elsewhere. But Bass saw something in Bryant, as much for his potential and intangibles as anything he witnessed on the court in high school.

"He was intriguing," Bass said. "He was athletic, still figuring out the game. Highly intelligent. I thought he could be a piece to what we were building that year. Come to find out, he was a great piece to that team. He bought into what we were trying to do. He knew his role on the team, and he fit in on and off the court on the team and in the St. Joe's community."

Bryant continued to put up modest numbers at St. Joe's, averaging 3.0 points and 3.5 rebounds as a freshman in 2002–03 when he came off the bench in 29 of 30 games. But it really didn't matter to him.

"I didn't care about my points or rebounds," he said.

What Bryant did care about was instilled in him by his father, also named John, at a young age. Whenever Bryant played, he was going to give everything he had and be the best teammate possible, just as his dad taught him.

"Essentially, he only said, 'Hustle and try your best every time you're on the floor,'" Bryant said of his father, who passed away in 2021. "When I played, I wasn't going to score 30. I wasn't going to grab 20 rebounds. But you certainly were going to get my best. I didn't take myself too seriously where I thought I should be doing those things. But I did take myself seriously being the best teammate I could be and the hardest worker on the floor."

He only wanted to hear one thing when people commented on his game.

"'He's certainly giving it his all,'" Bryant said, before laughingly adding. "It might not always be the outcome we want, but he's certainly giving it his all."

Bass was correct about Bryant's intangibles and intelligence. They have carried him far professionally, and he entered the 2024–25 NBA season as the top assistant coach for the Chicago Bulls. It would not be a surprise for him to be a head coach in the NBA one day. At the highest level, he has coached the game's top stars. But he also highly values players, like him, who don't get the mega headlines and do the little things to help the team win.

"I respect the guys who play hard every single night," Bryant said of current NBA players. "That was my role. If I can do something to make a hustle play that might spark something for our group, then I've done my job."

Just like Mallon, Bryant was perfectly content doing whatever he could to help the Hawks win. In 2003–04, that would mean taking over for Mallon as a starter. His job would be to set screens and do all the dirty work down low, not glamorous but what the team needed. And that was just fine by Bryant.

"I've been a part of a lot of teams since then," Bryant said. "Sometimes on teams, people are externally or internally motivated. I think about our team, it just was, it just was a team."

It was a team that would become great. And every great team plays great defense. And there likely wasn't another player in the country who enjoyed playing defense more than Tyrone Barley.

***

Barley wanted to go to Seton Hall. He grew up in Newark, New Jersey, just a few miles away from the Pirates' South Orange campus, where he'd often go to work out. That was his dream school.

"Not being offered a scholarship at Seton Hall didn't sit well with me," Barley said.

He also understood. He was on a great high school team at Seton Hall Prep, which sent four players in his senior class to Division I programs. But Barley didn't put up big numbers, averaging 10 points per contest, in part because there were other talented players on his high school team and in large part because he relished stopping opponents more than scoring points.

"I enjoyed that more than scoring, which is opposite," Barley said of playing defense. "Most people want to score."

Barley remembers a high school All-Star game following his senior year in which everyone but him was interested in putting on an offensive show.

"All I cared about was playing defense," he said. "I'm taking charges in the All-Star game. When do you ever see that? I didn't care. Whoever I was playing against, I didn't want you to score, even in an All-Star game."

Barley's defense and his just-enough scoring attracted the Hawks. He knew very little about Saint Joseph's and, unlike Carroll and Jones, knew nothing about Nelson. Very quickly, Barley found out about Nelson. They came in as freshmen together, and Barley eagerly defended his classmate and fellow point guard during the first week of practices. Barley, who had played against some of the best guards in the country in high school, had never seen anyone like Nelson before.

"I always took anyone scoring on me so personal," Barley said. "But [that first week of practices] I could not stop Jameer at all, like I don't understand it, he was incredible. Me and my pride, I was like I can stop anybody, anytime. I remember this one practice, he was just playing with me. How can this be? He threw the ball between my legs and got it back and stepped back for the three. The game for him, he had to see it in slow motion, or something. He was too advanced for his age at the time.

"When I say this never happens against me, it never happens. But that's when I knew this kid is so special."

Other than Nelson, no one would have success scoring on Barley during his four years at St. Joe's. As with most of his career, he came off the bench in 2002–03 as a junior and immediately locked down the opposition. Barley's tenacity helped the Hawks lead the nation in field goal defense in 2002–03, holding opponents to 37.2 percent shooting, while finishing seventh in scoring defense (59.5 points per game).

"Tyrone didn't want you to get a good shot," Brady said. "He never wanted you to be comfortable."

If anything, Barley was even more locked in heading into his senior season, not only defensively but offensively as well, thanks to a budding confidence in his new three-point shot that he and Brady worked on following his junior year. He looked forward to bringing his hard work in the offseason to a game.

Chet Stachitas also was known for his defense before college. Only, it was on the soccer field, where he excelled as a center back. That would change after a move to Florida that would set up Stachitas to be another key player for Saint Joseph's in 2003–04.

***

Like Barley, Stachitas did not have St. Joe's at the top of his college list. Unlike Barley, he had impressed recruiters with his offensive game. After relocating from the Philadelphia suburbs to Ponte Vedra Beach, Florida, Stachitas scored 2,505 career points and had his jersey retired at Nease High School.

Before moving to Florida, Stachitas was a big-time Pennsylvania youth soccer star, making the state's Olympic Development Team as a defender. In Florida, though, soccer and basketball seasons clashed, and Stachitas chose basketball, in part because college basketball offers full college scholarships, unlike college soccer. An excellent student whose parents both attended the University of Pennsylvania, Stachitas had his heart set on Stanford. But he was the second choice at his position on their list, and the Cardinal coaches did not have a spot for him after their top target, Dan Grunfeld, committed. Stachitas pivoted and decided between Penn and St. Joe's, ultimately choosing the Hawks.

As a freshman in 2002–03, Stachitas averaged 3.0 points in 10.5 minutes. Though a prolific scorer in high school, he was never a great shooter from long range. In fact, he had more of an archaic set shot from distance in high school. With Brady's help, he began to become a jump shooter from beyond the arc after arriving at St. Joe's. But he had marginal success as a freshman, shooting 26.3 percent from three-point range. Stachitas wanted more minutes and knew the only way would be to improve his jumper.

"I wanted to have a bigger impact on the team and contribute more, so I had to go to work," he said. "I just knew if I was going to contribute, I have an opportunity here going small with the four guards and really stretching out the floor and knocking down shots. It definitely was a point of improvement in my game."

Just like Barley, Stachitas put in work in the offseason before the 2003–04 season to better his long-range shot, and he was eager to display it. He knew his role would be as a contributor and hoped to get as many minutes as possible. However many he got, his mentality would be certain.

"I know I have half the game to bust my ass, basically," he said.

Dwayne Lee wouldn't get on the court anywhere near half the game. Not as Nelson's backup at point guard. Like Stachitas, though, he was going to make the most of every single minute.

***

More than anyone at St. Joe's, Lee knew all about what made great teams, having played at famed St. Anthony's in Jersey City, New Jersey, for legendary high school coach Bob Hurley Sr. As a senior, Lee averaged 12.6 points and four assists to help St. Anthony's win its second consecutive New Jersey Tournament of Champions title in 2001–02 when they ended the season ranked No. 2 in the country by *USA Today*.

In spite of his talent, which he would eventually showcase in his final two seasons on Hawk Hill, Lee could barely get on the court as a freshman with Nelson ahead of him, chipping in 1.3 points and 0.6 assists in 7.6 minutes per game. But Lee was going to do everything he could to help make the team better.

"My role was to be ready when my number was called, to really push these guys in practice," said Lee, who has gone on to become a successful Division I assistant coach. "I guarded Jameer every single day in practice. I saw my role as a guy who would just keep the guys sharp and make sure they were prepared for the game."

And whenever he entered to give Nelson a breather, or if Saint Joseph's star point guard got into foul trouble, Lee, the final piece of the Hawks' regular nine-man rotation, was determined to maintain Nelson's elite level.

"I didn't want there to be a drop-off," he said. "I wanted to build off the leads those guys were able to build and take it from 10 to 14 or eight to 12. I wanted to be a star in that role, really take a step back and not look at it selfishly because, honestly, we all are competitors and want to play. That's what I wanted. But you could see the season materialize into something special. It wasn't about me. It was about the group."

***

Lee had a team-first mentality, just like Carroll, Jones, Mallon, Bryant, Barley, and Stachitas. They all played hard. They all played for one another. They all played to win.

"We complemented each other with our games, just the role clarity and the buy-in from everybody," Carroll said. "There was nothing like it."

As a result of the acceptance of their roles in order to make the team better, the players developed a genuine chemistry with one another that can be hard to create.

"There were no cliques, we were all friends, everybody was cool," Jones said. "We hung out with each other off the court, we worked out with each other, we had class together. We were a very close-knit group, and we all had the same goal of wanting to compete. Nobody had an ego. And it was just all about us."

They all were excited to come together for the most anticipated season in Hawks history. There was just one potential problem: Jameer Nelson was considering playing in the NBA in 2003–04 and not on Hawk Hill.

CHAPTER 5

Jameer Nelson's Big Preseason Decision

Don DiJulia couldn't wait to see for himself what all the hype was about with Jameer Nelson. Now in the 15th year of his second term as St. Joe's athletic director entering the 2003–04 season, DiJulia knew as much about the 94-year history of Hawks basketball as anyone. The school itself wasn't big, but its passion for basketball was huge. In addition to producing many superb players, St. Joe's became a cradle of sorts of NBA coaches, having sent seven former players to lead NBA teams. After topping the nation in scoring (23.4 points per game) as a St. Joe's senior in 1943, George Senesky went on to a playing and coaching career with the Philadelphia Warriors. He coached the Warriors to the NBA title in 1956. And, in 1977, former Hawks coach and alumnus Jack Ramsay led the Portland Trail Blazers to the NBA title with another previous St. Joe's coach and alumnus, Jack McKinney, on his staff. DiJulia was a member of Ramsay's famed 1964–65 Hawks team that went 26-1 in the regular season. DiJulia either played with, or knew practically everything about, every single player ever to wear a Hawks jersey.

So, he was eager to compare Nelson to the greatest former Hawks. DiJulia, as anyone who has ever encountered him will attest, is not one to boast. But, like assistant coach Monté Ross, head coach Phil Martelli, and *Philadelphia Daily News* college basketball writer Dick Jerardi before him, DiJulia was blown away the first time he saw Nelson play. DiJulia's initial look came on November 17, 2000, when Nelson tallied 11 points, eight assists, three rebounds, and two steals in 24 minutes against Western Carolina in his debut as a freshman. After Nelson followed that with 12 points, nine assists, and five rebounds in the next contest against South Carolina State and then netted 15 against Vanderbilt in his third game, DiJulia started to think back to every prominent guard in Hawks history for context.

"Who were our guards that were outstanding at St. Joe's?" DiJulia thought. "Can he do the things that they did? Obviously, we've had a ton."

DiJulia settled on Jim Lynam, Matt Guokas, and Dan Kelly as three to whom to compare Nelson. The AD couldn't think of anything any of those stellar Hawks did any better than Nelson.

"I'm watching Jameer play two or three games and I'm thinking, 'Yeah, he can do what they did,'" DiJulia said. "'Oh my goodness, this guy hasn't played four games yet as a freshman, and he might be one of the best players we've ever had.'"

As is his way, DiJulia was keeping his thoughts close to his inner circle, if not to himself. Martelli, though, continued to promote Nelson with even higher praise than before, telling Jerardi in mid-November that the freshman was even better than he thought when he recruited him.[13] The coach's words proved to be true, as Nelson's brilliance helped the Hawks win 14 of 16 Atlantic 10 games and finish 26-7 overall in 2000–01, losing a 90-83 thriller in the NCAA tournament to top-seeded Stanford to end their season. Nelson had 14 points, nine rebounds, and nine assists in that second-round game, which was highlighted by Marvin O'Connor's 37 points for St. Joe's.

Nelson continued from there. By the time he completed his junior season, Nelson was unquestionably one of the best players in school history, if not the best, after accumulating 1,435 points and 543 assists while starting 93 games (missing one due to a funeral) and leading St. Joe's to a 68-26 (.723) overall record and 38-10 (.792) mark in the A-10. He finished his junior season in 2002–03 by dazzling the country with 32 points in a first-round NCAA loss to Auburn.

Nelson no longer was a secret. Far from it. Martelli didn't have to shout his star guard's merits from a megaphone—though the coach would continue doing so—because everyone saw what Ross witnessed at a high school gym in 1997, Martelli and Jerardi saw at Villanova in the District 1 final in 1999, and DiJulia marveled at in the first three games of the point guard's St. Joe's career in 2000: Jameer Nelson was a special player. Everyone knew it—including NBA scouts.

**

In 2003, the NCAA had a rule that prospects could work out for NBA teams and still maintain their college eligibility as long as they didn't hire an agent. It was a no-brainer for Nelson to test the NBA waters after his junior season, and the Hawks coaching staff supported his decision.

"No one was like, 'Jameer, come back, come back, we need you,'" St. Joe's assistant coach Mark Bass said. "It was like, 'Go test it, man. See what they say.' No one was upset. It was an opportunity for Jameer and his family. Everyone bought in."

Nelson flew to Chicago for the NBA predraft camp, held June 3–6 at Moody Bible Institute. Things got off to a rough start for Nelson when an elbow from future NBA guard and head coach Willie Green cracked a tooth and required two stitches to mend a cut on his jaw.[14] Nelson brushed off any pain this caused and performed admirably in three games, averaging 10.3 points and 6.3 assists.[15] Although Martelli said NBA types provided positive feedback about Nelson's showing in Chicago, the Hawks guard had two things working against him in his quest to be a first-round pick and earn a guaranteed contract: the abundance of talented point guards available for the 2003 NBA draft and, as with his college recruitment, his height.[16]

Nelson's game usually made people forget about his height, but the measuring tape could not be swayed. In Chicago, he came in an inch shorter than his previously listed height of 6 feet.[17] It also didn't help Nelson that so many players who played his position were vying for NBA scouts' attention. In fact, nine point guards, led by Kirk Hinrich (No. 7 overall) and T. J. Ford (No. 8), would be selected in the first round of the NBA draft on June 26, 2003. Nelson held one final workout at St. Joe's for the Orland Magic, the Trail Blazers, and the Detroit Pistons on June 16, just three days before the June 19 deadline to withdraw from the draft or lose your college eligibility. As late as the night before the deadline when Jerardi called him for comment, Nelson still wasn't sure whether to pursue the NBA or return to college. "It was *that* close," Jerardi said. Ultimately, the lack of assurance that he would be a first-round pick and his comfort with St. Joe's led Nelson to choose a return to college for his senior season over early entry into the NBA.

"I just wanted to be put into a situation to be successful," Nelson said. "I didn't feel like I was ready for the NBA, for whatever reason. I'm sure I could've figured it out. But I really enjoyed college and really enjoyed playing in front of the St. Joe's community and fans, my family, and friends."

Nelson told his coaches and teammates on June 19 that he would be back. While everyone wanted what was best for Nelson, obviously they all were elated to get the news that he was returning for his senior season.

"It was like, 'OK, now let's get everybody together, get working, and continue to get better for the season,'" Bass said.

There certainly was no shortage of confidence for what the Hawks could accomplish in 2003–04. The loss to Auburn, with St. Joe's playing shorthanded due to a hobbled Delonte West, not only showed them what they could accomplish but left them with a bad taste in their mouths.

"All we were talking about was making a run," Dwayne Lee said of the upcoming season.

The run West was thinking about wasn't just about an A-10 title or another trip to the NCAA tournament. He talked about winning a national championship and going undefeated when the Hawks met in an upstairs shared space at the Fieldhouse, known as the Hall of Fame room, to discuss preseason expectations.[18]

"I remember," Hawks assistant coach Matt Brady said, "Delonte said in his very quiet demeanor, 'No reason why we shouldn't go undefeated.' I remember him saying that exactly. There were no real snickers. I'm not sure we believed that would happen, but I do think that portrayed that confidence that that group had in themselves. They did believe they had the right team and the right guys on the team."

That confidence started with Jameer Nelson.

***

Like West, Nelson was thinking big as the 2003–04 season approached.

"I knew we had a really good team that could hopefully create some buzz for the program but also some unfinished business," Nelson said. "We made it to the [NCAA] tournament my junior year and lost to Auburn. I thought we could've gone further, so I wanted to try to win a national championship. It was a healthy arrogance that I had for the team and the expectations."

Chet Stachitas immediately felt the sense of assuredness that oozed throughout the program from Nelson on down.

"I remember someone said [before his freshman season in 2002–03], 'We can go the whole year without losing back-to-back games,'" Stachitas recalled. "As an incoming freshman, you see some big names, Boston College, Villanova. I remember feeling like, 'If these guys believe that, I've got to believe that, too, and don't care what the name says across the chest of whoever we're playing. OK, we can compete with anybody.' If these guys believe that before the season even starts, I'm going to believe that now. That kind of set the tone."

Stachitas's confidence was riding even higher entering 2003–04 thanks to an offseason of work on his jumper, hoping it would lead to more minutes as a sophomore. Tyrone Barley was feeling similarly good. Not only had he been refining his jump shot, but Barley was inspired by attending an Alicia Keys concert in Philadelphia over the summer.

"I was sitting there pretty close to her, and I just saw perfection," Barley said of Keys, the R&B star. "I just saw her craft and how much she probably had to put into it to be as talented as she was. And I'm like, 'Hold up, I'm going out, I'm doing this, I'm staying up all late, I ain't working out.' Why? Work harder. Do things. Stay in the gym. That really was a moment where I said, 'I gotta do better.'"

Barley went to work, putting up even more long-range jumpers to hone his new form. Lifting even more weights. Dedicating himself completely to basketball.

This mentality was nothing new to West. But West had extra incentive, too, something he and high school coached Glenn Farello discussed over the summer after Nelson announced his return.

"We talked and said, 'Look, you have a great opportunity this year with Jameer,'" Farello recalled. "He wanted to get to the next level from the circumstances he was in as far as a financial standpoint. He was very motivated."

Barley and West couldn't wait to get on the court. In a preview of what was to come, the pair helped their Gray team rout the Nelson-led Crimson squad in a publicly held preseason scrimmage, known as Hawk Hoops Hysteria, on November 8, 2003, just six days before the season opener. They each scored 16 points in their 71-47 victory, with Barley draining four of seven shots from three-point range and helping Gray hold Crimson to just 38.2 percent field goal shooting with his typically tough defense.

The Hawks were eager to get on the floor for real. In a rarity for a St. Joe's team in the preseason, Associated Press voters placed the Hawks in the Top 25. They came in at No. 17, but it didn't add any pressure.

"That's the sign of a good team," Bass said of the ranking. "It was just like, 'That's a number. Let's go out and play basketball and do what we do. Let's lace them up and play who we have to play.'"

Everyone was feeling good, including athletic trainer Bill Lukasiewicz.

"I was definitely excited coming off the previous year," Lukasiewicz said. "We had everybody back. We were healthy going in. Monté Ross would say to me, 'If you do your job, we'll be alright.'"

And then an injury hit the Hawks. Dave Mallon went down in practice the day before Hawk Hoops Hysteria and learned two days later that he would be sidelined for three to six weeks with a stress fracture in his right foot that would hamper him all season.

"It was devastating," Mallon said. "I felt good about my role on the team. I felt like I was good at it at the time. Then, that injury happened. To be told you have broken bones in your foot, that hurts."

After the injury, Mallon also got a taste of just how big of a story the Hawks were. He was reclining at home the evening of his prognosis watching sports on television when he saw his name scroll across the ESPN screen.

"Somebody took the time to type my name and let people know we were injured," Mallon said. "We must be on to something."

Unfortunately for Mallon, when the Hawks tipped off the 2003–04 season, he was going to have to sit and watch—like seemingly every person who had any connection to St. Joe's. Not only were they playing the rubber match of a scintillating three-game series against West Coast Jesuit power Gonzaga, but the Hawks were opening on one of the world's biggest stages at New York City's Madison Square Garden. And no one with ties to the school or the program wanted to miss the start of what they all expected to be a magical season.

CHAPTER 6

Game 1: An Opening Statement

Friday, November 14, 2003
Madison Square Garden, New York
No. 17 Saint Joseph's vs. No. 10 Gonzaga

The excitement for Saint Joseph's 2003–04 season was boiling over from the moment Jameer Nelson announced he was returning for his senior season on June 19. Now, it was finally time to see the Hawks take the court for a real game, and no one associated with the school wanted to miss it.

Three days before its highly anticipated season-opening matchup against No. 10-ranked Gonzaga at Madison Square Garden, St. Joe's announced that it had sold 3,600 tickets to set an individual school's box-office record for the Coaches vs. Cancer Classic, eclipsing the previous mark of 3,200 tickets by UConn and 3,000 by Duke. By Friday night's game, the number of tickets sold exceeded the school's entire undergraduate enrollment of 3,850, as 4,100 tickets were bought through the school.[19] And many others in St. Joe's gear would just show up in New York on game day.

In the lead-up to the game, Hawks athletic director Don DiJulia scoured the campus to find anyone willing to drive a school bus of students to New York. He secured 15 drivers, each of whom received free admission in exchange for their service.

"We had to depend on a lot of volunteers across campus," DiJulia said. "Who wants a ticket to the game? Count [the students] when they start and make sure they're all on the bus on the way back."

Bill Avington, a 1994 Saint Joseph's graduate, didn't ride a bus up to New York; rather, he joined many St. Joe's supporters on New Jersey Transit trains that run from Central Jersey directly to Madison Square Garden. Avington's trip felt like a chartered train for Hawks fans.

"I remember seeing St. Joe's gear, hats, sweatshirts everywhere you looked on the New Jersey Transit train," he said.

Once he arrived, Avington saw even more Hawks attire.

"It was like a St. Joe's reunion up there," he said. "I remember being stunned by the amount of fans. The Garden is a big place. A third of the arena was St. Joe's people."

Philadelphia Daily News college basketball writer Dick Jerardi estimated that six thousand St. Joe's fans were in attendance.[20] "Our whole universe felt like they were in Madison Square Garden," DiJulia said.

Ray Parrillo, St. Joe's beat writer for the *Philadelphia Inquirer*, felt similarly. "The entire school and every St. Joe's alum in the country seemed to be there," he said.

The players also could feel the support.

"It literally felt like we were at the Fieldhouse," said Rob Sullivan, a sophomore walk-on in 2003–04. "That was the first moment of, 'Holy smokes, this is big-time national college basketball, and St. Joe's is part of it.'"

If the game was anything like the last two meetings between the teams, all of those Hawks fans—and everyone else in New York—would be treated to an evening of hoops that they wouldn't soon forget.

***

St. Joe's and Gonzaga had played on New Year's Eve each of the previous two seasons. Gonzaga, located in Spokane, Washington, is a Jesuit school like St. Joe's. Both had built powerhouse programs, overcoming their "mid-major" status in the process, and the many similarities were not lost on the players.

"We were the West Coast version of them, or they were the East Coast version of us," Cory Violette, a senior center for Gonzaga in 2003–04, said. "Small school, no football program, just basketball. We looked at them like they're built like us. You assume they're going through what we're going through."

Another thing in common was that both played their home games in buildings that had limited capacity and were incredibly tough on opponents, as each would find out. On December 31, 2001, Dan Dickau drained a three-pointer from the right wing with five seconds left at Alumni Memorial Fieldhouse, the Hawks' cozy, on-campus home, to lift the Zags to an 83-80 victory. A year later on New Year's Eve, Nelson scored 34 points and hit a running layup with eight seconds remaining in overtime to lead St. Joe's to a 79-78 victory that ended Gonzaga's 29-game winning streak at its 6,000-seat on-campus home, The Kennel. Just four total points separated the teams in a pair of contests that were both won in the final seconds.

All eyes were on the rubber match in New York, to see what would happen next in this thrilling series and to find out just how good the Hawks really were.

"It's like, 'OK fellas, let's go out there and see what we have,'" St. Joe's assistant coach Mark Bass said. "And see do we really belong?"

Among the St. Joe's contingent eager to find out was first-year Hawks radio play-by-play voice Tom McCarthy. Today, McCarthy is one of the top broadcasters in sports, as the television voice of the Philadelphia Phillies and a national college basketball and NFL announcer. Then, he was still building up his résumé and shifted from radio voice of Princeton basketball to the same position with the Hawks to further establish himself in the Philadelphia media market. The atmosphere and the buildup left McCarthy pinching himself over his new role.

"What the heck am I doing here?" he said. "This is amazing."

Perhaps the only person not full of adrenalin and excitement as tipoff approached was Hawks sophomore Dave Mallon, whose right foot was in a boot after sustaining a stress fracture in a preseason practice a week before the opener. His role for this game would be to cheer on his teammates from the bench, definitely not the role he had envisioned while working on his game all summer.

"It stunk," he said. "The Garden is filled in. This is the stage of all stages. I wanted to show I've been working and can do something here."

Mallon needed a pick-me-up, and his teammates would give Mallon and the 6,000 Hawks fans who turned Madison Square Garden into a very large, raucous Fieldhouse a lot to be happy about.

***

As the players were ready to jump center, Avington was thinking about the opportunity in front of the Hawks. With Nelson, St. Joe's had emerged as a legitimate force for the last three seasons. But Gonzaga had sustained success for even longer, winning at least 24 games in the previous six seasons, and had become a regular NCAA tournament team. The Zags had been particularly dominant in the two preceding seasons, going 53-13 (.803) overall and 25-3 (.893) in the West Coast Conference (WCC).

"Gonzaga was the standard-bearer for our kinds of schools, a Jesuit school that was a national program," Avington, a former sports editor of *The Hawk* student newspaper, said. "This is what we want to be, what we could be maybe."

The Hawks were ready to show Avington and everyone that an East Coast Jesuit powerhouse was possible, too. They gave Avington and thousands more St. Joe's fans plenty of reasons to cheer.

"I remember every basket sort of felt like it was at the Fieldhouse," Avington said.

Helped by this virtual home-court advantage, St. Joe's used a 16-4 run to start the second half to take a 50-42 lead that they wouldn't relinquish, eventually winning 73-66.

The Zags would be helped more later in the season by Adam Morrison, who scored 10 points in his college debut against the Hawks long before he would emerge as one of the nation's best college players and the No. 3 overall pick in the 2006 NBA draft. They also would eventually get back a healthy Ronny Turiaf, who managed just two points in five minutes while being hampered by a stress fracture. The 6-foot-10 Turiaf would go on to play 473 NBA games over nine seasons.

On this night, Turiaf was only slightly less of a spectator than Mallon, both watching Nelson's magnificent opener.

Nelson was just what Phil Martelli was telling anyone and everyone. If not the best player in America like his coach proclaimed, then Nelson at least was the best one on the floor this night. He had 20 points, 10 assists, eight rebounds, two steals, and just two turnovers in 27 minutes. ESPN's Dick Vitale, as is his way, was screaming superlatives into the microphone about Nelson.

"Get your tickets early!" Vitale yelled on the ESPN broadcast. "It will be the Jameer Nelson basketball show in Philadelphia!"

St. Joe's point guard's performance didn't surprise the Zags.

"We were nervous about him, and the coaching staff was nervous about him," Violette said. "We did not have anybody we thought could really guard him. The whole scouting report was team defense. Try to be there for guys because we knew he was going to get by us. We thought maybe we could take advantage of him on the other end, but he's a lot stronger than your typical point guard. You can't really go 'mouse in the house' with him because he can keep guys out of the [painted] areas."

If it were just Nelson doing damage, Gonzaga might have been able to pull out the victory. But the Hawks also got 16 points from Delonte West and 12 each from Pat Carroll and Tyrone Barley. The trio combined to make 11 of 17 shots from three-point range.

With his new form, hard work in the offseason, and inspiration from the Alicia Keys concert, Barley opened his senior season by making four of five three-pointers. Entering the year, he had missed 78 of 114 attempts from long range. He was a different offensive player now, and it showed.

"It was just a confidence that I had now that I could just let it go," Barley said. "Before it was like, 'I don't want to shoot at all. There's no point.' You know you can make it if the form is right. Just keep everything simple and whatever happens, happens. As opposed to thinking, 'Dang, can I make this shot?' It's a completely different game when the thought process is wiped away. Alright, the form is fine. Now, you live with the result."

One area of Barley's game that didn't change was his defense. It still was stellar. His late steal of WCC reigning Player of the Year Blake Stepp helped seal the win. Barley and the Hawks held Stepp to just eight points on two of 12 shooting while limiting the Zags to 36.4 percent field goal shooting overall. St. Joe's also got a big boost defensively from Dwayne Jones, who used every bit of his insight and added muscle from his redshirt season two years prior to block six shots.

"Dwayne Jones was a monster in that game," Violette said. "I remember him being a tough guy to get around. He was a real rim protector."

Even more than 20 years later, the reserved Jones remained humble about his performance.

"It was just competing and wanting to win and help my teammates out," he said. "As the last line of defense, that was my way to impact the game. Try to pay attention, read stuff, and just try to erase things."

Jones let his game do the talking. And so did his teammates, giving Bass the answer to his pregame question about the Hawks.

"Yeah, these guys belong," Bass said. "We played to our expectation that night."

The Zags were impressed, too.

"We were pretty upset about losing, but we also felt like we got beat that game," said Violette, who had 13 points and 15 rebounds. "It's different than when you get that feeling you gave a game away. They were just a really good team. They came in there and beat us that night."

The performance, and the way in which the Hawks did it, left Gonzaga with nothing but respect for its opponent.

"There were a few teams where we didn't want anything to do with after the game, but St. Joe's was not like that," Violette, today a financial planner for Merrill Lynch in Washington, said. "We had a healthy respect for those guys. They just came out there and handled business. They didn't talk trash. They spoke with their game."

Violette and the Zags would recover quite well from their opening defeat, ending up with a 28-3 overall record and 14-0 mark in the WCC, making St. Joe's victory that much more impressive upon later reflection. However, nobody at the Garden needed to wait until the end of the season to put this win into perspective. To those in attendance or watching on TV, the feeling was clear that these Hawks were off to the start of a special season.

***

Avington, like other Hawks fans and objective observers, knew that beating Gonzaga would be a statement victory.

"St. Joe's wins that game and you're like, 'OK, this is something,'" he said. "It woke up a lot of national eyes who either didn't know what St. Joe's had coming back or said, 'Show me.' And St. Joe's definitely went up there and did that. It was one of the moments where you knew this could be special."

Father Timothy Lannon felt similarly to Avington. Unlike Avington, Lannon hadn't seen much St. Joe's basketball in the last two decades. But he had seen some elite basketball lately. Lannon was in his first year as president of Saint Joseph's after serving in the same role at Marquette, which reached the Final Four in 2003 in Lannon's final days as president.

"I was watching great basketball back in Milwaukee," Lannon said.

And he saw more of it in New York to start the 2003–04 season.

"We played so well," Lannon said. "I was kind of stunned how well we played. I knew we were good. That's where I thought to myself, 'We are going to have a great, great season.'"

Jerardi had seen every great college basketball player and team up close since taking over the city's college basketball beat for the *Philadelphia Daily News* in 1987. Right away, he knew this Hawks team was different.

"I called Phil the next morning and said, 'Phil, I just looked at your schedule, and I'm not sure you're losing any games,'" Jerardi said.

Hawks fans were similarly optimistic.

"I remember I didn't get home until two in the morning, and I could barely sleep because of all of the excitement of that game," said Brian O'Connell, who attended every St. Joe's home game with his father, Bill, a 1971 graduate.

Owen Patterson, from his courtside seat at MSG, was amazed by St. Joe's performance.

"That was an incredible night," Patterson, a 1980 graduate, said. "It was like, 'This is legit.'"

Martelli, who earned his 150th career victory with the win, was elated with his team's showing in a game that he said had the feel and intensity of one in March rather than November. However, he was not surprised by the way his team played. From the moment he laid eyes on Nelson, Martelli knew that the point guard would lead the Hawks to high places. Remember, his first words after Nelson committed were, "Yes! We're going to the Final Four. Thank you."

So, the St. Joe's coach wasn't being flippant when Vitale praised him afterward.

"Vitale stopped me and said, 'This is going to be unbelievable,'" Martelli recalled. "I said I knew."

Martelli's Hawks showed Vitale and everyone how good they were on the biggest stage in New York with a national television audience watching. Their next test would be much, much different, on the road in front of just several hundred fans in a tough environment. And St. Joe's would be playing against a rare opponent who did have prior success defeating Jameer Nelson.

CHAPTER 7

Game 2: West, Barley, and Body Blows

Tuesday, November 25, 2003
Case Gym, Boston
No. 13 Saint Joseph's at Boston University

A lengthy layoff after Saint Joseph's impressive season-opening victory over No. 10-ranked Gonzaga at New York's Madison Square Garden in front of thousands of Hawks fans and a national television audience did nothing to cool Phil Martelli's confidence. Martelli wasn't being arrogant when he told ESPN's Dick Vitale that he knew this was going to be an unbelievable season. The St. Joe's coach legitimately felt that way ever since Jameer Nelson decided to return for his senior year, and the Hawks point guard's performance against Gonzaga kept Martelli's spirits sky-high.

Joe Sullivan sensed this right away when he met Martelli and the Hawks on Monday, November 24, 2003, the night before their second game of the season against Boston University at Case Gym. Sullivan is a 1972 Hawks graduate and had worked in the sports department of the *Boston Globe* since 1994, becoming sports editor in 2004. Whenever the Hawks played in New England, Sullivan made sure to meet up with them. On this trip, he was unable to attend the game, but Martelli invited him to the pregame dinner. St. Joe's hadn't played in 10 days, yet the coach was still feeling good.

"That night, he told me how great he thought they were," Sullivan said. "'The speed is unbelievable with this team,' Phil said. He's always outward, and all that, but he just seemed exceptionally confident that night talking about how good the season could be. He was supremely confident, you could tell."

With Nelson, Martelli had reason to feel good. Also, he couldn't help but be confident after the strong week of practices from Delonte West, who was beginning to resemble the player who was so explosive before a stress fracture limited him in the final eight games of the 2002–03 season.[21] Martelli knew that while Boston University was good, the Terriers had no one like Nelson or West. And the coach also knew that he had the role players who could provide support to Nelson and West as needed.

"They were well-coached, but we were just going to wear you down," Martelli said. "I didn't know where it was going to come from. Tyrone [Barley] off the bench. Or was it going to be Pat Carroll? Or Chet [Stachitas]? The knowns were the knowns. Nobody that we played had anybody like Delonte and Jameer until the end. But in those games, I knew we had enough guys to deliver the body blows. We were just going to weaken their knees."

If the Terriers were going to pull off an upset, they had three things going in their favor: there could be a letdown for St. Joe's with such a huge drop-off in atmosphere at Case Gym compared to MSG; the Hawks could have some rustiness from such a long stretch without playing; and Boston University was actually a very, very good team.

The Hawks' home court, Alumni Memorial Fieldhouse, wasn't even as big or as modern as many high school gyms; however, its capacity was almost double the 1,800 that squeezes into Case. Boston University's home court doesn't even have any seats behind the baskets. And with Thanksgiving just two days away, there were even fewer people there than might have been on, say, the previous Saturday night. The announced attendance was 1,669, and Dick Jerardi reported in the *Philadelphia Daily News* that there was little to no atmosphere that night from the home fans.[22] It was quite a change from the circus-like environment that had greeted the Hawks in New York against Gonzaga a little more than a week prior.

"It was a November game, so the crowd was a November crowd, and we had just come off this unbelievable crowd with Gonzaga," Martelli said.

As for the layoff, based on Martelli's confidence and West's preparation leading up to the game, that wasn't likely to be an issue. But what could be an issue was the fact that the Terriers were really good, and Case usually was tough on opponents. Boston University was two years removed from an America East Conference title, clinched on their home court, and a berth in the NCAA tournament. They had combined to win 42 games in the previous two seasons, and they would go on to finish 23-6 in 2003–04 and earn a postseason spot in the National Invitation Tournament (NIT). Though it might look like it on paper, this was not a cupcake matchup.

"We felt like we had a solid mid-major team that year," Terriers senior Ryan Butt said.

The Terriers had one more thing going for them in their upset bid: Ryan Butt knew what it took to beat a Jameer Nelson-led team.

***

Butt, a native of Lancaster, Pennsylvania, is still the all-time leading scorer at Hempfield High School, which is about an 80-minute drive west of St. Joe's. He scored 1,612 points in high school and helped Hempfield to an easy victory over Nelson's Chester High squad in the 1998–99 season when both were high school juniors. That was the Chester team that would go on to win the PIAA District 1 Class AAAA final over Pennsbury at Villanova.

"We had a really good high school team, and he obviously did too at Chester," Butt said. "Things just clicked for us in that game. We played a phenomenal game. I played pretty well, and all the guys played pretty well."

Even in victory, Butt came away thoroughly impressed with Nelson.

"He wasn't super tall, but he was strong and strong on the ball," said Butt, who today is a math teacher at Donegal High School, which is just seven miles from where he starred on the court in high school. "He had a great feel for the game. He wasn't a super loud, outgoing type of guy. You just knew that he had that look in his eye that he could play. He was just a strong leader the way he played. I knew early on, even as a junior when we played him, that he was a phenomenal player."

Butt also knew from experience that Nelson was beatable but that it wouldn't be easy. On this night, though, it wasn't Nelson who would do the most damage against the Terriers. Picking right up where he left off in practice, West had a team-high 20 points, along with five rebounds and four assists.

"It was usually Delonte West," Butt said. "He was the one guy that hurt us the most. I thought we played pretty well against Jameer [13 points]. Delonte was always the guy making the play that got them going again. He doesn't look physically dominating, but he was just so quick and had kind of a crafty type game where he was able to get his shot off. At that point, Jameer had the bigger name, but [West] definitely was the guy that we struggled to defend."

In addition to West, the Hawks also got a big lift off the bench, both defensively *and* offensively for the second straight contest, from Barley. Just as Martelli expected, one of St. Joe's role players came up big. Barley finished with season highs in points (15) and three-pointers (five). His remarkable transformation from a player who was reluctant to even shoot a long-range jumper to one who practically couldn't miss from beyond the arc continued. In 90 career games entering 2003–04, Barley had made 36 of 114 attempts, or 31.6 percent, from three-point range. In just two games thus far in his senior season, he had drained nine three-pointers on just 14 attempts for a spectacular 64.3 percent make rate. Incredibly, Barley had more than doubled his three-point percentage.

"My form was terrible," Barley said of the first three seasons. "No matter how many times I shoot, I'm not getting better."

After Barley's junior season, Hawks assistant coach Matt Brady adjusted his shot by moving the point at which Barley released the ball from near his right ear to out in front of him and closer to his right eye and forehead. It made all the difference.

"Drastic improvement," Barley said. "It changed my whole shot. Just by me picking up the little things Matt Brady taught me, I can transform anyone's shot because it's all about technique."

It also took lots of hard work and repetition by Barley in the offseason for the change to stick.

"He really wanted to be good," Brady said. "He was very determined."

Barley's improvement on his outside shooting not only benefited him but also the entire team. It forced defenders to stay close to Barley on the perimeter for the first time in his career, thus opening up even more space for Nelson and West to operate.

"Being able to stretch the defense with a significant jump shot unlocks everybody's power," Brady said. "It helps every individual player, and then it creates the space everybody needs to play in when you want to drive [to the basket]."

Even with strong play from West and Barley, the Terriers showed how good they were and kept the game tight for most of the first half. Then, St. Joe's went on a 13-2 run to end the opening half, and the Hawks coasted from that point, winning 71-56.

"Every time we made a run, they had a bigger run back at us," said Butt, who scored a career-high 20 points. "They had an answer every time we seemed to string things together and start playing well."

Like Martelli predicted, the Hawks were able to deliver enough body blows. The coach didn't mean it literally, but Butt took a hard shot that resulted in a broken nose when John Bryant inadvertently elbowed him square in the face as the two battled for a rebound. Bryant also got nicked up in the game—possibly on the same play, though he wasn't certain about that more than 20 years later—cutting his upper lip severely enough that the scar still can be seen today. While Butt left the court physically hurting a bit, his confidence and that of the Terriers was not damaged. In fact, they felt good about how they had performed against the Hawks.

"We got some confidence that if we could hang with those guys, that going back into our conference we'd be pretty competitive," Butt said. The Terriers did just that, going 17-1 in league play before getting upset in the America East Conference tournament.

Once again, the Hawks won a game that would look even better by the end of the season. This time, though, unlike after beating Gonzaga, hardly anyone noticed or celebrated a victory that was expected. It was early, but the Hawks were undefeated, just as West said he thought they could be at the preseason team meeting and Jerardi told Martelli they could be when he called him following the Gonzaga game. In their next contest at Old Dominion, though, the Hawks would need some late-game heroics if they were going to save any talk of an undefeated season practically before it even started.

CHAPTER 8

Game 3: A Long Shot and
a High Standard

Saturday, November 29, 2003
Ted Constant Convocation Center, Norfolk, Virginia
No. 13 Saint Joseph's at Old Dominion

Tyrone Barley and Chet Stachitas weren't the only Hawks players working on their long-range games in the offseason. In preparation for the longer distance of the NBA's three-point line, Jameer Nelson was also focused on becoming a better outside shooter. He wanted to extend his range from beyond the arc. Working with Philadelphia native and former NBA guard Doug Overton, Nelson put up countless shots in the summer before his senior season, with each one a little farther from the basket. Later, Golden State Warriors star Steph Curry and the emergence of analytics would make shots from well beyond the three-point line more commonplace. Then, Nelson just wanted to add more to his game to make himself a better player and pro prospect.

"When you look at analytics now, the farther you are the better because there's more spacing," Nelson said. "I just wanted to increase my range."

As late as the day before the Hawks' third game of the season, at Old Dominion at the Ted Constant Convocation Center on Saturday, November 29, 2003, Nelson was still practicing making jump shots from near half-court using his normal form.[23] And, man, would this ever come in handy. Bigger, stronger Old Dominion dominated St. Joe's in the second half and nearly erased a late, 14-point deficit on Isaiah Hunter's steal and layup that pulled the Monarchs within 72-70 of the Hawks with 46 seconds remaining. The Monarchs would get the ball back at least one more time and needed a defensive stop to keep the contest a two-point game. They almost got a gift from St. Joe's.

Delonte West was dribbling just over the time line on the right side of the court. Everyone was wondering why he was being so casual. West had mistaken the game clock for the shot clock. Thinking he had plenty of time, he was in no rush. Nelson recognized West's mistake.

"Jameer is screaming at him for the ball," said Joe Cabrey, a 1974 St. Joe's grad who attended every Hawks game in the 2003–04 season and was sitting behind the visiting bench this night.

West was trying to figure out why Nelson was yelling. "He was completely oblivious to the shot clock," Phil Martelli said.

Finally, just before the shot clock was set to expire, West obliged Nelson and tossed the ball to his teammate. The problem was that Nelson was standing in the center circle with two Monarchs about to converge on him. While the situation seemed frantic, neither Nelson nor Martelli was excited. The coach had an inordinate calm at the end of games with Nelson as his on-court leader. It took only a couple of contests in Nelson's freshman season for Martelli to see that everything he thought about Nelson when he recruited him was true—and even more so—thus creating a serene feeling for the coach.

"I already knew he was going to be extraordinary," Martelli said, but in those first two games Nelson was even better than the coach expected. "This is way different than I thought." The Hawks would play at Vanderbilt in Nelson's third career game, losing 78-76 on November 19, 2000. Like Martelli's description of Barley's newfound shooting success, that Barley's belief in his new shot was what was making all the difference, the coach's belief in Nelson was key. Even though the Hawks lost to Vanderbilt, Martelli's confidence in Nelson was so great that he believed the Hawks would be victorious.

"I just thought he was going to steal the ball, and we'll win the game because of him," Martelli said of the Vanderbilt game.

So, at ODU, when West passed to Nelson and the coach saw the shot clock about to expire with the ball at half-court, he wasn't overly concerned. "You didn't shrug," Martelli said.

Nelson was calm and confident when he received the pass, in part because that was who he was and in part because he had practiced this exact shot for hours and hours with Overton. He caught the pass facing West, who was to Nelson's right. Nelson quickly swung his right leg forward, providing momentum for the long shot, and with both feet on the face of the Monarchs' lion logo at half-court, unleashed a normal-looking jumper with nine seconds remaining.[24] Accounts say the shot was from 38 feet, but watching the replay makes it appear that it was from even farther away from the basket.[25] Just as the ball neared the hoop, Nelson thrust his right hand confidently into the air. When the ball incredibly splashed through the net, he calmly backpedaled to the defensive end as if he had just made a simple, early-game free throw. All of his preparation had paid off in the most crucial of moments.

"I didn't know I would hit that, but I was prepared for it," Nelson said. "It wasn't a shot where it was like, 'Oh man, this is a once-in-a-lifetime shot.'"

Ken Krsolovic was on the St. Joe's radio call that evening. Krsolovic had been the Hawks' play-by-play announcer for the previous 15 years before accepting a position as athletic director and head baseball coach at Division III Lake Erie College in Ohio in the summer of 2003.

"I remember distinctly that summer that Jameer was in the gym one day, and he came up to me and said, 'You're leaving?'" Krsolovic recalled. "I'm like, 'Yeah, I have a chance to be an AD and a baseball coach.' He's like, 'You're going to miss a really good year.' I said, 'I know.'"

Because Tom McCarthy had a prior commitment for the Old Dominion game, Krsolovic filled in against the Monarchs. He was elated to have the opportunity to call Nelson's half-court shot, which he remembers describing as a 40-footer.

"I was thrilled I got to do that one," Krsolovic said.

The Monarchs managed a meaningless layup to close out the game but didn't have time for any more points. St. Joe's won 75-72 to improve to 3-0. Old Dominion, likely the better team this night, was shocked.

"I'm thinking, 'Oh sweet, we just got a possession back here. We're about to take over here,'" Alex Loughton, ODU's leading scorer that season, said. "It hits the bottom of the net, and I'm just like, 'What the heck was that? How the heck did this dude shoot a jump shot without looking like he strained any kind of effort into it?'"

Monarchs coach Blaine Taylor sensed trouble as soon as Nelson let go of the ball.

"When he jumped up, you would've thought he was shooting a 12-footer," Taylor said. "I remember muttering under my breath, 'Dammit, that son of a gun is going to make that.' He made it, and they're off the hook."

St. Joe's assistant Matt Brady had counseled Nelson on his form, as he had West and Barley. Brady coached Nelson to shoot positioned more "straight up and down" rather than leaning to one side or the other. A near half-court shot like this one, though, takes more than just good mechanics.

"That shot was 100 percent Jameer and his mental fortitude and toughness," Brady said. "We could've easily lost that game if Jameer wasn't ready for the moment. But he was ready for the moment because he prepared himself."

Taylor could only shake his head. "He just defied logic sometimes," ODU's coach said of Nelson.

The Hawks' victory also defied logic. Old Dominion dominated St. Joe's, still without injured 6-foot-10 forward Dave Mallon, on the interior, outrebounding the Hawks 49-25, including an incomprehensible 23-4 advantage on the offensive glass. The Monarchs only shot 38.6 percent from the field but nearly won because they put up 70 field goal attempts to the Hawks' 55, as St. Joe's was unable to get many rebounds. Loughton, a 6-foot-9 sophomore center from Perth, Australia, where today he runs a basketball program for children, called Loughton 40 Hoops, was practically unstoppable with 24 points and 15 rebounds. ODU outscored St. Joe's 43-36 after halftime.

"On that day, we were as good as them," Taylor said.

The game would pay dividends later for the Monarchs. Like Boston University had four days earlier, ODU gained confidence from its performance. Taylor was in his third season at the helm and would build ODU into a Coastal Athletic Association (CAA) power that would reach the NCAA tournament in four of the next seven seasons after 2003–04.

"It wasn't a bunch of jokers that showed up one day and decided to play good," Taylor said. "We were a legitimate group with a future. So that game was good for us."

The game was good for the Hawks, too, as it allowed Martelli to harp on playing to a standard. The coach was thrilled to see Nelson's shot fall, of course, but he was steaming mad afterward because of the way the Hawks played.[26] The postgame locker room felt as if the visitors had been blown out.

"I don't remember much about my personal game that game," said Stachitas, who came off the bench for 11 points. "I do remember the feeling that we were lucky to eke out of there with a victory. It wasn't a great locker room. That's where it started that season that we were playing to a standard and not necessarily the team we were playing against."

It wasn't the Hawks' best game, by any means. Nelson finished with 24 points, and West, other than losing track of the shot clock, had a strong game with 23 points. Barley cooled after his fast start in the first two games, missing six of seven three-pointers, and Pat Carroll went scoreless for the only time in the season. Besides the stats in the box score, St. Joe's didn't play to its own high standards and those set by Martelli. In spite of this, the Hawks pulled out the victory, something assistant Mark Bass believed was a positive.

"The sign of a good team is you just figure out a way to win," Bass said. "At Old Dominion, we figured out a way to win. You're not going to play your best every night. But you find a way to get a stop, or find a way to hit a big shot. That's the sign of a good team."

Although they didn't meet their standard, the Hawks definitely were a good team, as Bass said. But they weren't celebrating like one afterward. The Hawks quietly packed their bags in a somber locker room, readying for a bus ride of five and a half hours back to St. Joe's. Finally, the Hawks would be returning to their cozy, on-campus court for the first time this season. And they weren't about to disappoint their home fans with another lackluster performance that would have to be saved at the end by heroics from Nelson or somebody else. They made sure of that right from the start.

CHAPTER 9

Game 4: Home Sweet Home, Alas

Tuesday, December 2, 2003
Alumni Memorial Fieldhouse, Philadelphia
San Francisco at No. 12 Saint Joseph's

It had been 166 days since Jameer Nelson announced he was returning for his senior season, and 18 days since Saint Joseph's opened the most anticipated season in school history with a convincing upset victory over 10th-ranked Gonzaga. Finally, the Hawks were back on campus, in front of their passionate fans and in one of the coziest, to put it nicely, venues in all of NCAA Division I.

Alumni Memorial Fieldhouse hosted its first game on November 26, 1949. A little more than 54 years later, on December 2, 2003, when the Hawks were set to welcome the University of San Francisco in the fourth game of the 2003–04 season, not much had changed about the Fieldhouse. If there were any upgrades, it certainly didn't feel that way. There was nothing modern about the Fieldhouse. The biggest issue with the Hawks' home facility was that it was too small. Everything was cramped. There was nowhere to put anything. Everything had to be shared.

Phil Martelli's office, with its thick cinder-block walls, tight quarters, and low ceiling, felt more like a closet. There was no practice court. The Hawks worked out on the same floor on which they played their games. On some days, that floor would be used by students playing five-on-five, and Martelli and his players had to wait to practice on their own court. Brendan Prunty remembered one such time during his sophomore year in 2003–04. Prunty and some friends headed to the Fieldhouse for a pickup game. When all of the courts in the rec gym were taken, the supervisor directed Prunty's group to the main court. As Prunty's five-on-five game was being played, in trots Martelli and some pretty talented spectators named Nelson, West, Carroll, Jones, Mallon, Bryant, Barley, Stachitas, and Lee.

"We're playing and the team walks in," Prunty, who would go on to cover the Hawks and college basketball for NJ.com, remembered. "Everyone stops. I knew Phil was a nice guy, but we're on his court. I'm expecting him to be like, 'Get the heck off the court.' And he looks at his watch and goes, 'You guys have another six minutes.' Someone was like, 'No, no, no, we'll get off.' And Phil said, 'No, we don't have the court for another six minutes. You guys are free to play.'"

It was no different in the weight room. Neither the basketball team nor any of the school's athletes had a dedicated place to pump iron. If they wanted to lift, they had to take turns with whoever else was in there, whether other athletes, undergraduates, professors, or even the general public.

"It was unbelievable," Hawks athletic trainer Bill Lukasiewicz said. "Jameer might say to some random guy, 'Can I work in here?'"

The locker rooms were so tiny that Dayton coach Brian Gregory, later on in the 2003–04 season, would ask school officials to find him another place to address the Flyers at halftime because he couldn't pull his team together to face him in the visitors' dressing room. The best St. Joe's could do was put Dayton in a space with a bunch of cubicles that was used by the school's athletic coaches and staff. That turned out to be a bad idea for Gregory and Dayton, as the area also was doubling that night as the dressing room for mascots participating in a halftime contest. And so it went at the Fieldhouse.

Visitors often couldn't believe it when they learned that St. Joe's practice court also was where the home games were played. Like in high school gyms, folded-up wooden bleachers were pulled out when it was game time.

Former Atlantic 10 commissioner Linda Bruno was at the Fieldhouse one day to watch her niece, who played for Iona, when former Gaels coach Tony Bozzella had a question for her. "'So, where do the men play?'" Bruno remembers Bozzella asking. "No, this is it. 'Really?' he said. Really, this is it."

Ray Parrillo, the Hawks' beat writer for the *Philadelphia Inquirer*, heard the same exact thing from a visiting reporter from *Sports Illustrated*. "He came up to me and said, 'You cover this team on a daily basis. Where do they play their games?'" Parrillo recalled. "I said, 'Well, you're standing on the court.' He said, 'Really? This doesn't look much bigger than a high school gym.' I said, 'This is it.'"

Martelli never harped on what the Hawks didn't have. Part of that, surely, was because recruits or current players would feed off of any negativity. And, frankly, part of that was because the coach really didn't know anything else, having been the Hawks' head coach since 1995 and a St. Joe's assistant for 10 years before that.

"We never apologized for it, we never talked about it," Martelli said. "I was never stomping my foot saying, 'Yeah, but.' It was never a topic."

As a result, it wasn't a problem for the players—though they were aware of its disadvantages then and today.

"Our facility, it's crazy," John Bryant said. "If people saw our facility now, they'd laugh. There's no way we should've been as good as we were. Like no way. But that's because Coach Martelli made it so we saw past it."

As much as the Fieldhouse, which finally was renovated in 2008, didn't stack up to most Division I facilities, there were some similarities that were exactly like the rest, including venues at college basketball blue bloods like Kentucky, Duke, and North Carolina. Just as there, the main court's dimensions were 94 feet by 50 feet. The free throw line was 15 feet from the basket. The hoops were exactly 10 feet above the hardwood floor. The court and the baskets didn't care how expensive or lavish everything around the home floor was; it only mattered if you could play. And, when they rolled out those creaky, wooden bleachers, man, these Hawks could play.

Oh, and one other thing: Whenever the Hawks were good, like in 2003–04, and the Fieldhouse was packed, there likely weren't many bigger home-court advantages than their tiny gym. The noise of 3,200 fans who were seemingly right on top of you sounded like 32,000—or more. Parrillo told that *SI* reporter something else. "This place gets really crazy when they play," he said. And crazy wouldn't even begin to describe what San Francisco was walking into for the Hawks' on-campus opener.

***

Martelli sensed before tipoff that his team had gotten his message after their lackluster showing three days prior at Old Dominion. Nelson had rescued St. Joe's with a near half-court shot, but the overall performance left Martelli seething afterward. The Hawks would not let that happen again.

"I remember thinking we're going to be really hard to beat," Martelli said, feeling a little sympathetic for his opponent. "This team came all the way across the country."

With Prunty and his buddies debuting their "Wild, Wild West" fan club getup, in honor of Delonte; 3,200 rabid fans stomping on those wooden rollouts and letting loose all of the pent-up excitement that had been building for five and a half months with cheers so loud that opposing players were unable to communicate with one another; and the Hawks eager to make amends for Old Dominion, St. Joe's came out furiously fast. The Hawks scored the first 10 points, then 29 of 33, before settling for a convincing 46-18 halftime lead. Game over.

"Those were the kinds of things that team did," Martelli said.

The final score was 84-52 but could've been 184-52 if needed. So many impressive numbers jump out of the box score that it's hard to settle on just a few. More amazing than any statistic, though, was the three-quarter court bounce pass that Nelson threw to West for a layup. Later in the season, television networks would be wrestling over TV rights to Hawks home games. On this night, unbelievably, the game wasn't even televised. The highlight of Nelson's assist is from the grainy coaches' tape. But, boy, it is a pass the likes of which you might never see again—and, because the contest wasn't on TV, a precious few probably have seen even once.

Helplessly watching from the Dons bench was John Cox, the brilliant scorer from Philadelphia's George Washington Carver High School of Engineering and Science who was a senior at San Francisco. Cox had spent many days working out at the Fieldhouse, both before entering college and with West and Nelson in summers when he was back home in between semesters. He had an affection for Martelli during the recruiting process but wanted to head west after high school, following in the footsteps of his father, "Chubby" Cox, another great Philly guard who played at San Francisco. John Cox could play. He scored 1,798 points in high school, netted 1,540 at San Francisco, and would represent Venezuela in the 2016 Summer Olympics. Martelli scheduled the game as a homecoming for Cox. Unfortunately for Cox, he couldn't help the Dons on this night after spraining his knee in their season opener.

"They hit us really good," said Cox, who is an assistant at La Salle today. "It was a great atmosphere, and I was bummed not to be playing in that."

He wasn't surprised by what he saw on the floor from Nelson, who had 18 points, six assists, five steals, and zero turnovers in 22 minutes, or from West, who had 13 points, seven rebounds, and five assists in 26 minutes. When he wasn't playing with his cousin, Kobe Bryant, Cox was likely practicing at the Fieldhouse with Nelson, West, and others in the summer. Nelson's floor game and leadership and West's competitiveness struck Cox in the summer before the 2003–04 season.

"He got good at the pick and roll," Cox said of Nelson. "You could see he was a combo, how good he can shoot, how he could hit the roller, make the right reads. I thought he got so much better that summer before doing it. I'm guarding him and he's like, 'John, I'm going to pick you apart on this pick and roll.' He was way ahead of me in figuring out how to do that offensively. I was really impressed with that. He had that edge to him. That doesn't jump out to you, like he's yelling all loud. He worked hard. He knew how to run a team and lead a team."

With West, Cox had the same experience as Dave Mallon when their side lost what Mallon thought was a casual Saturday pickup game. As Cox attests, there was nothing casual when West was involved in a game.

"Ultimate competitor," Cox said. "Lose, run it back. He'll play one-on-one all day, two-on-two all day, three-on-three all day. That's what gave him the edge. He had that, and he was a smart player."

In addition to strong games from Nelson and West, Chet Stachitas contributed 13 points off the bench in a second consecutive solid outing. St. Joe's also got 13 points and 12 rebounds from Dwayne Jones. It was one of four double-doubles on the season for Jones, who made six of seven field goals. Rebounding, like blocking shots, was just another way to help the team—and to help himself in the process.

"It was just about effort," Jones said. "For me, that was the way that I scored. I knew I wasn't going to get many opportunities and, like all guys, you want to try and score. It was just attacking the glass, timing, understanding where my teammates shot from, where their shots would miss, and just trying to put myself in a position to win the rebounding battle."

When they weren't scoring, the Hawks were turning up their defensive pressure against San Francisco a game after Old Dominion had scorched them for 43 second-half points. The Dons would pay, as St. Joe's forced 24 turnovers, accumulated 13 steals, and held the visitors to three of 14 shooting (21.4 percent) from long range.

Martelli and the rabid Fieldhouse fans went home happy. Father Timothy Lannon, St. Joe's president, received likely the loudest "Happy Birthday" serenade of his life on his 53rd birthday. After everyone cleared out and the court went silent, staff members pushed back those wooden bleachers into neatly stacked columns off to the side. St. Joe's would need its practice court back. There was a lot of work to do. Martelli knew their next contest would not be easy. Big 5 games at the Palestra never are. And any matchup against a team coached by Fran Dunphy requires the ultimate preparation.

CHAPTER 10

Game 5: Big 5, Palestra, and Dunph

Saturday, December 6, 2003
The Palestra, Philadelphia
No. 12 Saint Joseph's at Penn

With the wooden bleachers folded up neatly and out of the way after their dominating victory over San Francisco at the Fieldhouse, Phil Martelli and the Hawks had three days to prepare for a Big 5 matchup against coach Fran Dunphy and Penn at the Palestra. After learning from his first year coaching high school, Martelli never wasted a minute of practice time anyway. And he certainly would use every moment at his disposal to prepare for the always challenging Dunphy-led Quakers. Martelli's excitement level was raised even more because the contest was at the Palestra, a venue he had revered ever since those childhood trolley rides there from his Southwest Philadelphia home.

"There were juices flowing," Martelli said. "Always in that building, always in the Big 5, and, obviously, with Dunph."

The Big 5 was formed on November 23, 1954 by the athletic directors of La Salle, Penn, Saint Joseph's, Temple, and Villanova. Very quickly, the unique collection of five Philadelphia Division I schools located within a radius of just 17 miles playing a round-robin series became one of the toughest tickets in town and one of the greatest traditions in college basketball. City basketball fans, like Martelli and Dunphy, packed the Palestra for Saturday night doubleheaders that often were extensions of rivalries of the best players coming out of Philadelphia's Public League and Catholic League. Undergrads rolled out banners with catchy mocks of their opponents, threw streamers onto the court after the first made basket, and helped to create a scene that made a sellout of 8,722 people one of the noisiest, coolest, and best atmospheres in sports. The Palestra is regarded with such reverence that it has been nicknamed the "Cathedral of College Basketball."

By 2003, the Big 5 had lost much of its luster. There are many reasons for this, including that many of the best area players whom Philly fans grew to know and idolize no longer were attending Big 5 schools with the same frequency as in the past. Many Big 5 games were still played at the Palestra, but some schools chose to play their home games on campus beginning in 1986.

The round-robin series halted briefly in 1991 before returning in 1999. Part of the reason for the pause was that scheduling was becoming more difficult in college basketball, and finding a spot for four nonconference games wasn't always easy. Also, and undoubtedly a greater reason for the shift away from facing all four teams every season, is the reality that every Big 5 game is a potential loss regardless of either team's record or status in college basketball. In fairness, schools trying to lessen their participation in the Big 5 and build a strong résumé for the NCAA tournament were in a no-win situation because computer metrics, talking heads, and selection committees have never properly valued the Big 5. Nationally, a loss to an Ivy League school like Penn, which does not award athletic scholarships, would be considered a so-called bad loss come March. Locally, everyone understood that beating the Quakers in a Big 5 contest was a well-earned victory. This was especially the case during Dunphy's tenure at the school.

***

Nicknamed "Dunph," Fran Dunphy began coaching Penn in 1989. He quickly turned the Quakers into one of the most consistent and dominant teams in relation to one's conference in college basketball. Over his 17 years at the helm, Dunphy led the Quakers to 10 Ivy League titles, nine NCAA tournaments, and 310 total victories—the most of any Penn coach. Amazingly, Dunphy directed a 48-game Ivy winning streak between 1992 and 1996, with the Quakers finishing undefeated in the league in 1993, '94, and '95. Penn was coming off consecutive NCAA tournament appearances and 47 combined victories in the previous two seasons entering 2003–04. Regardless of what the computer metrics, talking heads, and selection committees said, this would not be an easy game for the Hawks.

And Dunphy certainly knew it wouldn't be easy for the Quakers, either.

"They were led by a guy who is an all-time Philadelphia Big 5 great in Jameer Nelson," Dunphy, still coaching, said in 2023 after leading his alma mater La Salle to a win over Howard. "And then you back that up with a Delonte West and so many other guys that they had that were just terrific players. And Phil did a tremendous job with that group. That was a special, special team."

The reserved Dunphy and outspoken Martelli are close friends but opposites in personality. But both are fiery competitors with a shared love of basketball, Philadelphia, and the Big 5. Not that they would have talked in the lead-up to their matchup at the Palestra on December 6, 2003, anyway, but Dunphy never felt the need to call his good friend with assistance that week or that season. With Nelson, Dunphy figured Martelli was doing quite alright without any outsider's input.

"He didn't need any pointers from me," Dunphy said. "He had so much trust in Jameer. It was a great relationship those two had. [Martelli] didn't need any help from anybody other than Jameer being the leader on the court. When the time came to have good possessions, Jameer got that done. And, obviously, Phil did a great job of molding that group and recruiting that group. It was an honor to play against them."

Though always respectful today and then, Dunphy wanted nothing more than to beat his good friend, especially after the Hawks had gone 4-0 in the Big 5 in 2002–03 for their first outright title since 1980. Martelli understood. It was the nature of the Big 5. Everyone involved knew that, even outsiders like Jeff Schiffner. Schiffner came to Penn from North Jersey and quickly got what the Big 5 was all about. In essence, it is like a sibling rivalry: You want to beat your siblings in everything but never want to see your siblings lose to anyone else.

"It was a source of local pride," Schiffner said. "In the Big 5, you always want to kick the other teams' asses. But there's always certainly a camaraderie with Philly teams that doesn't exist in other parts of the country." In St. Joe's fifth game of the 2003–04 season, Schiffner nearly kicked the Hawks' asses all by himself.

***

In 2002–03, Phil Martelli Jr. helped Pat Carroll finish the season ranked seventh in the country in three-point percentage, boosting Carroll's confidence by telling him he was the best shooter in the country after every warm-up shot. In fact, Schiffner was the best three-point shooter in the country that season, making a remarkable 49.3 percent (74 of 150) of shots from beyond the arc. And Penn's senior guard would barely miss against the Hawks in their fifth game of the 2003–04 season, draining seven of 11 three-pointers on his way to 23 points.

"Obviously that game, I was feeling it a little bit," Schiffner said. "I certainly felt the hot hand."

Penn also got 12 points on four three-pointers from Charlie Copp.

"When you think about our offense and what we were trying to do, that's what we were aiming for," Schiffner said of the long-range shots.

Against most teams, that kind of production likely would've been enough. But the Hawks weren't most teams. They had Jameer Nelson.

Nelson was a force everywhere on the court against Penn, finishing with 23 points, six rebounds, four assists, and a career-high eight steals.

"The thing that set him apart is he just really, really knew how to play the game and had an innate ability to be in the right place at the right time on the offensive and defensive side of the ball," Schiffner said. "When the ball was in his hands, you always just felt like something good was going to come out of it. And, by the way, when you reverse that and play defense against him, it's like, 'Oh God, the ball's in his hands. Something good is going to happen.' There were not a lot of other guys out there like that. He was an unbelievable talent."

As great as Nelson played, this was a Big 5 game at the Palestra. Wins are never easy. Leads are never safe. The Hawks were in a tight contest throughout the second half, and the Quakers were within three points with 46.4 seconds remaining before St. Joe's iced the game at the free throw line, improving to 5-0 with a 67-59 victory that, as expected, was never easy. Dunphy heaped praise on Nelson afterward at the postgame press conference and still was doing so more than 20 years later.[27]

"He was smarter than most and tougher than most, and he knew exactly who he was," Dunphy said in 2023. "He worked hard at every aspect of the game. While he was a great player, I think always his best attribute is his leadership. Phenomenal leader. Even today. He was mature when he was a freshman. When he was a senior, it was ridiculous how mature he was."

Schiffner, like Nelson a senior in 2003–04, also had seen the development of both Nelson and the Hawks.

"Every year it felt like they added another component," said Schiffner, with phones ringing off the hook in the background at his Goldman Sachs offices in New York. "What you saw was that team year by year coming into its own, and that year was their big year."

In addition to Nelson, Delonte West (15 points) and Tyrone Barley (10 points) chipped in with double-digit scoring games against the Quakers. Carroll had a quiet seven points but always was a threat from the outside. Schiffner said the Hawks' perimeter players, both offensively and defensively, posed a great challenge for any opponent.

"Our matchups on the perimeter were, one of us was going to take Delonte, one of us was going to take Jameer, and the other was going to end up with Pat Carroll. We always laughed," Schiffner said. "I don't think there was a team that put more pressure on you from a perimeter standpoint than that team. I can't even imagine one. It was 40 minutes of just grind to just get the ball up the court on offense and to keep them in front on defense. That's the one thing I'll always remember."

For Martelli, every Big 5 game at the Palestra was one to remember. But he and the Hawks probably wanted to forget about their shooting performance from outside against the Quakers, as they hit a season-worst 15.8 percent from beyond the arc, making a woeful three of 19 tries from long range. Alas, they wouldn't have much time to even think about that, as they would be back at the Palestra in just three days for a home-away-from-home game against Boston College. Any concern Martelli had about his Big East Conference opponent evaporated when he saw Boston College enter the gym.

CHAPTER 11

Game 6: BC Checks Out,
Bryant Checks In

Tuesday, December 9, 2003
The Palestra, Philadelphia
Boston College at No. 12 Saint Joseph's

Shortly after taking over as Saint Joseph's head coach in 1995, Phil Martelli implemented a program policy that the Hawks would not check out of hotels until after games. Too many times, Martelli had noticed players distracted in the hours before tipoff by packing, figuring out phone bills in the pre–cell phone era, or doing something else that caused delays in leaving hotels. Players were not focused when tipoff arrived as a result. The coach quickly saw a positive impact on performance from the new checkout policy.

In their sixth game of the 2003–04 season, the Hawks were not staying in a hotel prior to their contest against Boston College, so the checkout policy was not in place. But St. Joe's would have to travel for its home game, making the 20-minute drive from campus to the Palestra because BC coach Al Skinner refused to play at the Fieldhouse. As a member of the Atlantic 10 Conference while coaching Rhode Island for nine seasons, Skinner had no choice but to play Rams road games there. Now that he was coaching in the Big East Conference and had a say on the nonconference game's location, Skinner wanted no part of the Fieldhouse's wooden bleachers, the 3,200 screaming fans right on top of you who sounded like 32,000, and the tiny locker rooms that barely could accommodate BC's tall and strong frontcourt players.

"They weren't going to play at the Fieldhouse because of Al's experiences," Martelli said.

So, after the Eagles hosted St. Joe's the prior season, Martelli agreed to move the Hawks' return home game in 2003–04 to the Palestra. The game was scheduled for the evening of December 9, 2003. But then Penn and Villanova also scheduled a game at the Palestra on the same evening. As guests on the Quakers' campus, St. Joe's didn't have much say. The Hawks either could move their game to the Fieldhouse, which Martelli would have loved but Skinner would have vetoed, or they could change the game time. So, the time was shifted to a rare 4:00 p.m. weekday start, with Penn and Villanova to follow at eight o'clock. The Hawks bused to the Palestra, arriving at 2:30—one and a half hours before tip, per their usual—to get ready for a matchup of unbeatens. Soon after, Boston College came walking into the Palestra. Martelli noticed right away that the Eagles not only had their basketball gear but also their luggage in tow. Apparently, Skinner did not have the same checkout policy as the Hawks coach. The Eagles had already checked out of the hotel, and Martelli also felt that they already had checked out of the game.

"I knew the game was over because BC came in with their bags," Martelli said. "I was thinking they must have a flight out of Philadelphia. They're thinking about their flight. They ain't thinking about this competition. I knew that it was over then."

**

If it wasn't over before the referee's opening whistle, as Martelli felt, John Bryant and Delonte West made sure that it would end in the Hawks' favor by the time things became official.

Bryant, admittedly, was not going to fill up a box score with points. What he was going to do was give everything he had and be the best teammate he could be for every second on the floor, just as his dad had taught him. Normally, Tyrone Barley was given the assignment to defend the opposition's best player. Against BC, though, the 6-foot-1, 185-pound Barley was no match physically for the Eagles' 6-foot-7, 265-pound Craig Smith—though Barley believed he could stop anyone and would not have turned down the assignment had Martelli asked. But the coach didn't turn to Barley to stop Smith, who entered averaging 16.8 points per contest. The important and difficult task went to the 6-foot-7, 220-pound Bryant.

"Tyrone was normally our defensive everything, and he still is arguably the top five defenders I've seen in my lifetime, and I've seen a lot of really good defenders at a high level," said Bryant, who became the Chicago Bulls' top assistant coach in 2024. "I was given that assignment that night, and the coaching staff was really big and adamant on how I needed to stop him, how I needed to be physical with him, cover him throughout the game."

Bryant knew that his value to the Hawks was in assignments like this. He never expected the ball, never needed shots, an unselfish mentality that helped make this St. Joe's team so great.

"I felt like on the defensive side was one of the ways I could really make an impact on our team because Jameer and Delonte never passed the ball to me," Bryant said without animosity. "I say that with sincerity and a little bit of humor because I was going to miss the layup anyway. I wouldn't pass it to me. It was a cool challenge for that game. He was probably already stronger than me and certainly more talented than me. But that was our team in a nutshell. You do what was required in that moment to help our team win."

Smith had the body and the game of a power conference player. A-10 schools, like St. Joe's, rarely get those types of players. Entering the game, Martelli was concerned about Smith, whom he thought was the second-best freshman in the Big East in 2002–03 behind Syracuse's Carmelo Anthony. Smith had picked up right where he left off as a sophomore after earning second-team All-Big East honors as a rookie. Later, he would go on to a very successful NBA career, earning more than $9 million over six seasons and 403 games after being selected No. 36 overall in 2006. On this night, though, Bryant pestered Smith into one of the worst games of his life, as the BC star netted just two points while making only one of seven field goals with four rebounds and three turnovers in 31 minutes.

Bryant's defense on Smith helped the Hawks go on to a 67-57 victory to improve to 6-0 while dropping the Eagles to 6-1. At the postgame press conference, Martelli didn't mention BC's luggage; rather, he gave credit for the victory to Bryant.[28] Smith also complimented Bryant.[29] For his part, as is his way, Bryant deflected praise.

"It's not like after the game, I was like, 'Yeah man, I did that,'" he said. "It was just what was required in this game, and that to me was the ultimate. We all accepted our roles. Everyone had a role on our team. We played our role well."

***

West's role against the Eagles was different. St. Joe's needed him to score. Through hard work and an unmatched competitive drive, West had just kept getting better and better ever since high school coach Glenn Farello told him he needed to develop a midrange game. And he was finally feeling healthy after the late-season stress fracture in 2002–03 and a sprained ankle in preseason practice before the 2003–04 campaign had limited him.[30] Against the Eagles, a team used to stopping some of the best players in the country in the always challenging Big East, West displayed all of the ferocity and skill he had developed from practically living in the gym, carving up defenders inside and outside, and finished with 27 points. He also added nine rebounds and five assists.

Brian Jesiolowski had been on the receiving end of that type of performance many times in late-night workouts with West at the Fieldhouse. Jesiolowski was a talented athlete and a very good scorer at Lebanon Catholic High School in Lebanon, Pennsylvania, which is about a two-hour drive west of St. Joe's campus. The 6-foot-7 wing had several offers to play Division II and III but wanted to go to college in Philadelphia, so he chose Saint Joseph's, where his dad also had attended. He continued playing basketball once he got to campus, starting with pickup games in the Fieldhouse's rec gym, then as a member of the Hawks' JV, which was not a school-sanctioned NCAA team but played competitively against area junior colleges. He then earned a spot on Martelli's roster in 2002–03 as a walk-on in his second attempt trying out.

Jesiolowski and West became fast friends. Jesiolowski marveled at West's many talents, from basketball, to art, to music, to his handiness. West did not have a car on campus and sometimes would borrow Jesiolowski's 1993 Oldsmobile Cutlass Ciera. The sound system in the car was broken, and Jesiolowski took West up on his offer to fix it. A talented actor and comedian now living in Los Angeles, Jesiolowski delivered every line of the West part of the following story in a startling impersonation of West's voice.

"He was like, 'Yo youngin, we gotta fix this,'" Jesiolowski, sounding exactly like West, said. "'I can't be riding down here and this CD player is skipping all over the place. You buy the CD player and I'll install it.' He stops midway through and goes, 'Alright, young, you want me to hook this up so every time the bass bumps, your lights flicker? I can cross the wires, so it's going to be pimping.'"

Jesiolowski paused to laugh.

"I was like, 'Nah, man, just hook the CD player up,'" he continued. "He got it to work. It was amazing. He was a great dude. He had a big heart. He cared about people. He said, 'If I don't make it to the NBA, and I'm going to make it, I can be a rapper, I can be a painter. You gotta be able to do multiple things.' I remember after that conversation I dropped him off in the gym and he slept in the locker room."

West was going to do everything he could to get better, even if it meant catching just a few hours of sleep in the Fieldhouse's cozy locker room so he could get up even more shots. On nights when he wasn't dropping West off at the Fieldhouse, Jesiolowski often was playing one-on-one against him in the wee hours of the morning.

"He was the smoothest, silkiest dude I ever saw play," Jesiolowski said. "When you see him play, you see how smooth his game is. But when you play against him, you realize how intense he is. He was like poetry in motion the way he glided across the court. He would seem like he was moving so slow sometimes, and he'd be past you. When you're on the court with him and you feel his strength and you feel how he rips the ball out of your hands and you feel his intensity, you're like, 'Oh, this is why you're able to get past people. This is why you're able to score on a 6-foot-10 dude and you're 6-foot-4.' He had a perfect combination of soft touch, power, and intense all the time."

Jesiolowski fondly recalls those one-on-one matchups. He loved being in West's company. And loved playing against him, even though there was never, ever any letup from his good buddy.

"I'm bigger than him, I weigh more than him, and he would beat me 11-1, 11-0," Jesiolowski said. "I couldn't get shots off, and I couldn't stop him. He was on a whole other level of strength and skill and talent."

On this late December afternoon at the Palestra, the Eagles got a taste of exactly what Jesiolowski experienced in those late-night workouts and what Farello saw coaching from the sidelines in high school.

"He just had every combination," Farello said. "Toughness, chip on his shoulder, intensity, plays defense, passing and shooting. But his basketball IQ, you don't see the combination and wrap that up with toughness. He became unguardable because you just can't read him a certain way."

West also was the beneficiary of many perfectly placed assists from Nelson. Against Boston College, Nelson threw a pass to West with 13:33 remaining in the second half that not only set up a three-point play but gave Nelson 581 career assists, breaking the school's all-time record set in 1994 by Rap Curry. Nelson finished with a typically strong all-around game of 13 points, seven assists, six rebounds, and three steals. With Bryant and West's performances, however, the Hawks didn't need Nelson to play the hero role on this day. In their next game, though, Martelli knew that everyone would need to be ready for whatever role was needed. Their opponent, city rival Drexel, would not be checking out early from any hotel. And their coach, James "Bruiser" Flint, certainly would have his players ready for the competition. However, even Flint would have never thought that he needed to put Chet Stachitas at the top of his scouting report.

CHAPTER 12

Game 7: Stachitas Steps Up

Sunday, December 14, 2003
The Palestra, Philadelphia
No. 12 Saint Joseph's at Drexel

Unlike what Phil Martelli felt about Boston College, Drexel would not be distracted for its game against Saint Joseph's at the Palestra on Sunday, December 14, 2003. For one thing, Drexel's campus is just two city blocks from the Palestra, so the Dragons would not have any luggage in tow from an early hotel checkout. Mostly, though, Drexel would just be ready to play. Teams coached by James "Bruiser" Flint always were.

After finishing as the runner-up to Martelli for the St. Joe's job in 1995, Flint helped UMass reach the Final Four as an assistant to John Calipari in 1995–96 in Martelli's first season leading the Hawks. When Calipari left UMass for the NBA following the season, Flint was promoted to head coach after seven seasons as an assistant. He reached two NCAA tournaments in five seasons, but following Calipari was never going to be an easy task, and Flint resigned after the 2001 season despite reaching the finals of the Atlantic 10 tournament that year after upsetting No. 1-seeded St. Joe's in the semis.

Flint then took over at Drexel in 2002 and would build the Dragons into a conference powerhouse in 15 seasons at the helm. Flint's biggest problem at Drexel was that nobody wanted to play him. When the Dragons did get rare opportunities to compete against higher-level teams, they often beat them, for example winning at Louisville, at Syracuse, at Villanova, and at Creighton. In 2011–12, Flint led Drexel to 29 victories, but the Dragons didn't make the NCAA tournament that season because their out-of-conference schedule wasn't strong enough as a result of limited opportunities from higher-rated teams.

Martelli, from his own personal experience trying to become a head coach and professional experience with teams unwilling to play the Hawks, knew the feeling of being on the outside looking in. Because of this and because Flint is a St. Joe's graduate, a good friend of his, and Drexel is a Philadelphia school, Martelli would always give the Dragons a game. Even though Drexel wasn't in the Big 5 then, belatedly being admitted in 2023 in a move that was long overdue, the contest had a similar feel to the previous weekend's game against Fran Dunphy and Penn at the Palestra.

"It was always special because it was a Philadelphia game, and Bru, and Bru's connection with the Atlantic 10," Martelli said.

Flint, known as "Bru," has a wonderful personality. Off the court, he has the most radiant smile and an infectious laugh. He is great company. Between the lines, though, he is much, much different. As warm as his smile is outside of the lines, his intense glare on the court can be downright scary. Much like former Temple coach John Chaney, you didn't want to be a player who missed a defensive assignment or a guard who turned the ball over under Flint's watch. Flint had the ultimate respect for Martelli, St. Joe's and, obviously, Jameer Nelson, whom he coveted out of Chester High School during the recruiting process. But neither he nor his players would be in awe or play scared of the No. 12-ranked and favored Hawks. It was no surprise to anyone who knew Flint or had competed against him that the two teams were engaged in a tussle for much of the first half, with Drexel going blow for blow with the Hawks.

"I thought we actually didn't play bad against them to start," Flint said.

But neither the Drexel coach, nor any of the 5,223 fans at the Palestra for the noon start, nor the many more watching on television could have ever expected what would happen next when Chet Stachitas entered the game.

***

Stachitas was a prolific scorer in high school in northern Florida. At 6-foot-5, he had the size and athleticism to dominate at the high school level. He also had built confidence in his game by playing on the AAU circuit for Fastbreak USA in Orlando, where he teamed with future six-time NBA All-Star Amar'e Stoudemire. After Stanford, his top choice for college, informed him that there was not a spot for him, Stachitas selected between Saint Joseph's and Penn. Stachitas's parents, Len (track) and Martha (field hockey, lacrosse, and fencing), had played sports at Penn. He knew the school and the Palestra well but decided to commit to Martelli and the Hawks. Once at St. Joe's, Stachitas realized his high school game didn't exactly work at the NCAA Division I level.

"I used to play above the rim," Stachitas, who also cleared 6-foot-6 in the high jump as a high school senior to finish second in Florida, said. "I used to dunk on people in high school. I have a great high school highlight tape. It just didn't translate to the college game, which is much bigger players."

After averaging only 3.0 points in 10.5 minutes as a freshman in 2002–03, Stachitas knew that he'd have to figure out other ways to score, most likely farther from the basket. The problem was that in high school he was never much of a three-point shooter, something that played out at Hawk Hill when he made just 26.3 percent from beyond the arc as a rookie. He had an old-school set shot from long range that wasn't effective when he got to college, and assistant coach Matt Brady helped him part with it.

"That was a big adjustment I made to become a three-point shooter, which really wasn't in my history up to that point," he said.

Stachitas started feeling more and more comfortable with his new jump shot from long range in the summer before his sophomore season, and he saw some decent results early on in 2003–04. Through six games prior to playing Drexel, he had made six of 15 shots from three-point range, a much-improved 40 percent, and had netted 6.0 points per contest. That was better production than his freshman season but not exactly statistics that would cause Flint to single out Stachitas on his pregame scouting report. So, Drexel's coach couldn't have been too worried when Stachitas checked into the game against the Dragons midway through the first half with the Hawks clinging to a four-point lead.

Stachitas himself wasn't planning to come in and do much damage right away, either. But Jameer Nelson had other plans for him. Nelson knew St. Joe's needed an offensive spark in the tight contest, and he pressed Stachitas to provide one for the Hawks, though Stachitas was a little surprised by this request.

"We're waiting for the TV timeout to come back, and I'm going to inbound to Jameer," Stachitas said. "We're just chatting before the play resumes, and he told me, 'Alright, we need you to come in and score and shoot.' I remember saying, 'Jameer, can I just run up and down the court first?' He's like, 'No, we need you to score now.' That was the confidence he would instill in other people. Like, 'No, we don't have time for you to run up and down the court. We need you to shoot the ball.'"

Stachitas followed Nelson's instructions exactly and quickly hit a three-pointer. Then another. And another. And then, finally, one more. Amazingly, he drained four of four shots from long range in just a three-and-a-half-minute span, scoring 12 points during a 19-2 St. Joe's run that made the score 36-15. The unexpected, red-hot performance by Stachitas was yet another example of Nelson's leadership, something that Fran Dunphy cited as the point guard's greatest quality, which is saying something considering his tremendous basketball skill set.

"He knew how to communicate," Stachitas said. "He talked to everyone a little bit differently based off his relationship with them. I don't know if he knew that's what I needed to hear because I was such a team guy. That's why we were so good, always looking for the extra pass, or who had a better opportunity than myself. Sometimes though your team needs you to shoot when you're open and stop looking for the extra guy."

Nelson knew that was exactly what the Hawks needed during the game-changing spurt against the Dragons. Drexel tried but never was going to come back from that 21-point deficit.

"It was him who killed us a little bit," Flint said of Stachitas. "I was like, 'Oh, wow.' I don't think we played that bad. They went on an unbelievable run, took control of the game, and that was it."

The Hawks coasted to an eventual 92-70 victory to improve to 7-0. Flint was impressed with what he saw.

"Just great chemistry, great guard play," he said. "Jameer was the key to it. As good as they were on offense, they were good on defense."

Flint thinks highly of Martelli, the 2003–04 team, and Saint Joseph's, in general. His father, also named James, who passed away later in the 2003–04 season, continued attending Hawks games long after Flint left Hawk Hill. James Flint Sr. loved Martelli, and father and son bonded over St. Joe's as James Flint Sr. lived out his final days. All of this is said to put into context Flint's postgame comments that raised some eyebrows when he stated that his 1985–86 St. Joe's team was better than the 2003–04 Hawks.[31] Flint was a junior on that team, led by Mo Martin (17.8 points), Rodney Blake (13.5 points, 7.1 rebounds), and Wayne Williams (13.0 points), which won the Atlantic 10 tournament and reached the second round of the NCAA tournament. He also made the remarks just seven games into the season.

More than 20 years later, Flint explained that he felt like his 1985–86 Hawks might not have gotten the respect that they deserved.

"You talk about the great players in the history of the school, you're going to put Jameer first and Mo second or third," Flint, who was honored four times as CAA Coach of the Year while at Drexel, said. "That team we had in '86 was bigger and probably a little deeper. Their 2003–04 team was a great team. At the time, I was telling everybody, 'Don't shortchange us.' That '86 team, at that time, was probably one of the better teams they ever had at the school. One of the things I wanted everybody to know was that we had a really good player, too. Mo Martin was a special player, and I wanted to point that out."

Martelli, who never has been shy about pointing out how great his players and teams were, gets it with Flint. There were never any hard feelings.

"Whenever it didn't have anything to do with that competition," Martelli said, "you know he was out there praising and praising and proudly walking around saying, 'They're my guys. They're my guys.'"

Flint still has a fondness for St. Joe's and Nelson, with whom he keeps in regular contact.

"You know *The Hawk Will Never Die*," Flint said.

The school's mantra is embedded in every Hawks player and coach, past and present. And that attitude would come in handy for St. Joe's in its next game. The Hawks were matched up against a young, tough, and talented team three time zones away. Their early undefeated mark was on the line, and they would need Jameer Nelson to summon some late-game magic once again.

CHAPTER 13

Game 8: A Tough Test

Saturday, December 20, 2003
The Arena, Oakland, California
No. 12 Saint Joseph's at California

Phil Martelli got a lot of phone calls after Jameer Nelson announced on June 19 that he was returning to Saint Joseph's for his senior season. For a change, among the calls coming in, Martelli was fielding scheduling requests for events that he had always wanted to play in but for which he rarely received an invite. He was delighted to schedule a game against California as part of the Pete Newell Challenge in Oakland, California. The Hawks would face the Golden Bears in the second half of a doubleheader on Saturday, December 20, 2003, with Stanford and Gonzaga meeting in the opener.

"We were always looking for those kinds of opportunities, and no one ever offered us these special games," Martelli said. "Since you have Jameer, you can now come."

The Pete Newell Challenge was in its seventh year and was a big deal in Oakland to honor the Hall of Fame coach, who led California, San Francisco, and Michigan State, and ran a popular big man camp. Among the teams who had played in previous editions were Kansas, Duke, North Carolina, Michigan, and Michigan State.

"They always brought in great teams every year," said Jonathan Okanes, who was then a sportswriter covering the event for the *Contra Costa Times*. "As a writer, that was something I always looked forward to. That event was always huge."

Okanes was particularly interested in the 2003 edition of the showcase event so he could see Martelli, Nelson, Delonte West, and the Hawks. Word was out about St. Joe's, but the Hawks had only appeared on national television once, in the season opener against Gonzaga. And this was the pre–social media days, so basketball fans on the West Coast weren't scrolling through reels or posts to see Nelson or Hawks highlights. They had to rely on whatever they could get on *SportsCenter*, which might be a highlight here or there. So, there was genuine excitement and intrigue about the Hawks.

"I was very familiar with how they were doing, especially Jameer, and was looking forward to covering them and watching them," Okanes said. "I remember thinking at the time that this was going to be a treat covering this game. This is pretty cool that I'm seeing one of the better teams in the country, one of the better players in the country, and probably the best backcourt that year. That was one of the top storylines in the nation and as a college basketball writer and college basketball fan, I was following them pretty closely. I was definitely dialed in."

Martelli also recognized this and was eager for the Hawks to make a good showing.

"We're playing in a tournament that has Pete Newell's name, and these guys from another part of the country are going to see our team and start to spread the word," Martelli said. "The word was out but not all the way out."

Martelli also knew that the opponent would not be easy. Cal was coming off three consecutive NCAA tournament appearances and at least 20 victories in each of those seasons. The Bears had lost much to graduation but reloaded with a heralded freshman class of four talented and tall rookies: Leon Powe (6-foot-8, 240 pounds), Marquise Kately (6-foot-5, 220), Ayinde Ubaka (6-foot-4, 200), and Dominic McGuire (6-foot-9, 200).

"Highly touted recruiting class," Okanes said.

The Bears' size and strength was going to be a challenge for the Hawks.

"I remember hearing leading into the game, 'This is going to be a tough one,'" said Dwayne Jones, who, at 6-foot-11, was one of few Hawks who could match the Bears' physicality. "'This is going to be our first loss. Their frontcourt is this. Their frontcourt is that.'"

St. Joe's would get some help in the contest with the return of 6-foot-10 forward Dave Mallon, who agonizingly watched the first seven games from the bench after sustaining a stress fracture in his right foot in a practice a week before the season opener.

"The wins start piling up, and I'm starting to get nervous because I'm missing something special here," Mallon said.

There was some thought about redshirting, and chances are good that in any other year Mallon would have sat out the entire season to get healthy. But he just had to be a part of what he had been seeing in street clothes.

"I can't sit this one out," he said. "I just gotta get out there. I'm glad I did. I didn't want to miss this."

Missing seven games had been hard enough on Mallon.

"It was emotionally challenging," he said. "You're finally starting to climb the ladder, and you're not a part of it."

Mallon was in uniform and available against the Golden Bears, but he wasn't quite himself that night. He never would be that entire season, describing the feeling like he was playing with a "twinge in your foot."

"You don't feel comfortable running or planting," said Mallon, who today lives in South Jersey and works as an insurance broker for Apex. "I'm not a fast guy, and if I lose a gear, I'm even worse. It definitely hobbles you a bit. It's always in your mind, too. You should be able to run seamlessly and when you have something holding you back, it wears on you."

Still, Mallon would rather be on the court even if he wasn't quite 100 percent physically, doing whatever he could to help, than sitting idly on the bench. And the Hawks certainly needed another big presence against the Golden Bears.

"That was a really, really, really tough game," Martelli said.

Other than Nelson, who was keeping them afloat, the Hawks struggled to find any offensive rhythm against the bigger, stronger Bears. Luckily for St. Joe's, Cal wasn't making many shots, either. The teams had combined to miss 23 of 29 three-point attempts with the game tied at 57 and the ball in Nelson's hands as the seconds dwindled.

This time, Nelson wouldn't need to launch from near half-court, as he did against Old Dominion when his 38-footer—unofficially, probably from at least 40 feet—helped the Hawks avoid an upset in the third game of the season. Nelson settled for a jumper from just inside the three-point arc on the right wing, right in front of the Hawks bench. He drained the 18-foot pullback jumper to give St. Joe's a 59-57 lead and then went sprawling on his backside back toward half-court. Nelson was glad to have made the shot and, he hoped, to have pushed aside Cal.

"It was tough, it was physical," Nelson said. "They were bigger, they were stronger, they were more athletic. And they made it tough on us. It was probably one of the closest teams that I played that had professional size and athleticism. And when I made the shot, I think I actually fell. I hit the ground like, 'About time. Get these guys off my back.'"

The clock showed 4.3 seconds remaining when Nelson's shot went through. After a timeout, the Bears threw the ball in from near midcourt. Unbelievably, Ubaka was wide open in the corner and put up a three-point attempt that would have won it for Cal. But it was yet another missed shot from long range, and the Hawks escaped with a win.

"It was a pretty good look," Okanes said. "I remember in the postgame presser [Ubaka being wide open] was the only question I asked Martelli. I remember his answer, and I'm paraphrasing, 'That was the subject of great conversation in the locker room.' Everyone kind of laughed."

Nelson finished with a game-high 19 points on a night when every other Hawks player was off offensively.

"That game was a real struggle," said Ray Parrillo, who was covering for the *Philadelphia Inquirer*.

West netted a season-low six points, missing 11 of 13 shots, and it would be the only time all season he didn't reach double digits in scoring. Pat Carroll's eight points were next-most after Nelson. Mallon did get into the contest, played five minutes, and scored his first points of the season on a dunk.

"I was just happy to be out there again," Mallon said. "That was an exciting game. Jameer hit that step-back. Just an awesome first game back. I felt whole again."

Martelli was not upset at all by the Hawks' struggles. Quite the opposite, he was impressed by how they gutted out the victory.

"It was an important trip for the grittiness of this group," he said.

The Hawks boarded a commercial jet for home, probably with plenty of ice packs on various body parts. They would have a few days to rest before getting just the medicine they needed: a return to the cozy confines of the Fieldhouse for the second time this season.

CHAPTER 14

Game 9: Revenge at the Fieldhouse

Saturday, December 27, 2003
Alumni Memorial Fieldhouse, Philadelphia
Pacific at No. 10 Saint Joseph's

After a long trip and tough game in the Pete Newell Challenge against California in Oakland, Saint Joseph's was happy to be back at the Fieldhouse for the second time this season. The Hawks were set to host Pacific at four o'clock on Saturday, December 27, 2003. Under normal circumstances, with students on break between the fall and spring semesters, the Fieldhouse might be half full, at best, for a nonconference opponent during this time of the year. The section behind the basket reserved for students might have a smattering of undergraduates mixed in with some adults. But this was not normal circumstances. This was not a normal season. The gym was packed to the rafters, and the students were ready and in full throttle well before tipoff.

"I remember specifically them having a student section right behind the basket where they filled up all the students in that small, older gym," Tyler Newton, a junior at Pacific in 2003–04, recalled more than 20 years later. "It was a phenomenal atmosphere. The students were there early when we were warming up, super loud and heckling."

The students weren't the only ones ready to go. In the previous season, St. Joe's headed to the West Coast for its highly anticipated game against Gonzaga at The Kennel on New Year's Eve. The Hawks needed a warm-up game and scheduled Pacific on December 28, 2002. St. Joe's was 7-0 and rolling. Pacific, located in Stockton, California, would finish 12-16 overall in 2002–03 and was not a great team by any means. But the Hawks, possibly looking ahead to their big showdown against the Zags, got beat by Pacific, 62-50.

"They were going up to Gonzaga to play, and I think we caught them thinking that we couldn't beat them," longtime Pacific coach Bob Thomason said.

Judy Martelli was in attendance at Pacific and remembers feeling disappointed after that defeat, only to be consoled by a Tigers fan.

"We were kind of down and a fan from Pacific comes over to me and says, 'Cheer up, don't worry about it, nobody goes undefeated,'" Judy Martelli said. "I was like, 'Oh yeah, I guess you're right.'"

Well, maybe. Or maybe not.

Fast-forward 364 days and the Hawks were undefeated once again, at 8-0, and still in play to realize Delonte West's preseason declaration and Dick Jerardi's similar message to Phil Martelli in a phone call after the season-opening win over Gonzaga that St. Joe's could go undefeated in 2003–04. There would be no looking past Pacific this time.

"They were ready for us," Thomason said.

Thomason also would have his team ready. He had learned a valuable lesson during the Tigers' first of five NCAA appearances in his 25 years at the helm in 1997 when they lost to St. Joe's in the first round in Martelli's second season. Thomason had studied the Hawks on tape and had his team well prepared from a technical standpoint. But what the tape couldn't transmit was the sheer intensity and emotion of St. Joe's. From that point forward, whenever Thomason's teams played an opponent from the East Coast, or anyone in the NCAA tournament, the coach treated the game like it was against Pacific's biggest conference rival.

"We had a scouting report, but it wasn't a personal fight," Thomason said of that 1997 contest. "[After that loss] we're going to make it personal, like a league game. And I think that helped us. It's hard when you're playing an East Coast team. It's not like you're playing a league team that you really hate. We tried to make it that way. I learned from that first St. Joe's game."

Thomason and the Tigers knew the challenge in Philadelphia would not be easy. Besides the fact that the Hawks were playing in their cozy, raucous gym with revenge on their minds, they had a couple of other advantages, as Newton recalled years later.

"I remember the mascot and the students and, of course, Jameer Nelson and Delonte West," Newton said.

Thomason had prepared his team for Nelson and West from the tape the best he could. The Tigers also would bring emotion, something they would do now whenever they played against any East Coast team. They also knew from experience the previous season how much fight they would need against the Hawks' talented and tough backcourt.

"They were athletic and had a toughness about them," Thomason said. "They could put the ball on the floor and score. Delonte could shoot, Jameer ended up becoming an even better outside shooter. Jameer was one of the best guards in college. When you have one of the best guards as the point guard, you're always in good shape as a basketball team."

At 6-foot-11, Newton was a full foot taller than Nelson. But he knew Nelson wouldn't give even an inch.

"You think Jameer can't do this or that because he's a smaller guard, but he was very explosive and tough," Newton said. "I remember for his size he could rebound the shit out of the basketball."

Besides West and Nelson, Newton was going to have to deal with the rowdy students for most of the evening after missing a fast break dunk early in the contest.

"I got on a breakaway," he said. "I was a pretty athletic guy and had put some people on posters in my time at Pacific. I'm running down and Delonte West starts chasing me down. Right before I'm about to take off to dunk, he runs right in front of me. I get nervous he's going to undercut me, don't get a very good jump, and end up hitting the front of the rim. And the whole crowd was riding me for the rest of the half. I was hearing it every time I touched the ball."

Newton remembered finishing another dunk in the second half. By then, the Hawks had built a comfortable lead on their way to an easy 73-55 victory. As expected, Nelson and West had big games, with Nelson getting 15 points, seven rebounds, six assists, and three steals. West led all scorers with 22 points, along with six rebounds and three steals. Chet Stachitas came off the bench with another important contribution, making four three-pointers on his way to 14 points. Stachitas clearly felt comfortable with his new jump shot and had drained 55.6 percent (15 of 27) of his attempts from beyond the arc through the Pacific game. Tyrone Barley also helped out on defense, as per usual, chipping in with four of the Hawks' 14 steals.

St. Joe's had not taken Pacific lightly this time around.

"They just had all of the pieces and had a lot of confidence in themselves," said Thomason, who won 437 games at Pacific and racked up five Big West Coach of the Year honors. "I was really impressed with them. Sometimes in coaching, it's just getting the most out of what you have. And they did."

The Hawks' win not only avenged their defeat at Pacific from a year earlier and moved them to 9-0, but the game also helped to kickstart the Tigers on their most successful stretch in school history. The defeat dropped Pacific to 4-6 on the season, and the players got together afterward to reset.

"We did not get our ass kicked very often, and that was one of the worst losses we took," said Newton, a successful entrepreneur in California today with businesses including a Kona Ice and a kickboxing gym who had 11 points and five rebounds. "We were a very competitive ball club, but they put it on us that day. After taking a beating like that, it was like, 'Hey man, we have to look each other in the eye. If we want to accomplish the goals we set out for ourselves this year, we need to buckle down and start doing what we need to do.'"

The Tigers did just that and went on to win 21 of their next 23 contests, including the Big West Conference tournament title and a first-round upset as the No. 12 seed of fifth-seeded Providence—using Thomason's strategy to bring the fight and conference rival mentality to an East Coast team—in the NCAA tournament. The

2003–04 Pacific team was inducted into the school's Hall of Fame in 2024. And the Tigers weren't done, either. The core of the team that lost to St. Joe's at the Fieldhouse would win 27 of 31 contests overall in 2004–05 and go 18-0 in the Big West before Pacific ended an amazing three-year run with a 24-8 overall mark and 12-2 league record in 2005–06. The Tigers made the NCAA tournament in all three of those seasons and were 47-3 in the Big West.

Some of the credit for that successful stretch goes to the defeat to St. Joe's at the Fieldhouse.

"I think we came together a little more after that loss and went on a real special run," Newton said.

The Hawks had their own special run going. In three days, they would look to finish out the calendar year before entering conference play with 10 wins to start the season. And they would be looking to Dwayne Jones for a spark.

CHAPTER 15

Game 10: Jones Shows Attitude, Dominance

Tuesday, December 30, 2003
Bob Carpenter Center, Newark, Delaware
No. 10 Saint Joseph's at Delaware

On the court, Dwayne Jones cast an intimidating presence. At 6-foot-11, he is tall, strong, and muscular. Jones also is a fierce rim protector, as Gonzaga found out in the season opener when he blocked six shots. Off the court, though, Jones is quiet, easygoing, and mild-mannered. Entering the 10th game of the 2003–04 season at Delaware on December 30, 2003, Phil Martelli had a talk with Jones about bringing some more meanness to the court.

Martelli loved Jones's selflessness. "He had no need to be featured in any way," he said. But the coach also had witnessed Jones taking over in practice. "There were dominant signs, whether it be shot-blocking, or finishes at the rim," he said. And Martelli wanted Jones to bring that to the game. Speaking in the postgame press conference at Delaware, Martelli said he talked to Jones in the lead-up to the contest about bringing attitude into the game.[32] More than 20 years later, neither Martelli nor Jones recalled that exact conversation but didn't doubt that it happened.

"I don't remember challenging him, but it doesn't surprise me that I did," Martelli said. "Some of that was selective, like trying to find guys who could make a difference. In that game, he could make a difference because he's bigger than them and better than their guys."

Jones understood the coach's mission and message.

"I don't remember that conversation exactly, but I do remember times when Coach would bring me into his office, or some of the other coaches would talk to me about just leaving my imprint on the game and bringing attitude and nastiness in my own way," Jones said. "I'm kind of a quiet, reserved person. But when it comes to being on the floor, I'm ultracompetitive."

In addition to the motivation from Martelli, Jones was spurred on against Delaware by two other factors: He believed he wasn't rebounding the way he should to that point in the season, and the Blue Hens were talking trash during the contest. Jones felt like he wasn't leading the team in rebounding. In fact, at 7.1 rebounds per contest, he did have a slight edge over Jameer Nelson (5.3) and Delonte West (5.1) through nine games. It's possible that he didn't remember that more than 20 years later. It's also possible in the moment that he told himself he wasn't leading the team in rebounding as a way to motivate himself, as athletes sometimes do in order to improve their performance.

"I just remember it being very competitive for me personally with the matchups," Jones said. "Delaware guys were talking trash a little bit, and it just kind of fired me up. I wanted to prove myself because I wasn't leading us in rebounding, and it kind of bothered me. Like, 'I'm the starting five [center]. I should be leading my team in rebounding.' During that stretch, I took it personally to just attack the glass and show that I could be one of the main factors on this team."

An inspired Jones unleashed the most productive three-game stretch of his career, leaving any part of his off-the-court Mr. Nice Guy persona outside of the lines. He hammered Delaware for 14 points, 11 rebounds, and two blocks in 34 minutes, making four of seven field goals. He followed that with double-doubles in the next two games, finishing a dominant three-game stretch by averaging 15.7 points, 12 rebounds, and two blocks while making 72.7 percent (16 of 22) of his field goals, many of which were dunks.

"I just think I was in a really good rhythm at the time," Jones said. "It was just me trying to put my stamp on the game and bring my attitude. Again, I'm not going to be out there talking much trash. But if I can get an offensive rebound, if I can block a shot, if I can run the floor, if I can get one of my teammates open that way … Just bringing my energy and effort."

After his college and professional career, Jones has gone on to coach. He has counseled players to star in their roles like he did against Delaware and throughout his career on Hawk Hill. He was a member of the Philadelphia 76ers' staff for seven seasons before joining his alma mater in 2023 as an assistant coach for the Hawks. While with the 76ers, he helped counsel players like Paul Reed, who served as All-Star center Joel Embiid's backup, about the importance of their roles.

"I was a role player and tried to be a star in my role," Jones said. "I try to use that messaging with guys, for example Paul Reed. I always wanted to do more, but you had to do what the team needed you to do. Just be a star in your role. Keep working hard and hopefully your role expands. Just do what's best for the team, understanding that if the team looks good, you're going to look good."

Jones more than did his part against Delaware, but the Hawks were surprisingly sluggish against the overmatched Blue Hens in the opening 20 minutes. Delaware was within just four points at halftime.

"That was one of two times they clearly played down to their opponent," said Joe Cabrey, a 1974 St. Joe's graduate who attended every Hawks home and away game in the 2003–04 season. "Phil got after them at halftime."

The Blue Hens recognized that St. Joe's didn't play to its standard in the first half, but they also felt that an upset was possible.

"It was a component of us playing good defense, but it was more them not hitting shots," said Mike Slattery, a Philadelphia native and Germantown Academy graduate who started at point guard for the Blue Hens that season as a junior. "When you're going into any game, especially against an opponent like that, your thought process is, 'If we can stay within striking distance, anything can happen.' I would be really surprised at halftime if we weren't like, 'OK, there's a chance here. Let's see if we can steal this one.'"

With Jones continuing his dominance inside and Nelson and West heating up from the outside, the Hawks didn't allow the Blue Hens' upset thoughts to last very long after the intermission. St. Joe's made its first five shots of the second half and scored 19 of the first 24 points after the halftime break on the way to a 75-54 victory. Nelson finished with 20 points, and West added 18 points, six rebounds, and six assists.

"I look up and Jameer has 20 points, and I felt like I was playing decent defense on him," Slattery said. "Delonte just decides he's going to take over, and he's doing whatever he wants in the second half. It was just a quick switch of offensive explosiveness. When a team like that gets on a roll at that pace, it's almost impossible to keep up. They turned it on when they had to. As good as our players were, we were just incapable to match up defensively to stop them over 40 minutes."

It was fun for the Blue Hens while it lasted, though.

"Any time you're playing a top 10 team, the vibe is going to be fantastic," Slattery said. "The people are going to be into it. We brought hope for the first half, and the Bob was rocking. For Delaware, it was just an awesome experience. The fact that we hung tight for a certain period of time made that a raucous house. It was a good time. Then they go on a run, and it deflated pretty quickly."

Slattery played on a very good Germantown Academy team that featured four other Division I recruits: Lee Melchionni (Duke), Ted Skuchas (Vanderbilt), Matt Walsh (Florida), and Rob Kurz (Penn). Slattery was disappointed with the result against the Hawks but happy to continue the competition against Philadelphia-area players, and he followed St. Joe's closely the rest of the way.

"Being from Philly, you want anyone from Philly who's making a run to try to win the whole thing," he said. "When you're in the heat of competition, you're not friends with anybody. You're trying to win and you're putting forth the effort to be a worthy opponent. When you compete against them and you feel like you had a good effort on your behalf, you feel like, 'OK, this is pretty cool. We want to support them to go as far as they can.'"

And the Hawks had their sights set on going far. Through 10 games of the nonconference schedule, they were still perfect. Up next, St. Joe's would be looking to continue their winning ways in Atlantic 10 Conference play. And they'd also be looking to do something that no team in school history had ever done.

CHAPTER 16

Game 11: A Record Start

Saturday, January 3, 2004
Alumni Memorial Fieldhouse, Philadelphia
George Washington at No. 10 Saint Joseph's

After recovering from a sluggish first half and fending off Delaware's upset bid, Saint Joseph's returned home to the Fieldhouse. The Hawks were set to open Atlantic 10 Conference play against George Washington at noon on Saturday, January 3, 2004. They also had a chance to make some school history, as no St. Joe's team had ever started a season with 11 consecutive victories. However, Phil Martelli was more focused on the game at hand and the beginning of league competition rather than the record books.

"I always throughout my career dealt with a game at a time, so I would never bring it up to them that this is a school record, that is a school record," Martelli said. "We were never defending the record. We were always playing that game. In my mind, everything that we had done could go like this"—Martelli snapped his fingers—"if you start out the league with a loss.

"Winning the league, that was a big deal to us. And starting at home, home games in any league are gold. That would've been the message I would've been delivering to them."

Mark Bass, who both played for Martelli and then worked for 20 years as his assistant, remembers the coach's consistent message as being focused on the task at hand.

"I just think we took the approach of, 'Let's get better, let's just get better,'" Bass said. "Phil did a good job with it. Who's our next opponent? Whose scout is it? How do we win that game? We really didn't talk about [records and being undefeated]. Then, when all of the reports started coming out and people started following, we still didn't get caught up in that. We still wanted to get better and be a good team."

Martelli might not have been talking about a record start, but many St. Joe's followers and interested observers were thinking about how a victory over George

Washington would better the 10-0 beginning by the 1964–65 Hawks. The style of play of that Jack Ramsay-coached team was different, with much more of an inside game than the perimeter-based 2003–04 edition. But there were many similarities between the two teams.

The 1964–65 Hawks, like the group with Jameer Nelson nearly 40 years later, had a star in 6-foot-4 forward Cliff Anderson. In 6-foot-5 Matt Guokas, Anderson also had a talented sidekick like Delonte West was for Nelson. Billy Oakes, a 5-foot-11 guard, 6-foot-5 forward Tom Duff, and 6-foot-6 forward Marty Ford also averaged in double digits in scoring like Anderson and Guokas and filled important roles. The 1964–65 team also had the intangible qualities of the Nelson-led Hawks.

"We gelled as a team very quickly," Guokas said. "We played together. We had to because we weren't super talented other than Cliff."

St. Joe's athletic director Don DiJulia was a reserve guard on that squad. He remembers the positive attitude of the group, which was reminiscent of what Dave Mallon said about Nelson, that if Nelson could do it, so could Mallon. DiJulia recalls reviewing the schedule with Guokas before the season, and they had the same thought as West almost 40 years later.

"We went through the whole thing and thought we could win every game," DiJulia said. "There was a confidence in some of those players, and that confidence just rubbed off to everybody else. Why not on a given day? If Clifford and Matty play their best, we know we're going to win. If they just play OK, we have enough other guys that if they compensate, we can play with all these teams. So, let's go."

In Anderson, St. Joe's had a down-low player who was practically unstoppable at times. He was playing in his first season at St. Joe's in 1964–65 and would finish his three-year college career with 1,728 points and 1,228 rebounds. Anderson once grabbed 32 rebounds in a Big 5 contest against La Salle. An All-American as a senior in 1966–67, Anderson still holds the school's single-season records for scoring (26.5 points per game) and rebounding (15.5). He later would play four seasons in the NBA. A Big 5 Hall of Famer, he was inducted into St. Joe's inaugural Hall of Fame class in 1999. Anderson passed away in 2021.

"Cliff Anderson was far and away our most talented guy," Guokas said. "He could score 20-plus a game, get to the free throw line, and was a terrific rebounder."

Like the 2003–04 Hawks, the 1964–65 players fell into very defined roles in which they starred.

"The rest of us had our particular jobs to do," said Guokas, whose long NBA career included five seasons as a player, seven as a head coach, and many more as a local and national television broadcaster. Included in his NBA stint was playing and coaching for his hometown 76ers. "Billy was a good outside shooter and scorer. Tom was a very underrated player. He did so much for our team. He was strong inside, a good jump shooter from about 15 feet, and a terrific rebounder. Marty blended in and filled in whatever we needed in a particular game. And we got good support from the bench. It just all worked together."

Guokas's Hawks got off to a fast start before stalling in their 11th contest when they lost to Providence, which was led by All-American and future NBA All-Star Jimmy Walker. The 1964–65 Hawks didn't lose another game until meeting Providence again in the second round of the NCAA tournament, where they were defeated once more by Walker and the Friars.

"Jimmy Walker was an outstanding player," Guokas said. "They proved they were a better team than us that year."

The 2003–04 version of the Hawks were set on proving that they were a better team than everyone, too. Like Guokas's squad, they already had beaten their first 10 opponents and were now just one of 11 unbeatens remaining in NCAA Division I. But George Washington would turn out to be a tough test, as conference games usually are. The Hawks led by just four points at the half, as GW found success scoring inside and at the foul line. St. Joe's finally got enough distance late in the second half, taking a 12-point lead with 5:13 to play, to have enough breathing room to go on to a 90-81 victory.

The win made St. Joe's 1-0 in the Atlantic 10 and 11-0 overall, breaking the 1964–65 record for victories to open a season. The 1914–15 Hawks also had started the season with 11 consecutive wins without a loss, but the school did not consider that the official record since that team competed against some club teams and high school teams.

"I was very happy for Phil Martelli," Guokas said. "He had been at St. Joe's for such a long, long time."

Nelson led the Hawks with 29 points, eight rebounds, and zero turnovers in 39 minutes. Dwayne Jones continued to play with the nastiness that started against Delaware when Martelli called on him to bring attitude to the court, finishing with a season-high 23 points along with 10 rebounds. West chipped in 18 points in a physical game that saw a combined 61 free throws.

Guokas didn't see the Hawks on this day, but he would go on to watch much of Nelson's career in the NBA from a front row seat. Nelson would spend 10 of his 14 NBA seasons with the Orlando Magic, where Guokas was the analyst for the local television broadcast. Guokas was thoroughly impressed by his fellow Hawk—both on and off the court.

"Jameer was a point guard who could score, had the three-point threat, could drive into the lane, and make a play," Guokas said. "He was an all-around point guard. He was so clever in the pick-and-roll game. He could pick, he could get all the way to the basket, and shoot little teardrops. Whatever. He was a great passer. He and Dwight Howard clicked very well. Jameer was outstanding.

"And he was a delight to be around. A great team guy. I could tell guys loved him. He had a great attitude and a smile all the time. He just loved being a basketball player and being in the NBA. It was fun broadcasting his games."

Guokas rarely broadcast college games but did call one St. Joe's contest, the Hawks' 83-80 home loss to Dan Dickau and Gonzaga at the Fieldhouse on December 31, 2001. Due to his conflicting NBA schedule, that was the only time he saw Nelson play in person in college. Guokas didn't think then or later that Nelson's lack of size would be an impediment at the next level.

"He's very gifted, very talented, and works hard," Guokas said. "Even though he's 5-foot-11, he's put together. He could take all of the banging and the bumping and that type of thing. [Defensively, in the NBA] he never seemed to get beat up by anybody. He held his own and played his position well."

The NBA would come later for Nelson. He still had work to do on the college level. With the school record for wins to start the season behind them, the Hawks set out on the road for their next league game. The opponent was one of the best defensive teams in the A-10, and St. Joe's would need Nelson to be on top of his game.

CHAPTER 17

Game 12: Another Challenge Answered

Tuesday, January 6, 2004
Robins Center, Richmond, Virginia
No. 9 Saint Joseph's at Richmond

With the school's record for most wins to start the season in hand, Saint Joseph's headed on the road for its second Atlantic 10 Conference game looking to build on the winning streak. But the Hawks would be doing it without John Bryant. In the five games following his game-changing defensive performance against Craig Smith and Boston College, Bryant had not garnered headlines. But, then, that was not his game. He was chipping in with some points and some rebounds here and there. Mostly, though, he was doing all of the dirty work by setting screens, battling down low, defending, and, of course, giving maximum effort and being a great teammate. But the physical nature of his role took a toll, and Bryant was in street clothes for the Hawks' contest at Richmond on Tuesday, January 6, 2004, with a back injury that would sideline him for three consecutive games.

"I feel like I was always in the training room just because of the nature of the way I played," Bryant said. "A lot of screens, a lot of dribble handoffs, a lot of pin-downs for Pat Carroll and Delonte West. So, you just put your body in harm's way, literally, every game."

Eventually, Bryant would need back surgery. That would come much later. Now, he was just trying to rehabilitate to get back on the court as soon as possible. Meantime, he felt like the Hawks would be OK without him.

"I remember thinking we're going to be fine," he said. "We have Dave Mallon. My first thought was that we have enough. I never thought I'm going to be the reason for us to lose. You never want to let the team down, but I felt like we had enough. Coach was masterful in giving us the confidence we needed that we had enough to keep going."

And, yes, Mallon was there to fill in for Bryant as the starting power forward.

And St. Joe's also had Jameer Nelson.

Nelson had been the Hawks' Mr. Everything practically from the moment he stepped on campus as a freshman. However, Phil Martelli had sensed recently that there was more for Nelson to give. Much like he did with Dwayne Jones before the game at Delaware, when the coach called on Jones to bring more attitude and nastiness to the court, Martelli pulled Nelson aside before the Atlantic 10 opener against George Washington and asked for more from Nelson. The Hawks point guard agreed with the coach's assessment that he could improve. Nelson was still filling up the box score, but he wasn't playing as well as he could. As an example, Nelson had combined for 15 turnovers in the three contests before the GW game. Both coach and player knew there was another rung to Nelson's game.[33]

Nelson responded with 29 points, eight rebounds, three assists, and zero turnovers in 39 minutes in the Hawks' record-setting victory over GW. And he remained in a zone at Richmond—even before the referee's opening whistle. Nelson had begun a warm-up routine around this time that Joe Cabrey said was as mesmerizing as the actual game at times. Cabrey remembers getting to his seat early just so he could watch Nelson warm up. He also recalls the absolute silencing effect the star guard's pregame routine had on often-rowdy student sections that were there early to heckle Nelson and the Hawks.

"Jameer would shoot three-pointers from one baseline to the other," Cabrey said. "Robert Hartshorn would feed him, and he would hit 35, 40, or 45 shots in a row in front of the student section. He never smiled or celebrated. He'd just do that until he got to the other corner. And people were like, 'Oh! My! God!' They go from that energy level to stunned because Jameer put on such a show. It was as entertaining as some of the games. He got into a zone. It was just ridiculous. Shot after shot after shot, he kept burying them."

To Cabrey's point, Martelli's first remembrance when asked about the Richmond game more than 20 years later was what Nelson did in warm-ups.

"It happened at other times, but that game his presence in warm-ups you were like, 'Oh yeah, this is different,'" Martelli said.

Spurred on by Martelli's words, like Jones before him at Delaware, Nelson was ready to carry his incredible pregame warm-up into the contest. But scoring points wasn't usually easy against the Spiders. Richmond was one of the best defensive teams in the league, if not the country, and featured eventual 2003–04 Atlantic 10 Defensive Player of the Year Tony Dobbins. Dobbins took turns guarding Nelson in coach Jerry Wainwright's aggressive man-to-man defense that was usually highly effective.

"All man, all the time," Mike Skrocki, a senior guard on Richmond in 2003–04, said of Richmond's defense. "Wainwright's philosophy was, 'We'll play anyone, anywhere, anytime. And we'll play man. Everyone has to help each other out. We'll give them our playbook.' He was very old-school. Wainwright saw zone as a weakness.

Mano a mano. It worked for us. When you instill that kind of philosophy and get the right guys to buy in, it works."

But no defenders, no matter how bought in, and no system, no matter how sound, were going to stop Nelson on this night. He picked up where he left off in warm-ups and torched the Spiders for 32 points to lead the Hawks to a 71-60 victory that improved them to 12-0 overall and 2-0 in the A-10. Nelson made nine of 14 field goals, five of 10 three-pointers, and nine of 12 free throws.

"It was just dominance," Martelli said. "And it was dominance through presence, not dominance through play, that sticks out to me."

Nelson scored 18 points in the first half to quiet the Robins Center crowd of 6,447 and help the Hawks take a comfortable 18-point lead at halftime.

"They steamrolled us early," said Skrocki, who would end the season as Richmond's leading scorer (16.0 points per game). "Our gym, packed crowd. I think Jameer probably just realized, 'Look, I can't let them hang around. Let's get them out of this early.' After halftime, we made a small run and then he squashed it. He just had that ability. We had played St. Joe's the last two years, and you could see the improvement and growth over the years. That last year [in 2003–04] he just kind of knew he was the man on that team. He was the engine. He just knew as I go, they will go. He just had that ability to know when he really needed to take control."

Ironically, Skrocki could have been teammates with Nelson. Martelli loved Skrocki's game and recruited him hard to St. Joe's. "He was so sound," Martelli said. Skrocki, a native of Howell, New Jersey, said he really liked Martelli, and it was a tough decision to choose the Spiders over St. Joe's and Davidson. Part of Martelli's recruiting pitch to Skrocki was the opportunity to play alongside Nelson, though Skrocki wasn't pulled in the same way as Pat Carroll and Jones would later be by Nelson's commitment to the Hawks.

"I remember Phil Martelli always talking about Jameer like, 'Aw man, we got Jameer coming, and you'll be great with him,'" Skrocki said. "'He'll be able to drive and kick to you. You guys will be a great one-two punch.' All this stuff. I had played AAU and all this, but I wasn't one of those guys who read all the reports and the rankings. I just go play. I hadn't really heard of Jameer at that point. I was just like, 'Who is this Jameer guy he keeps talking about?' He keeps telling me this Jameer guy is unbelievable, and I'm like 'Damn, I've never heard of him.'

"Here we are four years later playing each other, and I'm like"—Skrocki laughed—"'Yeah, this Jameer guy is pretty good. Pretty damn good. He's going to end up in the NBA and [college] Player of the Year. Yeah, I think he's alright.'"

Besides Skrocki, likely all college basketball fans now knew exactly who Nelson was after breathtaking performances like the one against Richmond. In addition to Nelson's phenomenal game, St. Joe's also got a huge contribution from Jones for the third straight contest. The Hawks center had 10 points and a season-high 15 rebounds along with three blocks. While the Spiders couldn't stop Nelson, they also had difficulty scoring because of Jones and St. Joe's guards.

"Jones is just eating up the paint, getting rebounds, blocking shots," Skrocki said. "It just makes it really difficult because you're either trying to shoot contested shots on the outside, or you're trying to drive by guys who are probably quicker than you, and then you have to deal with Jones on the inside who is probably going to alter your shot. They really had the right roster to produce that defense."

While the Hawks kept rolling with the victory, Richmond was barely above .500 after the defeat, dropping to 8-6. But the Spiders did pull positives from the contest. Sixteen days later, Richmond traveled to play No. 12-ranked Kansas at Allen Fieldhouse. And Wainwright used Richmond's experience against St. Joe's as motivation for the game against the always tough Jayhawks.

"Coach Wainwright just listed out on a whiteboard before we took the floor all of the good players we played that year," Skrocki, who was inducted into Richmond's Hall of Fame after scoring 1,408 career points and making 220 shots from three-point range, remembered 20 years later. "On that list was Jameer Nelson and Delonte West, future pro players we played. He said, 'Look, you played against the best players, so why are you scared of Kansas? They're just five other dudes. Here's a list of guys you played that are going to be in the NBA.' It kind of gave us the confidence to say, 'We've played the best, so we shouldn't go out there and be scared tonight.'"

Richmond didn't play scared at all, upsetting Kansas 69-68 to help turn around the Spiders' season. "That's what started it steamrolling for us," said Skrocki, who scored 23 points against Kansas. The Spiders would go on to receive an at-large bid into the NCAA tournament.

The Hawks had their sights set on more than just getting a bid to the NCAA tournament; rather, they wanted to win the whole thing. However, there was still much time and plenty of work to be done before the tournament started in March. And St. Joe's would get right to it after returning home from Richmond to prepare for another A-10 road trip. The Hawks had several days to practice. And, as always, the sessions would be extremely intense.

CHAPTER 18

Game 13: We're Talkin' about Practice

Saturday, January 10, 2004
Palumbo Center, Pittsburgh
No. 9 Saint Joseph's at Duquesne

Brian Jesiolowski played in 15 games in the 2003–04 season. As a senior walk-on, Jesiolowski's appearance meant the game's outcome was no longer in doubt. When he did enter a contest, though, Jesiolowski was expected to play with the same level of effort that had been drilled into all Saint Joseph's players during Phil Martelli's intensely competitive practices.

"One thing Coach Martelli always conveyed to us was that we were held to the same standard as everybody else," Jesiolowski said. And when Jesiolowski—or anyone else—didn't meet Martelli's demandingly high bar, he heard about it.

"There was never going to be a letup," Martelli said. "I never sat down. I didn't want them to think it was over. I didn't put them in the game just to dribble it out. You worked hard in practice. Go play. But play the way you've been taught to play."

At 6-foot-7, Jesiolowski was a valuable player in practice with his size and athleticism. When he did get opportunities to play in games, he relished them.

"Man, it was awesome," he said. "There was nothing like it, playing in front of crowds like that."

Jesiolowski got one of his coveted chances at Duquesne's Palumbo Center on Saturday, January 10, 2004. Jameer Nelson scored 19 of his 21 points in the first half; Delonte West added 20 points; and Chet Stachitas, still successfully firing away from three-point range, made all three of his attempts from the beyond the arc. With the game in hand, Martelli pulled Nelson and West with about 10 minutes remaining in the Hawks' eventual 78-61 victory that moved them to 13-0 overall and 3-0 in the Atlantic 10. Jesiolowski subbed in for the final minute and got a quick reminder of what was expected of every member of the Hawks.

"I got in and I'm kind of being lazy and foul a guy on a fast break," he said. An angry Martelli summoned Jesiolowski to the sidelines. "Coach calls me over,"

Jesiolowski said, "and is like, "'What are you doing?! You're held to the same standard as everybody else!'"

It was a teaching moment by Martelli for Jesiolowski *and* for every player who was watching from the court and the bench.

"Like Brian in that case, I never let it go in practice," Martelli said. "What do you mean you let him beat you one-on-one? We play one-on-one every day. In that situation, you're not going to let him dribble by you. The standard of competitive fire was in all that they did."

For Martelli, it didn't matter whether you were a future first-round NBA draft pick, like Nelson and West, or a future Hollywood actor and comedian, like Jesiolowski. The coach demanded competitiveness, effort, and intensity in practice and in games every day from everyone.

Martelli's approach was a far cry from former 76ers star Allen Iverson, who questioned how he could make teammates better in practice in an infamous press conference.[34] Making teammates better in practice is exactly what Martelli expected of walk-ons like Jesiolowski and Robert Hartshorn.

"Be prepared to show up to practice and play your ass off," Jesiolowski said. "[Martelli] conveyed to us that you are what makes our team better. The more you bring it in practice against the guys, you make our starters better. So, you have to bring it just as much as they are. We had to push ourselves to be in shape and be aggressive and be at that level so we can make everybody better."

Hartshorn was especially good at raising his teammates' levels in practice. The former St. Joe's cheerleader also was a talented athlete like Jesiolowski. But he helped to keep the energy high in practices as much with his mouth as with his game. Hartshorn's talkative nature was an unseen, unheralded role, but it was important to the success of the team.

"Our practice had a level of intensity, and if I could stay enthusiastic, energetic, and intense, that would help to drive practice," Hartshorn said. "I would see guys in the cafeteria and would say, 'Don't forget what's going to happen to you at 6:30.'"

Hartshorn's nonstop talking sometimes drew the ire of his teammates. During one practice, Nelson and Tyrone Barley got so annoyed with him that they picked up their defense on Hartshorn at full-court and would not let him dribble the ball past half-court. Eventually, Hartshorn just tossed the ball as far as he could and it landed in the second level of the Fieldhouse. The scene didn't allow the Hawks to go through the opposition's plays, but it brought exactly the type of intensity Martelli was looking for.

"They wouldn't let him complete a pass," an astounded Martelli said. "So, we couldn't go through the other team's stuff. That's how hard they guarded him. Because he wouldn't stop talking, they weren't having it that day."

"That's my way of, 'OK, you want to play, I'm not letting you breathe,'" Barley recalled. "I'm picking you up full-court."

Barley remembered another time when he got so mad at Hartshorn that he chased him around the gym. "I do remember Martelli giving [Hartshorn] a wink like, 'Good job,'" Barley said. That's what Hartshorn did for those Hawks. He aggravated them to help get the best out of them.

"We loved one another, and love is the sincerest form of understanding," Hartshorn said. "Every guy out there understood when we got between the lines, all bets are off. I'll knock your head off, but I'll hold my hand out and lift you up. Or if I take sweat and throw it in your face, that means you need to get up and stop being a punk because we have business to handle. And there were some practices that were like that.

"I could do that with Delonte, also a guy who lived on the edge of a lightning bolt, or with the nicest guys on the team. John Bryant almost took a swing at me. Dwayne Jones, the guy that never said anything to anybody, I had him cock back and want to swing on me. If I can get it out of those guys, I know I'm doing my job. I knew what our potential was, and I feel like there's nothing worse than untapped potential."

Hartshorn, who also provided constant, positive encouragement during games, helped to raise the level of competition in practice with his somewhat unconventional methods. And Martelli was all about competition. The Hawks didn't spend time in layup lines, or even doing wind sprints as you'd expect to see in a basketball practice. Every part of practice was scripted with the goal for there to be a winner and a loser, as if St. Joe's were playing an actual game.

"I believed in competition," Martelli said. "If you're doing a shooting drill, there should be a winner and loser. And it was intense. There was no stepping off it [by the players]. And, for that, I will always be grateful. We practiced every day like a team that hadn't won a game, not a team that had won every game."

Andrew Koefer noticed this right away and wasn't exactly thrilled. Koefer could have continued his basketball career on the Division III level after playing at Allentown Central Catholic but wanted to focus on school and the next part of his life, so he enrolled at St. Joe's with no intention to ever play competitively again. Early in his freshman year in the fall of 2003, however, Koefer joined an intramural basketball team mostly just to meet new people. Some of the other players said he should try out for the Hawks' JV, and he did well enough in an early Saturday morning session to be invited to the team. But there was more. Martelli was watching the practice and was looking to add some walk-on guards to help keep Nelson fresh. After a hard, three-hour workout with the JV, Martelli told Koefer to return in a couple of hours for a three-hour session with his team.

"You want me to come back and practice with the actual guys? That's not a good idea for me," Koefer thought.

And it wasn't.

"I got destroyed," he said. "It was awful. I hated it."

Koefer returned for two more sessions and had no intention of making the team.

"It was so intense, mentally, physically, and emotionally," he said. "I anticipated getting cut, and it was almost a mercy. I don't know if I can do this for the next five months. I would love it if they cut me."

But Koefer got an unexpected message from Martelli.

"He said to me, 'We want you to be part of the team,'" Koefer said. "I'm like, 'Holy shit, this is not kinda what I wanted.' But what idiot would ever say no to that? So, I'm like, 'Yeah.'"

On the way back to his dorm room, Koefer called his father to break the unbelievable news.

"They just offered me a spot," Koefer told his father. "My dad said, 'I thought you were saying how bad it was going.' I was like, 'It was going really bad.' He said, 'You gotta do it.' I'm like, 'I did do it.'"

Things didn't get any easier for Koefer in practice as an official member of the team.

"These guys are so fast that I just felt like I was playing on ice skates all the time," the 6-foot-2 Koefer said. "And they were strong, too. I couldn't believe how much grabbing and holding and shoving went on. That was just the defense at this level."

A few days into practice, Koefer figured out how he could be accepted and how he could help the Hawks. In pursuit of a loose ball, he didn't stop when the ball went over the boundary line nor when it was a few feet beyond it. He ran after it, diving well out of bounds to retrieve it.

"They were just cheering and yelling," he said of his teammates' reaction. "I realized I am not going to get their respect as a basketball player. I am not talented or gifted enough. But what I must do is fight and battle and just be a dog. What happened was they did start respecting me a little bit, not because they thought I could play but because they knew I wasn't going to let somebody walk all over me. I would've been such a better high school player if I would've had that nasty attitude."

That nasty attitude in practice permeated through every member of the Hawks, starting with the two best players.

West's dedication to practice, in formal team sessions, informal workouts, and just in the gym all by himself, was legendary.

"He never, never, never practiced at 99 percent," Martelli said. "It was always 100 percent, even when he worked out on his own. He practiced to exhaustion. He worked out to exhaustion."

Nelson practiced like he was trying out for the team and expected everyone to have that mindset. If sessions didn't go as well as planned, the Hawks' leader let his teammates know. It didn't matter how many preseason accolades, newspaper headlines, or compliments from Martelli or others Nelson got. He acted like just another guy trying to keep his spot in the lineup. If teammates didn't bring that mentality, he let them know about it.

"Phil brings everybody in at the end of practice and before Phil could say anything, Jameer said, 'Look, I want y'all to know we're all fighting for spots here,'" assistant coach Monté Ross remembered about one subpar practice. "Like, 'Nobody has no spots. We need to be working our tails off because we're fighting for spots.' You're talking about a guy who's 'Preseason Whatever' and 'All Everything.' That's the type of leadership he brought to the program."

Like Dave Mallon, who believed it when Nelson said that if Nelson could do it, so could Mallon, the Hawks followed Nelson's example.

"He played hard, everybody else played hard," assistant coach Mark Bass said. "He worked hard in the weight room, everybody else worked hard in the weight room. He was silly, everybody else was silly. They just gravitated to him."

Ross remembers another session that was supposed to be a simple walk-through that elevated to more because of Nelson.

"It turned into a full-fledged practice because the group was so competitive," Ross said. "It was just truly, truly amazing. Jameer was the leader of that."

To a man, every Hawks player credits the practices with helping to make the team great, even if it wasn't always fun in the moment.

"We practiced hard," Stachitas said. "I remember as a 19- or 20-year-old hearing of other programs that didn't practice as hard as us. And that sounds nice. But you sit here 20 years later and obviously you're thankful for it."

"The way we practiced, it pushed everybody and made everybody better," Nelson said. "It made us compete at a high level. Once we started playing in the game, we were like, not toying with guys, but we were flowing."

That was the thing about such intense practices. When the games started, they were relatively easy compared to what the Hawks were dealing with on a daily basis to prepare for those contests.

"They battled so hard in practice, they competed so hard in practice, that the games were easy for them," Bass said.

"Sometimes teams face adversity in the course of the game, but I think Martelli really tried to let us face adversity at practice," Barley said.

"How we competed with each other every day in practice, we were able to carry it over every day versus opponents," Jones said.

The intense practices also led to some heated exchanges between teammates, and not just from those who got tired of Hartshorn's talkativeness.

"It was kind of this interesting circus of competitive nature," Mallon said. "You'd get after each other on the court. Usually, it would blow over by the time everyone got to the locker room. But it was an intensity that to an outsider watching, you'd think, 'Oh my God, these guys don't get along.' But we're here with a goal."

"I just know that when we stepped on that court, we were really going after each other, trying to kill each other, but in the most respectful way possible," Dwayne Lee said. "Iron sharpens iron, and that was the mindset. I think Coach Martelli really enjoyed that part of it. He would pair the teams the right way. A lot of times, it was the top guys against the guys in a lesser role coming off the bench, and everyone has something to prove. That made it that much more special."

Emotions got high at times in practice but cooled afterward.

"They were competitive and we would push each other, but then we'd go back in the locker room and laugh our behinds off," Lee said. "On game night, we were all pulling the same direction as one."

"We were able to be super competitive and push each other in practice," Jones said. "Once practice was done, we were back to being friends again."

The nature of the practices helped to form an unbreakable bond.

"Did they bump heads sometimes? Yes, they did," Bass said. "But they knew when they had to come to battle, everybody had each other's back."

The Hawks certainly had each other's backs at Duquesne, where they rolled to an easy, though not perfect, 17-point victory. Following the win, they returned to Philadelphia for more practices. Martelli's sessions never were easy, anyway. After the second-half performance against Duquesne, in which St. Joe's, using a mixture of starters and reserves, got outscored 39-31 and allowed the Dukes to shoot 57.7 percent from the field, the coach certainly wouldn't be taking things easy on the players in upcoming practices. And, in the Hawks' next game, Fordham would pay for it.

CHAPTER 19

Game 14: A Reporter's Dream

Tuesday, January 13, 2004
Alumni Memorial Fieldhouse, Philadelphia
Fordham at No. 6 Saint Joseph's

After routing Duquesne but leaving Phil Martelli displeased with a lackluster second half, Saint Joseph's got back to work at practice to get ready for Fordham. Martelli, as he always did, would have St. Joe's intimately prepared for the Rams. More than that, though, the Hawks coach would be demanding that his players reach for their own high standard.

And due to their impressive standard of play and undefeated record to this point, St. Joe's was picking up more and more media attention, both locally and nationally. The Hawks rose to No. 6 in the Associated Press Top 25 poll one day before hosting Fordham at the Fieldhouse on Tuesday, January 13, 2004. They were now one of just six unbeaten teams in the country.

Fordham entered the contest having lost 28 consecutive games in Philadelphia. The Rams were seemingly forever rebuilding and were doing so again under first-year coach Dereck Whittenburg. The Fieldhouse's wooden bleachers and student section were packed. Press row was full of reporters who, like the fans, were squeezed tightly into the cramped gym. As the number of victories without a defeat continued to increase, the anticipation on Hawk Hill that already had begun at a fever pitch at the start of the season just kept growing and growing to inconceivable levels. Everyone at the Fieldhouse was ready to erupt.

"The Fieldhouse was just really jumping," Ray Parrillo, who covered the Hawks for the *Philadelphia Inquirer,* said, referring not just to the Fordham atmosphere but all home games in 2003–04. "It was electric in there."

In this contest, no one figured Fordham had much of a chance. As it turned out, the Rams had even less of one than anyone even thought beforehand.

Clearly, the Hawks had gotten Martelli's message in practice about not playing down to an opponent and not succumbing to second-half doldrums like at Duquesne. They easily defeated Fordham, 79-35. St. Joe's raced out to a 23-4 lead and finished the first half with a jaw-dropping 48-12 advantage. The Rams had more turnovers (13) than points in the opening 20 minutes. With most of the starters now watching, St. Joe's didn't let up in the second half like a game ago against the Dukes, outscoring Fordham 31-23 after intermission.

Jameer Nelson had 13 points, six assists, four rebounds, and three steals in just 23 minutes. Delonte West also played only 23 minutes and finished with 12 points, 10 rebounds, four assists, and three steals. Nelson and West watched the reserves preserve the large lead, leaving Martelli genuinely pleased.

"The response from that team to coaching was extraordinary," Martelli said. "To outside adulation, which can screw you up, they were just really focusing on play hard, play smart, and play together. That was just another example. That's an absurd college score, 48-12. And I don't mean this to be disrespectful, but you could play to Fordham or you could play to us. We played to us."

Artur Surov took advantage of the second-half minutes. St. Joe's freshman 7-footer netted a career-high eight points, along with two rebounds, against the Rams, though he wasn't boasting about it more than 20 years later.

"They were all garbage time minutes, of course," he said. "A freshman playing on a team of that quality. I wouldn't say it demanded any heroic effort to score those points or take those rebounds."

Regardless of the situation, Surov's teammates showed their appreciation for his effort.

"The most vivid memories are the reactions of our starters and how genuinely excited they were," he said. "I don't think I've seen such enthusiasm toward non-rotation players in other teams that I played on. That's a good example of the kind of team spirit we had and certainly contributed to us having such a successful season."

For Surov, it had been a whirlwind calendar year. Born in Estonia, he moved to Finland at six years old. Finland isn't exactly a basketball powerhouse, but basketball was a natural fit for the tall young man, who was 6-foot-6 at 12 years old and 7-foot by 16. Through a local connection, he came to the United States in January 2003 and played half of a high school season at Memorial Day School in Savannah, Georgia. He originally committed to the College of Charleston but wound up at St. Joe's after Charleston wanted him to redshirt. In January 2003, he had just arrived in a new country from one where basketball was an afterthought. In January 2004, he was playing 10 second-half minutes for the No. 6-ranked team in the country.

"It's so funny to think about where I was," Surov said. "It was such a huge jump, from a country that barely knew about basketball then. You couldn't see basketball anywhere. It wasn't on TV. Nobody at school cared that you played basketball. Basketball did not mean anything and, suddenly, it means everything to everybody."

With Surov's second-half help, the Hawks cruised to the victory to improve to 14-0 overall and 4-0 in the Atlantic 10.

Dick Jerardi and Parrillo rose from their seats on press row after the final whistle, took a few steps to their right and then another quick right under a tunnel, where a tiny room—as you would expect in the Fieldhouse—would be awaiting Martelli's postgame press conference. The coach filled up their notebooks with many positive reactions to the win.[35] Then, the two seasoned reporters headed to St. Joe's locker room to talk to the players.[36] Throughout his career, Martelli maintained both an open locker room for media and an open practice policy for anyone. This meant that reporters could talk to any player in the locker room after a cooling-off period, and both reporters and anyone else interested could watch Martelli's practices.

Back then, it was uncommon for reporters to be able to enter locker rooms in college basketball and talk to whomever they wanted. It was more common for teams to bring players to a staged press conference. Sometimes the media would request certain players; other times teams would bring out whomever they chose. The open locker room policy, as Martelli had, was something usually seen in professional sports 20 years ago. That also has changed somewhat. Although there are some exceptions, most postgame media access to players today in all sports usually takes place at an arranged press conference or in a group setting in the locker room.

And the open door for practices also was highly unusual, if not unique to St. Joe's. Other coaches might allow media or invited guests to view practice, but it would be hard to find others who would literally open the door and let anyone off the street come in and watch practice.

Martelli's welcoming media policy for the locker room and practices not only provided Jerardi, Parrillo, and others with easy access to the Hawks, it also helped to make covering the 2003–04 team a dream job.

"It was probably the most fun that I ever had in my job," Parrillo said. "I covered a lot of different sports and different events. I was working every day, but it didn't feel like that. I looked forward to going to practice every day. There were endless story ideas. There was a great group of guys on the team, and Phil made everything so accessible for us."

In many of Parrillo's other assignments, he would have to jump through hoops to do interviews.

"You have to make appointments, and coaches restrict access," he said.

But not at St. Joe's.

"It was just great to drive in and just walk in to practice," Parrillo said. "It was so enjoyable from a reporter's standpoint. It was a dream because you could pretty much do anything you wanted. You didn't have to run it through anybody. You could just come up with story ideas, and you knew you could get that story."

Parrillo was grateful for the entire experience.

"I just felt really, really lucky," he said. "Dick Jerardi and I would talk about it like, 'Boy, we're really getting paid to do this?'"

Martelli's openness to the media also made Marie Wozniak's job easier, as well. Wozniak was in her first season as sports information director, which is the conduit between the media and the team. It would be a whirlwind of a season, for sure. But accommodating reporters' requests and always being able to offer the option to talk to Martelli or players before practice—and even to stay and watch if they wanted—made Wozniak's first year not only manageable but also fun.

"The thing that really, really helped was Phil's practice policy," Wozniak said. "I could have media in every day. We could do 15 to 20 minutes, and the players could talk to the media before they went on the court. That helped an awful lot. It kind of also made the media work a little bit. It was like, 'Get over here and talk to them as much as you want.' That took away having to schedule Jameer on the phone or having to do a separate TV hit. That was great. Every single day, I was on the court before practice just managing that.

"Phil made it easy. If it was pulling teeth to do interviews and stuff like that, then that would've taken more out of me. But I was just in a routine with the nonstop emails and phone calls. It never got to the point like, 'Oh my God, I can't handle it.' It was almost like a challenge. Like, 'You're never going to deal with this again, or you might not. Just cherish this.' There are people in my profession that would kill to have a season and a coach like that."

Wozniak's role was the one Larry Dougherty held for the previous 15 years before departing for a similar position at Temple prior to the 2003–04 season.

"People were saying to me, 'You're leaving St. Joe's when they're looking like the greatest team in their history?'" Dougherty said. "I'm like, 'I know. This is a great opportunity for my family.' I love St. Joe's and now I love Temple. I have two schools that I really love and care about."

Dougherty observed the media firestorm from afar as Wozniak assisted Parrillo, Jerardi, and many others. That included Andy Schwartz, who was then a young sports reporter for Comcast SportsNet. Schwartz covered the 76ers' run to the 2001 NBA finals, the Phillies' trip to the 2008 World Series, and the Eagles' Super Bowl appearance following the 2004 season. But covering the Hawks hit him in a different way.

"St. Joe's had something special about it," Schwartz said. "There was something about being in [the Fieldhouse] that was different in all the best ways. It's an experience I'll never forget. It was so refreshing. To me, the best way to sum it all up is as reporters we're supposed to be objective. You're not supposed to root for the teams we cover. But these guys were impossible not to root for."

The Hawks were captivating more than just young reporters. Their story had become huge in Philadelphia and soon would become monstrous in the city and throughout the nation in a way that none before had or would after for Jerardi.

"For me," Jerardi said, "it was by far the best, long-running story I covered in 33 years at the paper. And there really isn't a close second. It was awesome."

Neil Hartman feels similarly. A longtime television reporter in Philadelphia now serving as the director of Rowan University's successful sports communications program, Hartman was granted inside access by Martelli to the Hawks program. Hartman's popular *Hangin' with the Hawks* series chronicled St. Joe's every move for Comcast SportsNet viewers.

"It was the most enjoyable experience in my career," Hartman said. "I've had the opportunity to cover every major championship, unique moments and athletes, and all that. But it was as close as a reporter can feel to being a member of the team and being locked into everything they are doing. We were a part of that team. And it all began with Phil. I'm just really grateful that Phil gave me the chance and the St. Joe's community embraced us the way they did."

All of the attention from Hartman, Jerardi, Parrillo, Schwartz, and many others would help bring notoriety to the school and the program. But it didn't change how the Hawks prepared or played.

"It got exciting, but it didn't faze the players as much," assistant coach Mark Bass said. "Give credit to Phil. He was out in front of it. Sports information people were out in front of it. It really helped with the team. We went about our business. It was about business and getting better."

For their next opponent, the Hawks would need to do just what Bass said, focusing on business and getting better, and block out any adulation coming their way. St. Joe's was headed to Xavier. And Xavier rarely lost to anyone on its home court. The media attention there would be even bigger for this game, as they would be playing in front of a national television audience. And those watching on television or in person would witness an incredible performance that they likely will never forget.

Jameer Nelson committed to Saint Joseph's over UMass and Temple in August 1999. The Hawks coaches developed a strong relationship with Nelson during the recruiting process, and he didn't like the thought of the drive through New York City to UMass, or playing behind good friend Lynn Greer at Temple. Nelson would compile a school-record 713 assists in his historic, four-year Hawks career. (Greg Carroccio/Sideline Photos)

Phil Martelli dreamed of coaching Saint Joseph's ever since eighth grade. He fell in love with the idea during childhood trips by trolley from his Southwest Philadelphia home to the Palestra for Saturday night Big 5 doubleheaders. After 10 years as a Hawks assistant coach, Martelli finally got a chance for his dream job a month shy of his 41st birthday when he was named St. Joe's head coach on July 20, 1995. (Greg Carroccio/Sideline Photos)

Delonte West was a lightly recruited prospect out of Eleanor Roosevelt High School in Maryland but transformed himself into a surefire, first-round NBA draft pick at Saint Joseph's with a work ethic and competitive drive not seen before or since on Hawk Hill. (Greg Carroccio/Sideline Photos)

Pat Carroll made 294 shots from three-point range in his four-year career at Saint Joseph's, helped greatly by assistant coach Mark Bass, who provided positive reinforcement and guidance on how to break free from defenders to find openings for long-range shots. (Greg Carroccio/ Sideline Photos)

Dwayne Jones packed on extra muscle during his redshirt year in 2001–02. He went on to have a stellar, three-year career at Saint Joseph's. Jones's voice was quiet, but his blocked shots and dunks echoed loudly in gyms and arenas. (Greg Carroccio/Sideline Photos)

Injuries hampered Dave Mallon in 2003–04, and he was crushed to have to sit out the first seven games of the season with a stress fracture in his right foot and the final four regular-season contests with an Achilles' injury. He did whatever he could to get back on the court so he wouldn't miss this special season, following Jameer Nelson's lead that if Nelson could do it, so could Mallon. (Greg Carroccio/Sideline Photos)

John Bryant wasn't recruited by any of the Division I schools in his home state of Virginia. He didn't put up big statistics at Saint Joseph's; rather, he was focused on giving everything he had and being the best teammate possible, just as his dad taught him. (Greg Carroccio/Sideline Photos)

Tyrone Barley was a defensive wizard but not a very good outside shooter during his first three seasons at Saint Joseph's, when he averaged 31.6 percent from three-point range. But assistant coach Matt Brady helped correct Barley's form, moving the point at which Barley released the ball from near his right ear to out in front of him and closer to his right eye and forehead, and Barley's hard work to make it stick made him a problem for opponents on both ends of the floor as a senior. (Greg Carroccio/Sideline Photos)

Chet Stachitas was a prolific scorer at Nease High School in Florida, where he also finished second in the state's high jump as a senior when he cleared 6-foot-6. Stachitas wasn't a great three-point shooter in high school but became one at Saint Joseph's, working hard to develop a consistent jumper from long range after entering college with an archaic set shot. (Greg Carroccio/Sideline Photos)

Dwayne Lee came to Saint Joseph's from one of the country's most successful programs, playing for Bob Hurley Sr. at St. Anthony's in Jersey City, New Jersey. As Jameer Nelson's backup, Lee didn't get many minutes in his first two seasons on Hawk Hill. But Lee did everything he could in practice to push Nelson and was determined to maintain Nelson's high level whenever he got an opportunity to play. (Greg Carroccio/Sideline Photos)

Saint Joseph's assistant coaches (left to right) Mark Bass, Matt Brady, and Monté Ross were keys to the Hawks' success. Bass assisted Phil Martelli for 20 years after playing at St. Joe's, where he made 225 career three-pointers. Brady was the Hawks' shooting guru and helped to transform Delonte West, Tyrone Barley, and Jameer Nelson into effective long-range threats. Ross became enamored with Nelson the first time he saw him, as a sophomore at Chester High School, by watching Nelson have the greatest impact on the court with the fewest points. (Greg Carroccio/Sideline Photos)

In 2003–04, Chris Bertolino continued Saint Joseph's long tradition as the full-scholarship student inside of The Hawk mascot costume. From the moment Bertolino put the beaked head on in the locker room until he took it off after the game, he didn't stop flapping his wings, doing thousands of one- or two-arm raises that embodied the school's mantra that *The Hawk Will Never Die*. (Greg Carroccio/Sideline Photos)

A former Saint Joseph's cheerleader, the loquacious Robert Hartshorn brought high energy and positive reinforcement to the Hawks. Hartshorn's nonstop talking in practices sometimes drew the ire of his teammates, though it achieved the desired effect of helping to raise the sessions' intensity. (Greg Carroccio/Sideline Photos)

As a walk-on, Brian Jesiolowski knew he wouldn't get many minutes in games. His role was to be in the best shape possible to push the starters and reserves during practice. Jesiolowski also developed a friendship with Delonte West, sometimes playing late-night one-on-one games with West at the Fieldhouse when he wasn't loaning West his 1993 Oldsmobile Cutlass Ciera. (Greg Carroccio/Sideline Photos)

Jameer Nelson and Delonte West were future first-round NBA draft picks who were surrounded by the perfect supporting cast. Individually, none of their running mates would be mentioned as an All-American candidate. Put all of the Hawks together, however, and you had a practically unstoppable force. (Greg Carroccio/Sideline Photos)

Athletic director Don DiJulia shakes hands with Jameer Nelson before the Hawks' game against Pacific early in the 2003–04 season. After watching Nelson play just three games as a freshman, DiJulia already thought Nelson was among the best Hawks guards ever. (Greg Carroccio/Sideline Photos)

Marie Wozniak (left) was in her first season as St. Joe's sports information director in 2003–04. Seated next to Wozniak is Atlantic 10 commissioner Linda Bruno. Wozniak was busy all season but was helped by Phil Martelli's open practice policy, which made coordinating interviews easier. Bruno negotiated a deal with Comcast that allowed ESPN to also televise the Hawks' final regular-season home game against St. Bonaventure. (Greg Carroccio/Sideline Photos)

Alumni Memorial Fieldhouse seated 3,200 fans and wasn't even as modern as many high school gyms. But it was loud, raucous, and a huge home-court advantage for the Hawks. (Greg Carroccio/Sideline Photos)

Phil Denne (right) assisted Marie Wozniak with media requests, like this interview of Phil Martelli by sportscaster John Clark of NBC10. (Greg Carroccio/Sideline Photos)

Father Timothy Lannon was in his first year as president of Saint Joseph's in 2003–04. Lannon was used to seeing good basketball after Marquette reached the Final Four in 2003 during his final days as president at the school. (Greg Carroccio/Sideline Photos)

Left photo: Delonte West (far right) teams with Dwayne Jones for a game of foosball against Jameer Nelson and an unidentified player during a visit to Ralph Maresco's house for dinner prior to playing Xavier at Cintas Center on January 17, 2004. As if he were playing one-on-one in the gym, West, to no one's surprise, wanted to win every single one of those table games. "Delonte was the most competitive guy I ever met in my life," Maresco said. Right photo: Maresco (standing center) looks over the scene in his dining room. (Photos courtesy of Ralph Maresco)

Dan Kropp heard Phil Martelli tell a Philadelphia sports radio station about the large crowds surrounding the Hawks. Soon after, Kropp was on security detail to help Jameer Nelson and St. Joe's navigate the increasing demand for autographs. (Photo courtesy of Dan Kropp)

Ryan Darrenkamp shaved his head to win a Phil Martelli lookalike contest in the preseason. His prize was a trip with the team to Fordham on February 18, 2004. (Photo courtesy of Ryan Darrenkamp)

Joe Lunardi talks to former Pennsylvania Governor Ed Rendell during a halftime interview. Lunardi also worked in public relations for the school in addition to his budding career as ESPN's bracketologist. In early January 2004, Lunardi was crunching numbers for his brackets and saw a track to an undefeated season and No. 1 seed in the NCAA tournament for St. Joe's. (Greg Carroccio/Sideline Photos)

CHAPTER 20

Game 15: A Perfect 24 Hours

Saturday, January 17, 2004
Cintas Center, Cincinnati
No. 6 Saint Joseph's at Xavier

Saint Joseph's had put on a show at home against Fordham, holding the Rams to just 12 first-half points on their way to a blowout victory that improved the Hawks to 14-0. Their next game, however, would not be easy. Playing Xavier never was. And playing on the road against Xavier had been an automatic loss for the Hawks.

Xavier joined the Atlantic 10 in 1995 and quickly became a dominant force in the league. The Musketeers won just 13 contests that first season before averaging 20.5 victories over the next seven seasons leading up to 2003–04. During that stretch, Xavier reached five NCAA tournaments and won two A-10 tournament titles. The Musketeers were almost impossible to beat at home, especially after opening the state-of-the-art Cintas Center in 2000. When St. Joe's traveled there for its 15th game of the 2003–04 season for a two o'clock tip on Saturday, January 17, 2004, the Musketeers had played 50 games in their new home arena and had lost only three times.

The Hawks were beaten in all five tries at Xavier since the Musketeers joined the A-10, and the games were not close. The average margin of defeat in those contests was 14.2 points, including a pair of losses at Cintas in 2001 and 2002.

Ralph Maresco knew all of this all too well. A passionate Hawks fan and 1983 St. Joe's graduate, Maresco closely followed the Hawks from afar after relocating to suburban Cincinnati. He was elated when Xavier, which is located in Cincinnati, joined the A-10 because it meant he'd finally be able to see his beloved team in person.

"I died and went to heaven when Xavier joined the A-10," he said.

The only problem for Maresco was that the Hawks rarely beat Xavier, winning only two of seven contests overall and never once in Cincinnati. So, Maresco would get constant ribbing from coworkers, friends, and random Xavier fans as he left the Musketeers' arena dejectedly after yet another St. Joe's loss.

"I was so conditioned to going down there, and we're going to lose," Maresco said of his experience watching the Hawks in Cincinnati. "But that's OK because that's my team."

In January 1998, prior to the Hawks' second trip to Cincinnati after Xavier joined the A-10, Maresco invited Joe Lunardi to his house for dinner. Lunardi is the Hawks' longtime radio analyst and was a classmate of Maresco's at St. Joe's. Over dinner, Maresco asked where the Hawks stayed during the trip and wondered if they might be interested in eating a pregame team meal at his house rather than at the hotel or a local restaurant.

"Joe said, 'If you invite them, they'll probably come,'" Maresco recalled.

Maresco had regularly corresponded with Phil Martelli since he became head coach, so Maresco's name was familiar to Martelli.

"I just loved the guy," Maresco said. "I loved him from the very beginning."

Maresco called Martelli and invited the Hawks over to his house for dinner prior to their next trip to Cincinnati during the 1999–2000 season. Martelli said yes, with two stipulations.

"He said, 'Yeah, we'll do this but no alcohol and a lot of desserts,'" Maresco said.

A tradition was born on March 4, 2000, when Martelli brought the Hawks to Maresco's house for dinner. It wasn't exactly a good-luck charm, though, as St. Joe's was crushed by Xavier the next day, losing 94-66. But Martelli enjoyed the experience enough to return in each of the following two seasons. And plans were all set for Martelli, Jameer Nelson, and the entire Hawks traveling party to dine at the Maresco house once again on Friday, January 16, 2004.

The dinner took a lot of coordination between Maresco, his wife, Michelle, and their neighbors. Michelle Maresco prepared chicken parmesan, a pasta dish, and homemade desserts. She put what she could fit in her own oven, and the neighbors helped with the rest.

"We would tell one neighbor, 'Put it in at this time, bring it over at this time,'" Ralph Maresco said. "Then, we'd tell the other neighbor, 'This is your job.' So, we had everybody set up. As soon as the bus left Cintas, it was 'Go' time."

Except on this occasion, the Hawks were stuck late at practice completing a free throw drill they often did to end the sessions. Because they weren't making enough free throws, practice was dragging on. Maresco, there to watch and to provide directions so the bus driver didn't get lost as in previous years, nervously looked on. Martelli had a very strict window from 7:00 to 9:00 p.m. for the dinner, and his host wondered if they'd even make it. ·

"I'm looking at my watch thinking, 'Oh my God, this is terrible, we are going to be late,'" Maresco recalled.

Eventually, the Hawks completed practice. Maresco directed the bus driver to Route 71 North for a 17.3-mile drive to his house that took 23 minutes. They did arrive a little after the intended start, but everyone had plenty of time to enjoy dinner and one another's company.

"There was no more surreal feeling than the bus pulling up to my house and everybody getting off," Maresco said. "They really enjoyed it. For the players, it was nice to do that and relax the night before the game."

Martelli was appreciative of the family's gesture.

"Ralph and his family had passion and love for the team and the program," Martelli said. "They were kind enough to invite us."

In addition to Ralph and Michelle, their four children joined the Hawks for dinner. When shown pictures of the evening more than 20 years later, Martelli paused when he looked at Dwayne Lee interacting with Katrina Maresco, who was three years old at the time.

"I'll always remember that right there," Martelli, pointing to the photograph, said. "These guys are so good. It wasn't staged. It wasn't like, 'Go spend time. Go watch a game together. Sit with their children.' They were just really good guys."

"It was pretty magical for them," Maresco said of his own kids' experience.

Martelli also was touched by how Katrina, Austin (who was six years old at the time), Meredith (nine), and Gabrielle Maresco (11) welcomed Phil Martelli Sr., who also was at the dinner.

"Here's what I really, really, really feel in my heart, the way they treated my father," Martelli said. "His children and the guests he had at that dinner treated my father like he was their grandfather. It was really cool."

In addition to enjoying homemade food and desserts, the Hawks relaxed by watching basketball in the living room and playing games, like Ping-Pong, air hockey, and foosball, in the basement. As if he were playing one-on-one in the gym, Delonte West, to no one's surprise, wanted to win every single one of those table games.

"Delonte was the most competitive guy I ever met in my life," Maresco said. "He would come upstairs sweating and bragging that he had beaten everybody in everything. The way he was laser focused playing those silly games in the basement, I just thought, 'This guy, he has the eye of the tiger. If you're this way playing Ping-Pong or foosball, what are you going to be tomorrow?'"

What are you going to be tomorrow? It would be special.

***

West and the Hawks departed the Marescos' well-fed and, in spite of their lack of past success in Cincinnati, feeling confident about the task at hand the following day against Xavier. They were not intimidated by Xavier's record at the Cintas Center, or the Musketeers' lofty status in the A-10.

"There wasn't a person in our group, not one person, who thought they're 47-3 [at Cintas], it's Xavier, they've kind of run the league," Martelli said.

Privately, the coach said as much to Lunardi before the game.

"I'm doing the pregame interview, and I would often turn off the tape recorder and go, 'What do you really think?'" Lunardi remembered. "He goes, 'Joe, I don't know much, but I know I have the two best players in the game. If you give any basketball coach worth his salt the two best players in the game, they should win.'"

As he settled with his family into his seats right behind the Hawks bench as a thanks for dinner, even Maresco was feeling positive despite all of the previous disappointing results.

"I remember thinking how many times I have been here, and we'd never won there," he said. "I'm thinking, 'This might be it. This might be the game.'"

The Hawks were not ahead on the scoreboard at halftime, trailing by six points, but they were playing with poise and confidence. And there was just something about West's game that looked and felt different. St. Joe's radio play-by-play broadcaster Tom McCarthy remembers recognizing immediately a locked-in focus on the St. Joe's guard. Broadcasting from the baseline under one of the baskets, McCarthy was struck by the way that West scored on a layup in the first half right in front of him.

"I remember it vividly," McCarthy said. "I remember Delonte coming in with his left hand. His eyes were so vivid and so expressive. He laid the ball in and I'm like, 'This is over. He's got it today. Oh my God, he's locked in.'"

Nelson also sensed that his backcourt mate was in a zone, and the point guard made it a point to keep passing West the ball.

"I just remember he was rolling," Nelson said. "With him rolling, we fed him the ball, but he wasn't selfish about it. I was like, 'This dude has it going on.' He was in some type of zone that was easy to see."

West kept making shots after halftime, from inside, from three-point range, from the foul line, from everywhere. One after another. Every single time he let go of a shot, the result was the same. One after another just kept going in the basket. One tough shot after another kept going in against a Xavier program that was the top tier of the league playing at an arena where they almost never lost.

Oh, and Larry Bird and Jerry West were courtside to scout Nelson and West for the NBA, taking away more of Martelli's attention than clearly West, Nelson, or any of the players.

"I'm just a playground rat from Southwest Philadelphia who has this unbelievable job, and Larry Bird and Jerry West are here to watch my team play?" Martelli said. "Chills. Chills."

And you could say the same thing about the feeling West's incredible performance left on Hawks supporters. When the game finally ended, West had scored 33 points and made all 12 of his field goal attempts, including each of his three three-point tries, and every one of his six free throw attempts.

A perfect game.

"That was one of the greatest individual performances I've ever seen," Ray Parrillo said.

That was a common reaction for anyone who witnessed it, including a national television audience on ESPN.

"To not miss a shot in a game in a road environment where the other team is desperate to beat us, that was a remarkable performance on the biggest stage under the brightest lights," assistant coach Matt Brady said. "That was just spectacular for Delonte and his family. I don't remember being aware of it during the game. I just remember every shot being important. And he made every shot."

Nelson also had a big game, scoring 28 points and making 11 of 18 shots. Nelson's two assists combined with West's five assists gave the pair a hand in every single one of St. Joe's 30 field goals, leading the Hawks to an 81-73 defeat of the Musketeers to improve to 15-0 overall and 5-0 in the A-10. It was the Hawks' first win over Xavier in Cincinnati since February 17, 1973. "I almost didn't know how to act," Maresco said.

Martelli was feeling so good walking off the court that he told athletic director Don DiJulia something that he would not let out to the players. "I said, 'Don, there's a chance we're not going to lose a game this year,'" Martelli said.

DiJulia agreed. "There's not going to be a harder game to win than what we just did," he said.

As the Hawks celebrated in the locker room, Maresco wanted to continue the joyride. Rather than head to his car, he led his family to the Hawks' bus at the rear of the arena.

"I didn't want this to end," Maresco said. "I said, 'Why don't we go on the bus and wait for them?' Which was the craziest thing. They came on and we were all clapping for them. When we got off the team bus, I said, 'Well, we really have to go home now.'"

It had been an unforgettable 24 hours for Maresco that was full of memorable moments. "It has to be in the top 10 in my life for sure," he said.

Maresco, Martelli, and West weren't the only ones who left Cintas feeling euphoric.

The Hawks also got two huge three-pointers late in the game from Pat Carroll, who was needed more in this contest with Chet Stachitas home to attend his grandmother's funeral. The sweet-stroking lefty had been struggling all season to find his form from a year ago. There was a feeling around the Hawks program, though, that those two shots might be just the spark Carroll needed to get going. And everyone would find out the answer when they returned home to a media frenzy and a game against UMass at the Fieldhouse.

CHAPTER 21

Game 16: A Media Storm and a Shooter's Form

Wednesday, January 21, 2004
Alumni Memorial Fieldhouse, Philadelphia
Massachusetts at No. 3 Saint Joseph's

After finally winning at Xavier, Saint Joseph's headed to the airport for a return trip to Philadelphia. Apparently, not everyone was following the story of Jameer Nelson and the undefeated Hawks.

"We were going through the Cincinnati airport and a woman checking us through said, 'Are you a basketball team?'" Phil Martelli remembered. "The players answered yes. And she got to Jameer and said, 'You must be the water boy.' And he said to her, 'Yes, and I'm the best damn water boy in the country.'"

Back in Philadelphia, where the Hawks would be readying for their 16th game of the season against Massachusetts at the Fieldhouse on Wednesday, January 21, 2004, there certainly would be no mistaking the 5-foot-11 Nelson for a water boy. Philadelphia sports fans already knew Nelson from his prolific careers at Chester High School and St. Joe's. With the media swarm that was about to descend on the Hawks, Nelson would become practically a household name in the city and across the country.

The Hawks had been a nice story from the moment Nelson announced in June that he would be skipping the NBA and returning to St. Joe's. There was the impressive season-opening win over Gonzaga at Madison Square Garden, Nelson's game-winning shots at Old Dominion and California, and, of course, the most recent victory at Xavier that featured Delonte West's perfect game. Sportswriters Ray Parrillo and Dick Jerardi were closely chronicling it. And there were others, too. But, as always is the case in Philadelphia, most of the media attention was focused on the NFL's Eagles. That all changed in the lead-up to St. Joe's game against UMass because the Carolina Panthers defeated the Eagles in the NFC Championship Game on Sunday, January 18, 2004. Suddenly, sports reporters needed stories to fill their print pages, garner clicks to their websites, and keep viewers tuned into their broadcasts.

Hello, Hawks.

"When the Eagles lost that game, there was a meeting at the *Inquirer* of the sports staff and how we were going to go forward and what we were going to cover," Parrillo said. "I remember the editor asking me, 'How good is that St. Joe's team?' And I said, 'They're really good. I think this is a team that deserves a lot of attention.' Other topics were brought up, and then he turned to me and said, 'We're going to depend on you to carry the sports section for the rest of the season.'"

At the *Philadelphia Daily News*, Jerardi heard a similar message.

"I remember [editor] Pat McLoone saying to me, 'You're up. Get us to the finish line,'" Jerardi said.

The message likely was the same at every print, digital, and television news outlet in the city because St. Joe's practice on Tuesday, January 20, 2004, the day before its game against the Minutemen, was packed with reporters and cameras. The Hawks were no longer a nice story; they were *the* story in town.

"We know what it's like when the Eagles are in season; that's the story," Marie Wozniak, St. Joe's sports information director, said. "Once they lost, you can picture the cartoon of everybody running the other way now and running to our campus. The gym was packed with media. The baseline was full of cameras. Now, Philadelphia is paying attention, and there are more people who are going to start paying attention. That was the realization that this could be something special."

Phil Denne was one of Wozniak's assistants and remembers fielding phone calls from reporters immediately after the Eagles' defeat.

"Things went absolutely berserk," Denne said. "The whole city just showed up because all of the sudden they had nothing else to do. Everyone was there."

"The level of attention ramped up a quadrillion," Joe Lunardi said.

When Wednesday night's game finally arrived, press row was overflowing with media, and photographers lined every possible inch of the court. The fans, like they had been all season, squeezed into every seat and every space on the wooden bleachers. The game had some added excitement, if that's possible, as the students had returned to campus for the spring semester and were geared up even more than they had been before. The whole scene created a massive home-court advantage.

"The noise in the Fieldhouse was just earth-shattering," Martelli remembered.

The Hawks would have a similar effect on the Minutemen.

St. Joe's blitzed UMass, starting the game by making five straight three-pointers. The Hawks led by 27 points at halftime, were up by 40 in the second half, and won going away, 92-67. St. Joe's, which had moved up to No. 3 in the Associated Press poll two days before the contest, improved to 16-0 overall and 6-0 in the A-10. As Parrillo reported in the *Inquirer* the next day, the Hawks and Stanford were now the only two undefeated teams in the country after Cincinnati lost to Louisville on Wednesday night.

Delonte West picked up right where he left off in his perfect game at Xavier, hitting his first seven field goals against UMass to stretch his streak to an astounding 19 consecutive made field goals. West finally showed he was human in the second half, missing a three-pointer with 13:08 remaining. He ended up with 19 points while making seven of eight shots to cap an incomprehensible two-game stretch where he scored 52 points in 60 minutes and made 19 of 20 field goals, including five of six from beyond the arc, and nine of 10 free throws. Nelson chipped in with 13 points and seven assists in 24 minutes against UMass.

"You just didn't know what to do with them," then-Massachusetts coach Steve Lappas said of Nelson and West. "They could be point guards or two guards. They were very versatile. They could shoot. They could play fast. They could play half-court."

Lappas also mentioned another weapon in the backcourt.

"And they had a great shooter on the perimeter," he said. "Those two guys could create so much that Carroll could just sit outside and just fire away. He was a great shooter."

***

Indeed, Pat Carroll was a great shooter. But he had not been playing to his lofty standards for most of the season. Although St. Joe's was winning every game, Carroll slumped to just 34.3 percent from three-point range entering the Xavier contest. He had made a mediocre and uncharacteristic 23 of 67 jumpers from beyond the arc to that point. This was a more than 10 percent dip from the previous season when he led the Atlantic 10 and finished seventh in the country by making 45 percent of his three-pointers as a sophomore.

"The first 14 games, it was almost like a cloud," Carroll said.

Always a player helped with a confidence boost, Carroll did not have Phil Martelli Jr., who had graduated, in his ear in 2003–04 telling him he was the best shooter in the country before every warm-up shot. There also were some questions about Carroll's confidence after he had airballed a potentially game-winning three-pointer the previous season against Auburn with 2.6 seconds remaining in overtime in the first round of the 2003 NCAA tournament that ended with a 65-63 Hawks loss.

"There were points in time where I wondered if the shot against Auburn had kind of weighed on him at all," Martelli said.

The coach didn't harp on the Auburn miss; rather, he encouraged Carroll to remain confident in a conversation with both the player and Carroll's father.

"It was more about staying with it," Martelli said. "I was not panicked nor were his teammates panicked."

Carroll also was hearing a similarly calming message from Hawks assistant coach Mark Bass.

"I was always there to say, 'Yo, you're a great shooter. Shoot your shot. Don't get down on yourself,'" Bass said. "It was more about him having the same confidence. That early-season struggle, he couldn't get out of his own way. He was pressing because he knew he could make shots. I was like, 'Pat, you gotta relax. You gotta relax.' We got in the gym and we're going to find this. I said, 'Pat, it's going to come. You just have to believe in it, believe in yourself, and believe in your shot. Just keep shooting your shot and you'll find your rhythm. It's going to come, man.'"

Carroll had complete trust in Bass. Unlike West, Nelson, Tyrone Barley, and Chet Stachitas, Carroll didn't need much technical help with his form from shooting guru and St. Joe's assistant Matt Brady. What he did need were positive reinforcement and advice on how to find openings for his shot at the college level. While all of the coaches helped Carroll, he leaned most heavily on Bass for both of his needs in all four years at St. Joe's. Unlike the 6-foot-5 Carroll, Bass was an undersized guard at 5-foot-9. Like Carroll, Bass was not the most fleet of foot and had to rely on craftiness and basketball IQ to find openings to shoot against faster defenders. And just like Carroll, Bass was a deadly three-point shooter. He passed everything in his bag of tricks on to Carroll.

"Not much needed to change with my form, but I needed help to be effective as a shooter at the college level," Carroll said of his transition from high school. "Mark Bass worked with me endlessly all four years throughout my time at St. Joe's."

Bass taught Carroll how to work off screens, how to fool defenders, and how to get open for shots. He was passing on strategies that allowed him to make 91 shots from three-point range as a Hawks senior in 1995–96 and 225 for his career, both of which were school records that Carroll would later break. Bass began by advising Carroll to develop strong relationships with Dwayne Jones, John Bryant, and other frontcourt players.

"I told Pat that I made a living being good friends with my bigs," Bass said. "Reggie [Townsend], Carlin [Warley], Will [Johnson], if they set a good screen, you're wide open. So, you have to be good friends with DJ and John. They understood if they set a good screen for Pat, Pat's going to be open and make it. If they set another good screen, their man's going to help, and they're going to get a dunk or layup. It worked both ways."

Bass also intimately schooled Carroll on how to free himself from defenders.

"It's all about feel for where the defender is at," Bass said. "It's all about separation. Sometimes you want to sprint off a screen, sometimes you want to stop, or sprint and stop. It's all about pace, how to use it, how to come off screens, and playing mind games with defenders. If a guy wants to cheat over the top [of a screen], you're going to fade to the corner. Guys ball watch, so once you pass, you cut. If you're off the ball and see the back of his jersey, you're cutting. You always want to be constantly moving and move with a purpose."

Eventually, Bass said, all of that guile and movement would free Carroll.

"I just told Pat, 'The ball will find you,'" Bass, who led the A-10 in three-point percentage (42.3 percent) in 1994–95, said. "'If you swing it and run to the other side, it will find you.' And that's what we constantly did."

All of the work with Bass and the coach's constant affirmation finally paid off for a relieved Carroll against Xavier. He made two three-pointers late in the contest, including one that erased a 71-70 deficit with 3:08 left and started a game-changing 10-0 Hawks run. Martelli and, most importantly, Carroll felt like those two shots provided him with the confidence he needed to escape his early-season struggles.

"Those were two big threes," Martelli said. "I do remember that now this was going to be the takeoff. Alright, he's back."

"The thing that really flipped the switch for me was the Xavier game," Carroll said. "I hit two key three-pointers late and something switched. I remember Coach Martelli telling me, 'Hey, this is a turning point.' And from then on, the stroke started coming."

Did it ever.

Carroll torched UMass from the outside, draining six of seven long-range shots that started a red-hot four-game stretch in which Carroll would shoot an incredible 74 percent from three-point range. Clearly, Carroll's confidence had returned. And the Hawks, as Lappas saw from one step off the court, had now gotten even more dangerous.

Bass was thrilled with Carroll's progress.

"It was great helping him to get where he was at and helping the team," Bass said. "The team enjoyed getting better and proved that you can do it if you work hard."

Carroll's return to form came at a perfect time, too. After UMass, the Hawks were entering a challenging, six-game stretch. The perilous run would start on a Saturday night in an overflowing gym that always has been one of the toughest venues on opponents in the Atlantic 10.

CHAPTER 22

Game 17: A Masterpiece and Controversy

Saturday, January 24, 2004
Reilly Center, Olean, New York
No. 3 Saint Joseph's at St. Bonaventure

Drive from Saint Joseph's about three hours north on Route 476 to Binghamton, make a left onto Route 17 for another two and a half hours or so and you will arrive in Olean, New York. As anyone who has ever been there can attest, the town that is home to St. Bonaventure University is remote, especially in the cold, snowy winter where there's not much else to do but go and cheer on the Bonnies at the Reilly Center. No matter how good or bad they are, year after year the Bonnies maintain one of the biggest home-court advantages in the Atlantic 10.

"It's one of the hardest places to play in the league," said Dwayne Lee, who served as a St. Bonaventure assistant coach from 2017 to 2019 after graduating from St. Joe's in 2006. "There are two 20-point [home] wins built into their schedule every year because of the weather and the travel and all that type of stuff."

On January 24, 2004, in St. Joe's 17th game of a thus far undefeated season, St. Bonaventure's home fans were ready in a way that even by their own intense standards was on another level. It didn't matter that the Bonnies were a season removed from a scandal that rocked the university and resulted in a new basketball coach and university president.[37] St. Bonaventure had won its previous two games, both at home, against UMass and Rhode Island, and the fans were riled up and ready for a Saturday night upset of the Hawks.

"This place was on edge," Steve Campbell, a longtime St. Bonaventure athletics administrator, said. "Students were back from break. You have your local community, the alumni, and a few hours to patronize the local establishments. It was loud and electric."

Unlike St. Joe's, St. Bonaventure didn't require students to have season tickets to attend home games. They just had to show a student ID, and they were in the door. No one wanted to miss this contest. As a result, students were jammed into the building until there was nowhere else to go but on the court.

"They were on the court," Phil Martelli said. "It wasn't even legally possible."

As the building rocked in the lead-up to the game, Martelli was in the locker room saying his pregame prayers when he got even more assurance from his assistant coaches.

"I remember before the game Monté [Ross], or Matt [Brady], or Mark Bass came in and said, 'We're good. Jameer just put on a show out there,'" Martelli said.

Nelson might have awed the crowd with his incredible pregame routine of draining one three-pointer after another—and, Martelli said, he also finished this warm-up with a rim-rattling dunk—but the fans were still ready to erupt when the teams jumped center to begin the contest.

"The place was an absolute madhouse. It was a fire marshal's nightmare," Joe Cabrey said. "Then the game started."

The Hawks quickly quieted the raucous crowd by scoring 15 of the first 18 points and continued to pad their first-half lead with a phenomenal performance that those there still marvel at today.

"You talk about taking the lid off the Reilly Center, it was like all of the air was gone," Campbell said. "They put on an absolute clinic. They were so fun to watch and so good, the way they moved the ball, the shots that they got. They could get any shot they wanted. It was an offensive and defensive clinic."

Jim Crowley also was there taking notes. A young coach of the Bonnies women's basketball team, Crowley wanted to see what all of the fuss was about over the Hawks.

"I was sitting down as a basketball fan," Crowley said. "It's not like today where you can watch every game [on television or streaming on the internet]. You know there's something good there, and you want to see what it's all about."

Crowley was mesmerized by what he witnessed.

"I remember sitting down and they just 'Tysoned' us," he said. "It was like getting ready for that big pay-per-view you paid 52 bucks for and in 32 seconds, [Mike] Tyson knocks the guy out. I remember it was evident very quickly that the game was over. You could feel it. The air came out.

"What struck me is how the ball moved for them. That ball just moved, man. It was side to side. It was inside out. It was offense without ego. They were spreading you out and moving the basketball and making the extra pass.

"I don't think anyone really understood what they were seeing. They were seeing a transformation in how the game was played. Credit to Phil to be comfortable with that, to have confidence in his own guys and his own ability to say, 'We're going to do this because we're good at it. It doesn't matter if other people don't think it's the thing to do. We're good at it.'"

With four guards on the floor at times, playing full-court pressure defense and launching three-pointers in a way that is common today but just wasn't something that was done in the early 2000s, the Hawks just overwhelmed St. Bonaventure. At halftime, the Hawks led 62-27 after nothing short of a masterpiece of a performance.

St. Joe's had made 20 of 30 field goals, including 12 of 18 three-pointers in the first 20 minutes. The game officially ended 20 minutes later with a final score of 114-63, improving the Hawks to 17-0 overall and 7-0 in the Atlantic 10. The victory also established a school record for consecutive wins, breaking the 1964–65 squad's 16-game streak.

"The dominance was just breathtaking," Martelli said.

And the dominance was captured for posterity. St. Bonaventure had a photograph from the game of the overstuffed Reilly Center, filled that night likely beyond capacity with an announced sellout crowd of 6,114, that was used in admissions brochures, media guides, and other promotional material for the university. The only problem for the school was that the first-half score could be seen in the photo. It's not exactly the message St. Bonaventure wanted to send to prospective students and potential donors.

"You're seeing this scene from the Reilly Center that was completely sold out," Campbell said. "Unfortunately, it had the score on the scoreboard and it was just brutal to have to see it. For years, we ended up trying to alter that so you didn't see the score and how lopsided it was. People would ask, 'Can that be right? That score can't be right.' Yeah, unfortunately, it's correct."

The Hawks, as Campbell said, had put on a clinic.

For the second time in three games, following Delonte West's brilliance at Xavier, St. Joe's would have a player finish with a perfect game. Nelson made six of six field goals, including four of four three-pointers, and three of three free throws and ended with 19 points and six assists in 26 minutes. West added 21 points, eight assists, six rebounds, three steals, and zero turnovers in 24 minutes. Pat Carroll's confidence from making two late three-pointers against Xavier continued, and the Hawks sharpshooter drained five of six three-pointers to make it a three-game stretch of firing at an unthinkable 81.3 percent (13 of 16) clip from beyond the arc.

It wasn't just the starters who impressed, either. With the outcome not in doubt, Martelli went deep to his bench and played 13 Hawks, 12 of whom scored. Lee chipped in with season highs of nine points and five assists, and Dave Mallon also contributed season highs of eight points and five rebounds. The Hawks finished the game with 29 assists and shot 66.1 percent from the field, neither of which would be topped by them in 2003–04.

"That was one of those games we were clicking on all cylinders," Lee said. "There was a belief growing amongst the team at that point of the season that we're doing something special here. We're starting to feel internally like, 'This train is starting to pick up speed.' And we really started to gain some confidence. We walked out of that arena feeling like, 'I know Bonaventure is down, but we played our asses off.' Unbelievable game. We got contributions from everyone. We won't play this well every night, but if we can continue to approach these games with the right mindset, the right chemistry among the group, we can do something special."

Crowley also was thinking about doing something special. Inspired by what he had just observed, he set out on a course to develop his program as close as he could to how the Hawks played that night.

"I appreciated how they played, how connected they were, how smooth everything was, how much trust there was between Phil and his players," Crowley said. "As a young coach, I'm thinking, 'Why can't we do that?' That stuff hit me really hard. Obviously, you are looking at pro level talent [with Nelson and West], but there was a whole other thing, just how [the St. Joe's players] elevated each other. The talent is what it is, but how do we get that?"

The St. Bonaventure women's coach began to construct his roster in a way in which players could pass, move, and shoot in a way similar to the Hawks.

"Space and ball movement was the equalizer," he said. "Now those big guys have to figure out how to guard you. That was something we thought we could do a little different. We weren't going to get these high-level recruits. But can we get [opponents'] higher-level kids to guard us? That is what ball movement does."

Crowley felt there was no reason the Hawks' style couldn't be duplicated. At the very least, he would try.

"Here's this little Catholic school, why can't we?" Crowley said.

It took several recruiting classes and lots of work, but Crowley used the blueprint he saw at the Reilly Center on a Saturday night in January of 2004 to build a dominant A-10 women's basketball program in the mold of the 2003–04 Hawks. It all culminated in 2011–12 when the Bonnies finished 31-4 overall, 14-0 in the A-10, and advanced to the NCAA Sweet 16.

"It was a season for the ages," Crowley said.

The Hawks were going through their own special season, something they all felt deeply after routing St. Bonaventure. An emotional Robert Hartshorn was moved to tears on the bus ride back to the hotel by the mastery and togetherness of the group in such a hostile environment.

"I high-fived every guy and started crying," said Hartshorn, the former cheerleader and walk-on who hit a three-pointer against the Bonnies. "I just love you guys and have a feeling in my heart that we're a team of destiny. It was a different feeling out there. I just don't feel like there's anybody that can mess with us. As long as we stick together, there's nothing that can stop us."

The Hawks players and coaches were elated with the performance. Those who watched, like Campbell and Crowley, also were awed. Yet, the talk afterward was not about St. Joe's sensational showing; rather, the focus was on a first-half exchange between Martelli and a fan sitting behind the Hawks bench.

***

It was called "55 Press," and it's how St. Joe's played the first half of every contest in 2003–04. Essentially, it was a full-court man-to-man defense. If Martelli wanted to turn the defense up a notch, he would write "55 On" on his whiteboard or call it out from the sidelines, a signal to his players to switch to a full-court trapping defense where two or more players converge on a dribbler. Against the Bonnies, though, Martelli didn't need "55 On" because "55 Press" was doing damage.

"We started every game the same way," Martelli said. "And what we were trying to do was check to see if you were willing to compete that night. And it also forced me to get substitutes into the game because no one could play like that for 40 minutes."

As the Hawks' first-half lead continued to swell with them playing their customary "55 Press" defense and hitting two-thirds of their shots on offense, a middle-aged Bonnies season ticket holder named Mary Palmer took issue with what she perceived to be unsporting behavior by the Hawks.

"I've heard everything, 'You're bald, you're this, blah, blah, blah,'" Martelli said. "Usually, I blank it out. For whatever reason, I could hear this voice through two timeouts about, 'Be a sportsman. Be a better person. You're pressing.'"

The account of what happened next was picked up by media outlets across the country, making headlines nationally in addition to in Philadelphia. Martelli turned around and shouted at Palmer. According to the Associated Press, he called her a "nitwit" and a "moron."[38] More than 20 years later, Martelli doesn't recall saying that.

"It's been reported that I said 'moron,' or whatever," he said. "I don't remember that, and I'm not trying to bail on it. What I said was, 'Worry about your own team. We're good.'"

Martelli didn't have any notion that he would be talking afterward about anything except the Hawks' amazing performance until being questioned about the exchange, which was overheard on press row.

"A younger reporter said to me, 'Is the pressure getting to be too much for you?'" Martelli remembered. "We had just won by 50 points, and I'm like, 'It's like this each game for us. Not pressure.' He said, 'Well, you yelled at a lady.' I didn't consider what I did yelling, but when I went back [and thought about it], maybe it was."

Two days after the game, Martelli apologized to Palmer and St. Bonaventure during his weekly A-10 media teleconference.[39] He also sent Palmer a fruit basket and invited her as the team's guest to Buffalo later in the season during the NCAA tournament. It bothered Martelli that he became the story that night.

"That performance should've been the story," Martelli said. "Jameer played [only] 20 minutes, and we scored 114. I never wanted anything to be about me and felt bad it was about me."

However, Martelli couldn't afford to let those bad feelings linger. He had to put all of his focus into the Hawks' next game. St. Joe's would be playing on the road against John Chaney and the Temple Owls. Martelli knew that to be a top-tier Atlantic 10 program, St. Joe's would have to beat the perennial league powerhouse Owls. The Hawks coach had become obsessed with solving Chaney's matchup zone, developing a unique formula to beat it. Now, with an undefeated team and arguably the best backcourt in the country, would the formula work?

CHAPTER 23

Game 18: A Formula Solves the Zone

Saturday, January 31, 2004
Liacouras Center, Philadelphia
No. 3 Saint Joseph's at Temple

Temple University and Saint Joseph's share a Philadelphia address. The Owls' home court, the Liacouras Center, is located less than six miles from St. Joe's on-campus gym. For the first four and a half years of Phil Martelli's coaching career, however, the schools might as well have been galaxies apart.

The John Chaney-led Owls owned St. Joe's during that stretch, beating the Hawks all 10 times in Martelli's first 10 tries as head coach. By then, Chaney had reached living legend status as the longtime leader of Temple's men's basketball program. He took over in 1982 and quickly transformed the Owls into a national powerhouse and regular NCAA tournament participant. After missing the NCAAs in his first season, Chaney led Temple to March Madness in 17 of the next 18 years. The Owls reached the Elite Eight five times over that period.

So, St. Joe's wasn't the only team losing to Chaney and the Owls. Far from it. For Martelli and the Hawks, though, it was a triply damaging defeat. As fellow members of the Atlantic 10 and Philadelphia's historic Big 5, which also includes La Salle, Penn, and Villanova (and, beginning in 2023–24, Drexel) playing a yearly series for city bragging rights, every loss to Temple was not just an ordinary defeat but also a lower spot in the A-10 and Big 5 standings. More than that, though, it was a pride thing. Losing to Chaney game after game was like Martelli and some childhood buddies from his home park at Finnegan Playground challenging some other kids from a rival neighborhood playground to a five-on-five game and having to come home and tell friends and family that they were defeated once again.

Martelli always had the utmost admiration for Chaney and Temple, but constantly coming up short grated on the Hawks coach.

"There was always respect, but there was no sense of fondness," said Mike Jensen, who began covering college basketball in the city for the *Philadelphia Inquirer* in

1988. "John Chaney was on top, and Phil was trying to get there. They are where we're trying to go, and they are preventing it. Simple as that."

To be a true contender in the A-10 and Big 5—and to regain St. Joe's pride and basketball standing in the city—Martelli knew he had to beat the Owls. He just *had* to. And the Hawks coach became obsessed with solving the Owls. Martelli studied them and studied them and studied them some more. Under Chaney, Temple did not foul opposing players with regularity, didn't allow many fast break points, committed very few turnovers, owned the rebounding battle, and regularly confounded opposing offenses with its vaunted matchup zone.

"Having watched so many times and looking at it, and I'm not analytical, but I just kept thinking, 'John Chaney has a formula,'" Martelli said.

So, Martelli devised his own formula that he thought could beat Temple. The recipe for a victory over the Owls, he thought, would include fewer than 10 turnovers and at least 10 offensive rebounds, 10 made free throws, and 10 made three-pointers.

"I went the other way and said, 'What's the number?'" Martelli said, explaining how he came up with the formula. "The threes, the turnovers, getting 10 foul shots meant you were in the mix. And offensive rebounds were something they would not allow. So that's where it came from. It [developed] over the course of time."

The coach began recruiting to the formula, finding players who would be a fit for it. He emphasized free throw shooting as a key for his team, often ending practices with "Win the Game," a drill to simulate the pressure of making clutch free throws they would need to hit against the Owls. Everything Martelli did was designed with defeating Chaney and Temple in mind.

"We had always heard for quite some time that Phil believed that all roads ran through Temple," said Dan Leibovitz, who was a Temple assistant coach under Chaney from 1996 to 2006. "He would recruit his roster and their style of play was ultimately to beat us."

The other important piece to top Chaney and Temple, Martelli knew, was figuring out the matchup zone.

***

Chaney's matchup zone defense confused opponents and was a major reason for Temple's long and sustained success. Unlike a man-to-man defense, where each defender marks an opposing player, defenders guard specific areas in a zone. Chaney resorted to this style of defense mainly to keep his frontcourt players out of foul trouble. Most of the time, Temple used either "Rover," a 1-3-1 zone, or "Eleven," a 1-1-3 zone. "Rover," with three players spread across the middle of the painted area, would be more effective against a perimeter-based team, while "Eleven," with three players spread across the painted area closer to the basket, would be better against interior-based offensive teams. While slightly different in scheme, the concepts of "Rover" and "Eleven" were the same.

In Chaney's system, guards were responsible for denying penetration into the lane. The middle man in the zone was a big, strong, and tall player whose job it was to contest any shots of players who broke through the guards. And it would draw the ire of the raspy-voiced Chaney when opposing guards got into the paint, especially if the middle man picked up a foul trying to stop their route to the basket.

"Coach never yelled at the big guy," Leibovitz said. "He yelled at the guard for allowing penetration."

The guards also had several other important responsibilities. Chaney was willing to live with long jump shots but never wanted to foul three-point shooters. So, in order to avoid fouling, his guards wouldn't jump to contest a shot from beyond the arc. They just raised their arms high. It's why Chaney recruited tall, long-armed guards, and why having the 5-foot-11 Jameer Nelson and the 6-foot-2 Lynn Greer on the court at the same time wasn't ideal for the coach's defense when Nelson was considering Temple out of Chester High School. The guards also had to do something Chaney called "stunting" the ball, that is to keep the ball on one side of the court. The weakness of a zone is that there always is a player open. If the Owls could isolate the play on one side of the court, it would be impossible to pass to an open player. A final piece of the puzzle was the relentless pressure the Owls put on ball handlers that made it feel like offenses were playing five against six.

Chaney's defense was called a zone, but it had the look and feel of a man-to-man defense. Or something much worse for opponents. It definitely wasn't what you picture a zone to be.

"You watch youth basketball and they say we're going to play a 2-3 zone, and they stand there with kids doing jumping jacks and nobody really exerts any pressure," Leibovitz said. "We were hell-bent on putting serious pressure on the ball wherever we could because we knew that in a zone, somewhere on the floor, somebody is open."

Martelli and all opposing coaches knew this, of course. It was just figuring out how to get the ball to the open man that was the challenge. That and having players who could make a long-range shot when it came to them. Teams would try to attack the Owls' defense in various ways. Sometimes they would place a player in the high post. Other times they would try to lob the ball over the top of the zone. Most of the time, opponents had specific zone offenses that the Owls staff could sniff out, especially against teams not overly familiar with Temple.

"Usually, we could find two to three zone offenses in our scouts," Leibovitz said. "It's part of the reason why we had success in the NCAA tournament because on a short prep teams were trying to prepare for us, and it was much easier for us to detect the two or three things they were going to do against the zone."

Martelli knew the Hawks would have to come up with a different way to attack the zone. Along with his formula, he devised a plan to make St. Joe's zone offense unpredictable. Rather than call specific plays against the zone, something Martelli called a "pattern," the Hawks coach taught general principles to beat the zone, something he called "concepts."

"The offensive idea was to attack them conceptually and not pattern-wise," Martelli said. "Pattern would be if I take this 'X' and this 'X,' you go here and here. Pattern, they would take it away. They were on a whole other level. The concept would be if I throw it here, you could throw it over there. We would play by concept because they would just eliminate pattern."

In essence, Martelli prepped the Hawks with options that they could have rather than rote, predictable movement. And he drilled it over and over and over until it became second nature for the players.

"It seemed like Martelli and the coaching staff had the cheat code for it," Chet Stachitas said of Chaney's zone. "We never had the challenge against it that most teams do because we had a plan against it. I remember the practices leading up to it. I remember where we had to be on the court specifically, no matter where we passed the ball. I could still draw it up today if you asked me where we needed to be against their matchup zone because we hammered it in practice."

There was one other thing that aided the Hawks.

"It certainly helps when the shots are falling," Stachitas said.

Against the Owls on Saturday, January 31, 2004, at the Liacouras Center, everything Martelli had preached—the formula, the concepts, and making shots—came together almost perfectly for St. Joe's.

The Hawks exposed the zone's every weakness by finding the openings on the outside and draining one long-range shot after another. Temple had no answers. St. Joe's lead was 16 points at halftime. The Hawks didn't let up after the break, and the advantage, inconceivably, got as high as 29 points with 8:44 remaining. When the final horn sounded, St. Joe's had won 83-71 to improve to 18-0 overall and 8-0 in the A-10.

The Hawks had more than 10 free throws, making 15, but didn't quite check off Martelli's formula boxes in offensive rebounds (six) and turnovers (13). But they more than made up for it in three-pointers, setting both a school and A-10 record by draining 20 shots from beyond the arc.

"I remember this is one of the games where they put it all together, and there was nothing we were going to be able to do about it," Leibovitz said.

Nelson and Delonte West each scored 21 points, making six and five three-pointers, respectively. Pat Carroll netted a season-high 20 points, hitting five three-pointers, and Stachitas came off the bench to drain four long-range shots. The four players combined to shoot 60.6 percent (20 of 33) from the arc.

"We had four shooters at all times, and it was kind of pick your poison," Carroll said.

The triumph was the culmination of Martelli's newfound success against Temple. He first defeated Chaney on February 29, 2000, breaking the 10-game losing streak to start his coaching career. The victory at the Liacouras Center made it six wins in eight tries for the Hawks over the Owls. St. Joe's dominance over Temple would continue. From that first win in 2000 until Chaney's retirement following the 2005–06 season, Martelli's Hawks won 11 of the 14 contests between the city rivals.

"Phil and John Calipari are the only people I know who figured out John Chaney's zone," said Dick "Hoops" Weiss, the longtime college basketball writer for the *Philadelphia Daily News* and *New York Daily News*.

It had taken time and recruiting the right players for his formula, and obviously having talents like Nelson and West would help against any team, but Martelli had succeeded in his quest to beat Temple.

"It was not like some All-Star team that was thrown together," Leibovitz said. "It was a well-constructed roster with some really talented guys who played unbelievably well together. I can't argue with the success of what he developed and the way they played. It was a really tough matchup for us on both ends of the floor."

While elated with the victory and the success against Chaney's zone, Martelli and the Hawks couldn't celebrate for long. In just 48 hours, St. Joe's would bus 6.9 miles westward on Lancaster Avenue to face archrival Villanova. The Wildcats had a young, talented coach and a young, talented roster and were in the process of building something special of their own. And the 2003–04 Hawks would show Jay Wright and the Wildcats more of what they needed to have future success.

CHAPTER 24

Game 19: An Important Lesson for a Rival

Monday, February 2, 2004
Pavilion, Villanova, Pennsylvania
No. 3 Saint Joseph's at Villanova

There is one game every season that every Saint Joseph's fan circles on the calendar. No matter the record, the expectations, or the matchups, Hawks fans want to beat Villanova every year. The heated rivalry between neighboring Catholic schools, dubbed by some "The Holy War," brings out all of the passion, the revelry, and the excitement that help to make college basketball so great. For the Hawks, beating the Wildcats is always a little sweeter than any other victory because of the notion that St. Joe's is on a lower rung than Villanova.

Part of that is on the court. As a member of the Big East conference, Villanova has a higher standing in college basketball than the Atlantic 10's Hawks. The Wildcats appear more on television, especially on national broadcasts, and as a result can attract higher-level recruits. And part of that is off the court. Villanova's location on the Main Line, a leafy, wealthy region of Philadelphia's western suburbs, and its broader reach for a student population that is much less local than St. Joe's creates a dynamic, fairly or not, of the haves versus the have-nots.

St. Joe's undergrads have been seen walking around campus with T-shirts broadcasting sentiments such as "Friends don't let friends go to Villanova." In the lead-up to games against the Wildcats, students have spray-painted bedsheets that say "Beat Nova" and hung them over the walking bridge that crosses City Avenue. For all of the pomp, the buildup, and the hope, though, the Hawks have had relatively little success against Villanova.

In the long history of the rivalry, the Wildcats have won 68 percent of the contests. Villanova's winning percentage is even higher since joining the Big East in 1980, as the Wildcats claimed 30 of the 40 matchups through the 2023–24 season. There have been some moments of elation for Hawks fans, like when students rushed the court at the Palestra after upsetting No. 22-ranked Villanova on December 18, 1994. Mostly though, it has been a one-sided rivalry with yearly disappointment for

St. Joe's supporters. That kind of continued losing creates an animosity that one can clearly feel in the stands at games, on internet message boards, and at social events.

Hawks fans did have reason to celebrate in a big way in the 2002–03 season when St. Joe's defeated Villanova 92-75 at the Palestra on February 3, 2003, a contest in which they led 40-9 with 6:29 remaining in the first half. And hopes were high for the Hawks again when they traveled the 6.9 miles to Villanova's Pavilion on Monday, February 2, 2004, for an eight o'clock showdown against the Wildcats on ESPN2. Under third-year coach Jay Wright, Villanova started a freshman and four sophomores as part of a rebuilding process that eventually would see the Wildcats become a national powerhouse. St. Joe's, on the other hand, had a talented, veteran, and undefeated team. For Hawks fans, it would be the ultimate cruelty for the first loss to come to Villanova.

"Of all the games, that was the one game they had to win," Dick Jerardi said.

As is often the case in the rivalry, there was consternation about the location of the contest. Originally, the game was slated for early December at the Palestra. But it was moved to early February at the request of ESPN as part of its "Rivalry Week." There was some thought about holding the game in South Philadelphia at the home of the NBA's 76ers, where Villanova hosts several Big East games each season, but the NHL's Flyers had a home date scheduled there for that night. Rather than stay at the Palestra, the Wildcats elected to host St. Joe's at their 6,500-seat on-campus court.[40] As a result, St. Joe's got the visiting allotment of 250 tickets, and Hawks fans squeezed into a tiny portion of the upper seating at the Pavilion. That just wasn't anywhere close to enough to accommodate the insatiable demand of St. Joe's fans, who were engrossed in a season-long, excited frenzy over the success of the Hawks.

"We had to figure something out," athletic director Don DiJulia said. "People wanted to see the game."

So, St. Joe's set up three large screens at the Fieldhouse and welcomed 2,500 fans into its on-campus gym for a watch party that had every bit the sound and feel of a Hawks home game. The Fieldhouse was rocking with excitement and optimism before tipoff. Phil Martelli was feeling good, too.

"Obviously, the Villanova–St. Joe's thing, you're a little bit more amped up," Martelli said. "But I can remember being calmer and, again not disrespectful, I just knew we were better than them. They were young. We were better."

There is no argument from Wright on this point.

"We had young guys," Wright, himself 43 years old at the time, said. "We felt like we were starting to get a little bit better, but we knew this is one of the best teams in the country."

And the Hawks showed why they were ranked No. 3 in the Associated Press poll and why they entered 18-0. Jameer Nelson had 23 points, four rebounds, and four assists in 38 minutes; Delonte West contributed 21 points, a season-high 11 rebounds, and six assists in 39 minutes; and Pat Carroll continued his can't-miss streak from long range, draining all four of his three-point attempts, and finished with 16 points. Carroll completed a spectacular five-game shooting display in which he made 22 of 30 (73.3 percent) of his long-range shots. The red-hot stretch started when he broke out of his early-season slump by nailing two late three-pointers at Xavier.

In spite of the outstanding performances by Nelson, West, and Carroll, the young Wildcats clawed and fought, keeping the game close until the final whistle, but St. Joe's prevailed 74-67 to improve to 19-0.

Of the Wildcats, Martelli was most impressed with freshman guard Mike Nardi, who scored 16 points and dished five assists when he wasn't hounding Nelson on defense.

"I remember how tough Nardi was that night," Martelli said.

The four Villanova sophomore starters, Allan Ray, Randy Foye, Jason Fraser, and Curtis Sumpter, combined for 31 points.

"You could already see that Villanova's young guys were going to be really good," Jerardi said. "I didn't think it was going to be then, but they gave them a hell of a game. They played really well. Villanova asked a lot of questions that night, and St. Joe's always had an answer. Always. At no time did I think they were ever going to lose the game."

Wright also felt like the Hawks were always in control.

"I remember every time we made a run, every time the crowd got going where it looked like we could get into the game, they always kept us at bay," he said. "Jameer Nelson would make a play, and not a spectacular play but the right play, to separate them. Delonte West would make a play, the right play, to separate them. And it was consistent. They would never get affected by the crowd. They came in very mature, very businesslike, no yelling at the crowd, no trash-talking. Nothing. Just business."

Villanova's coach would use the Hawks' performance as a reference point during the Wildcats' building process.

"We really learned a lot from them that game," Wright said. "We played great and we knew we played great. They were just better. We knew we played a great team. We said, 'If we're going to be a great team, this is what it's going to take.' We saw it right in front of us.

"It was such a great game for us. We just came out of that even more impressed with them, and their efficiency, their attention to detail, their maturity level, and their competitiveness. To be able to come into that environment on the road, they made all the right plays. They were a machine. That's what it's going to take. We have to be that efficient and be that attentive to detail."

Wright said in the lead-up to the contest that Nelson could score like the 76ers' Allen Iverson if he wanted to, but he chose to play a complete game.[41] Nelson's style of play also would be a model for Wright's point guards going forward.

"Every time it looked like we were going to be able to make a run, he'd make a steal or get a defensive rebound, or he'd have an open three but find [Dwayne]

Jones for a dunk," Wright said. "Instead of trying to single-handedly outscore us, which he could've done, he just made the right play. And that was something that we really talked to our guys about afterwards. It was something that we would always talk to them about, but it was right in front of us and something we experienced. It was really valuable for us."

He also liked the way in which the Hawks handled the victory.

"Of all the St. Joe's–Villanova rivalry games, I just thought it was so impressive that when they were at their best, they were humble and businesslike, and never put it in our face," Wright said. "I was so impressed with that. And I think it was the leadership of Jameer and Phil. I remember telling Phil that after the game. It was really impressive, as impressive as their talent."

With his young roster, Wright would finish out the 2003–04 season with an 18-17 overall mark and a 6-10 record in the Big East. The Wildcats had yet to have a winning record in the Big East under Wright, going a combined 21-27. But they were getting better and, helped by what they saw from St. Joe's, knew exactly how they wanted to play. The Hawks' model would help to propel Villanova into a dominant force in college basketball under Wright. The Wildcats made the NCAA tournament in 2004–05 for the first time under Wright and then went to the Big Dance in 15 of the next 16 tournaments, highlighted by a pair of national championships in 2016 and 2018 and two additional Final Four appearances (2009, 2022).

Between the 2004–05 season and his surprise retirement in April 2022, Wright's teams would dominate St. Joe's and the Big 5 in a way that had never been seen before. Over that stretch, the Wildcats won 60 of 68 contests against La Salle, Penn, St. Joe's, and Temple. Wright would claim six Big East Coach of the Year Awards and was inducted into the Naismith Hall of Fame in 2021. He retired with a 520-197 (.725) mark in 21 seasons at Villanova. It was unprecedented success that was boosted by that defeat to the Hawks at the Pavilion. Wright is not one to compare himself or Villanova to others but acknowledged the impact of that contest on the Wildcats program.

"The timing of our guys being [young], getting their butts kicked [on February 3, 2003], living in Philly and watching a great St. Joe's team after having felt it, the efficiency, the maturity, the businesslike approach, playing great [on February 2, 2004] and it still not being good enough, I'm sure that was impactful," Wright said. "It was perfect timing."

While the Wildcats would be one of the nation's top teams soon, St. Joe's was there right now. And the Hawks had yet another challenge ahead. Up next, they would be playing in another Big 5 game. This one would be at the Palestra, where leads are never safe and upsets all too common. And St. Joe's would be facing an assistant coach and former Hawk who knew their style intimately. If they wanted to remain undefeated, the Hawks just could not afford a letdown after Villanova.

CHAPTER 25

Game 20: Scouting Report? Dominance!

Saturday, February 7, 2004
The Palestra, Philadelphia
La Salle at No. 3 Saint Joseph's

For the first time since playing three straight games there in early December, Saint Joseph's returned to the Palestra for a Big 5 matchup against La Salle at two o'clock on Saturday, February 7, 2004. Phil Martelli fell in love with the gym, nicknamed the "Cathedral of College Basketball," as a kid growing up in Southwest Philadelphia when he took trolley rides there for Saturday night doubleheaders.

Jack Scheuer also loved the Palestra. A longtime sportswriter for the Associated Press, Scheuer is the answer to one of the greatest trivia questions in sports.

Q: Who is the all-time leading scorer in Palestra history? A: Jack Scheuer.

In fact, Scheuer's name doesn't appear in any record books. In reality, he actually has scored more points at the Palestra than anyone, as he hosted a longtime weekly media pickup game there. Scheuer's rules for the game were simple: He didn't care if you could play, only that you played the right way.

Scheuer, who passed away in 2020, was revered in Philadelphia college basketball circles. A Big 5 Hall of Famer, the respect for Scheuer was so great that, like the trivia question, he also is the centerpiece of one of the all-time great Philadelphia college basketball stories. One day, as Scheuer was leading one of his pickup games, coach Fran Dunphy brought his Penn team out of the Palestra locker room for practice on their floor. Realizing his mistake of scheduling practice at the same time as Scheuer's game, Dunphy apologized and took the Quakers' session to a side court in an auxiliary gym. That was the high esteem in which Dunphy and everyone held Scheuer.

Scheuer was a fixture at the Palestra. He just loved the place and could visit whenever he wanted, as he had a key to the gym. He celebrated his 75th birthday at the Palestra, where his family gave away T-shirts that said "Big 75" with a knockoff of the Big 5 logo and placing a "7" in front of the "5."

Today there is a plaque honoring Scheuer's memory outside of locker room No. 4 at the beloved place he affectionately called "my gym." Scheuer relished any chance to cover games at the Palestra and especially sold-out contests when 8,722 crowded into the building and created an atmosphere the likes of which you likely never will experience anywhere else. In those contests, Scheuer would lean over to a colleague and scribble the word "corners" on a piece of paper because every seat, including those in the four corners of the gym, was full. Palestra sellouts will be forever referred to as "corners" in honor of Scheuer.

When Phil Martelli exited locker room No. 4, the same one that today bears Scheuer's plaque and always was the preferred dressing room for Martelli's Hawks, he looked up and saw something much, much more than just "corners." The crowd was unlike anything he'd ever witnessed in his countless trips to the Palestra.

"There were no aisles," Martelli said.

Everyone wanted to be there to see the Hawks reach their 20th victory without a loss. And John Gallagher was going to do everything he could to deny them.

Gallagher was in his fifth season as a La Salle assistant coach after graduating in 1999 from Saint Joseph's, where he was a reserve player for Martelli. Known by everyone as "Gal," he has gone on to a successful career as a head coach. He took over at Hartford in 2010 and led the school to its first and only NCAA tournament appearance in 2022. In March 2023, Gallagher was named the head coach at Manhattan. In every stop of his coaching career, which also includes assistant stints at Penn, Lafayette, Boston College, and Hartford, Gallagher has brought with him valuable lessons learned from Martelli.

"You can break down my coaching in this way: My motivational stuff begins and ends with Phil Martelli," Gallagher said. "And it's based on unconditional love for players. He has unconditional love for his players. His organization is second to none. His detail on his motivation and themes for the year are second to none. Each year had a different theme. He never coached the same way the next year. He had different motivations."

Gallagher was recruiting a player following the 2023–24 season in the transfer portal when he explained an example of Martelli's influence.

"I just got done talking to a player who committed to us, and I said, 'I watched your film, and you look over at the bench,'" Gallagher said. "I said, 'If you look over at the bench, I'm taking you out.' You can turn it over, you can miss every shot, but I don't like guys looking at me. It's basketball. We're not curing cancer. This is supposed to be fun. 'Don't look over. I want you to play with unbelievable freedom and unbelievable belief. Do not look at me.' And that was from Phil. Play the game. It's basketball."

He also has modeled his game-day routine after Martelli.

"Every game has three offensive keys, three defensive keys, and three specials [like Martelli]," Gallagher said. "Foundationally speaking, that's how he's affected my coaching. He taught me to breathe as a coach. Even building my program at Hartford into a champion, his fingerprints are all over it."

Gallagher's admiration of Martelli began during his own playing days when he gained inside knowledge of how the coach runs a program. And, in the lead-up to the La Salle–St. Joe's matchup at the Palestra, he was going to use every single bit of that insight to put the Explorers in the best possible position for what would be a shocking upset.

"I scouted them," Gallagher said.

There were several pieces to the puzzle that Gallagher believed the Explorers would have to solve. First, he understood Martelli's substitution pattern intimately and would match the Explorers' scheme with the Hawks' personnel. Second, he knew St. Joe's was particularly effective on scoring and defending baseline out-of-bounds plays, so the Explorers would be ready for that. Third, for the Explorers to have any chance, Gallagher figured they would have to limit the Hawks to under 60 possessions, and preferably around 55. He went back through his memory bank, looked over every tape, and put all of his skill, wisdom, and everything he had learned into a scouting report for head coach Billy Hahn.

"If you just went out and played them, you had no chance to win," Gallagher said.

And, as they would show in dominant fashion, even if you scouted the 2003–04 Hawks with someone as talented as Gallagher who had inside knowledge of the program, it really didn't matter, either.

However, Gallagher's plan looked good early when the motivated and prepared Explorers took a 19-17 lead. But the Hawks closed the first half on a 29-13 run that ended with a backbreaking four-point play by Pat Carroll with 2.5 seconds remaining before intermission. The Hawks' lead eventually grew to 30 points in the second half before they settled for an easy 89-63 victory that upped their record to 20-0 overall and 9-0 in the Atlantic 10.

Sitting courtside, Scheuer would've written the letters "VGH" in his notebook to describe St. Joe's play. "VGH" stands for "Very Good Hoops," and it was rare to receive that lofty accolade from the high standards of Scheuer. Usually, he would write "GH" for "Good Hoops" when impressed. A poor performance would receive "BH" for "Bad Hoops." An awful game, also rare, would get "VBH," or "Very Bad Hoops."

There was no question about how to classify this one for Scheuer, as the Hawks once again had put on a clinic that epitomized "VGH." Delonte West became the 42nd player in school history to surpass 1,000 career points, finishing with 22 points, seven rebounds, and five assists. Jameer Nelson had 20 points and five assists. In an unusual statistic, the Hawks had more steals (12) than turnovers (nine). Through no fault of his, Gallagher's scouting report didn't work.

"Even when you tried to maneuver tactically against them, they were too talented," he said. "Of all the teams I've seen in 25 years, I've never seen a team that understood each other [as well] from a personnel standpoint. Never seen it. Still haven't. And they had the best player in the country and then a top 10 or 15 player as his backcourt mate.

"I thought we had a great game plan. The problem is St. Joe's was the greatest team I've seen at taking your game plan, figuring out what you were doing, and then manipulating against it."

An example of that was the possessions. La Salle did everything it could to slow the game down, but it didn't work. The Hawks went well over the 60 possessions Gallagher wanted to keep them under.

"It was around 64 to 66 possessions," Gallagher said. "It got too fast for us at times."

Martelli was thrilled with the performance, but he wasted little time turning the Hawks' focus to their next opponent. Inside of locker room No. 4 afterward, St. Joe's coach wrote the following on the board: "Dayton 66, SJU 56—Dayton 76, SJU 73."[42] Those were the results of the previous two meetings against Dayton during the 2002–03 season, a regular-season home defeat and a loss in the A-10 tournament semifinals. Like St. Joe's, the Flyers also were undefeated in the A-10 thus far in 2003–04, and they headed to the Fieldhouse for a midweek showdown of unbeatens. In addition to a traditionally tough opponent, St. Joe's would have to deal with something else. There would be media attention the likes of which the school had never seen before thanks to the little man from the little school that's beating everyone.

CHAPTER 26

Game 21: A Cover, a Crowd, and a Clinic

Wednesday, February 11, 2004
Alumni Memorial Fieldhouse, Philadelphia
Dayton at No. 3 Saint Joseph's

From the season-opening win over Gonzaga at Madison Square Garden until the 20th victory without a loss against La Salle at the Palestra, Saint Joseph's had been gaining more and more notoriety. Ray Parrillo and Dick Jerardi's articles had drawn large headlines in the *Philadelphia Inquirer* and *Philadelphia Daily News*, respectively, from Day One. As the winning continued, Parrillo and Jerardi were still there, but now they were competing for St. Joe's attention with countless other reporters as the story just got bigger and bigger, both locally and nationally. But it would explode to an entirely different level on the morning of the Hawks' 21st game of the 2003–04 season, at the Fieldhouse against Dayton on Wednesday, February 11, 2004.

On that day, newsstands displayed the latest copy of *Sports Illustrated*, the national weekly magazine that was a must-read for sports fans. Splashed across the cover was a confident-looking Jameer Nelson with his left hand on his hip and right hand holding a basketball at his side. Underneath in huge white capital letters were the words: "MEET JAMEER NELSON THE LITTLE MAN FROM THE LITTLE SCHOOL THAT'S BEATING EVERYONE." If sports fans didn't already know about Nelson and the Hawks, they certainly would now from the cover and the feature story on the inside pages.

"The reaction was like, 'How could this happen?'" athletic director Don DiJulia said. "It was astounding and astonishing."

In the previous week's edition of the magazine, Super Bowl hero Tom Brady graced the cover after leading the New England Patriots to a 32-29 victory over the Carolina Panthers. And, now, it was Nelson and the Hawks' turn.

"You had this little Catholic school all of the sudden in the spotlight," Atlantic 10 commissioner Linda Bruno said.

"The idea that happened is just remarkable," Joe Sullivan, a 1972 St. Joe's graduate who worked in the sports department of the *Boston Globe*, said. "That really sort of represents what they achieved nationally that they would be on the cover of that magazine. It didn't mean as much in 2004 as it did in 1974, but it was still very important."

There would be time later for the Hawks to digest the article and feel the cover's impact, but not now. Not with Dayton in town for a highly anticipated showdown. The Flyers always have been among the top tier in the A-10, and they entered this matchup, like St. Joe's, undefeated in the league. Unlike most opponents during Nelson's four years, Dayton had success against St. Joe's. The Flyers had defeated Nelson and the Hawks in four of the previous six matchups, including both games in 2002–03. They knew they could beat St. Joe's again and would not enter this game intimidated in any way.

"Everybody that's any type of competitor is looking forward to it like, 'We've got our shot. We get a chance to take a crack at them,'" said Keith Waleskowski, who was a senior for Dayton in 2003–04. "So, you get a little bit excited for that. You realize they're really, really good, too. So, it's not going to be the easiest task."

The defending A-10 champion Flyers were going to have to contend with more than just the opposing players, as the Fieldhouse was bursting with anticipation to see the undefeated Hawks again. That the game was a first-ever meeting between A-10 teams that both entered with 9-0 records only added to the raucousness.

"The noise, no one can withstand this noise," Phil Martelli said. "You can't. Mentally, psychologically it's impossible to overcome the noise."

As difficult of an environment and as loud as it was, Waleskowski actually embraced the atmosphere inside the Fieldhouse, which supposedly seated 3,200 fans.

"I'm pretty sure they crammed about 4,800 in there, which makes it an awesome atmosphere," he said. "It's packed, it's loud, everybody is just on top of you. The student section was three rows deep on the floor. They're on top of you. Any time we had to take the ball out under the basket, the ref had to part the seas like he was Moses. Then you just have the students in your ear saying all types of colorful stuff. You know you're going to hear, 'You suck!' And you know you're going to get cussed at and all that. But when they come up with better things to say, about your mom and your sisters and everybody else, that was always fun.

"Just everybody was super, super into it. It was a tense atmosphere for us as visitors. But those are the fun environments to play in. Not big, empty gyms. Those [St. Joe's games] were just fun games."

Waleskowski said the Flyers were able to block out the noise to a certain point, but it affected them when trying to communicate on the court.

"It becomes background white noise because it's kind of the same level except it's so loud," he said. "You're calling out a screen, and then I'm getting called out by my guards for not calling out a screen. I'm like, 'Dude, I'm yelling at the top of my lungs five feet apart. I can't yell any louder.' Home-court advantage, that's what it is. You can feel the noise."

The Hawks also made their presence felt on the court, taking control of the contest with a strong first half that ended with St. Joe's leading 36-25. The Flyers' troubles continued at halftime in the tiny visiting locker room.

"It was like a hallway," the 6-foot-8 Waleskowski said. "It was almost difficult to get in and out."

First-year Dayton coach Brian Gregory was animated and wanted to fire up the Flyers for the second half. But Gregory couldn't pull his players into a circle to address them because of the minuscule size of the locker room. Frustrated, he asked if there was somewhere else Dayton could go. Then, things went from bad to worse for the Flyers.

"They had some administrative offices beneath with more space, and they said we could use those offices," Waleskowski said. "But then we went in there, the halftime show must've been something to do with mascots and there were like 10 different mascots in there. It was a circus. It was like, 'What the hell is going on? Now we've got mascots at the halftime?'"

Things didn't get much better for Dayton after maneuvering past mascot costumes and copy machines back onto the court. Nelson and Delonte West were filling up the box score, and the Hawks were getting contributions from up and down the lineup.

"They had so many weapons," Waleskowski said. "Jameer and Delonte got a lot of publicity, and rightfully so. But they were super versatile. They weren't stars that were selfish and had to go out and get theirs. In games where they didn't get theirs, they wouldn't pout and try to force things. They found other ways to do it."

On this night, the St. Joe's stars did get theirs and so did many of their teammates. Nelson showed why he became an overnight sports sensation as *SI*'s cover choice, garnering 16 points, seven assists, six rebounds, and three steals in 37 minutes. West had 24 points and five assists, and the Hawks put forth another clinic on their way to an 81-67 victory that improved them to 21-0 overall and 10-0 in the A-10.

Tyrone Barley played his usual clamp-down defense while adding 14 points; Pat Carroll made all three of his three-point tries; Dwayne Jones had six points, eight rebounds, and three blocks; and Chet Stachitas contributed a season-high four steals. For the second straight contest in what would amazingly occur 11 times over the course of the season, the Hawks had more steals than turnovers.

The 6-foot-5 Stachitas relished his role of doing the dirty work, and particularly liked coming off the bench against the tall, physical Flyers and causing havoc while guarding a bigger, stronger power forward.

"I was undersized to play that role, but I was scrappy and knew I could out-scrap some people," he said. "I was kind of an unassuming, scrawny white kid coming in to guard their four-man. I liked mixing it up. But I also knew my minutes were limited, so I would go all-out on defense.

"I kind of liked banging down low and fronting in the post because I knew I had DJ behind me. I would typically try to front the pass. I could also hide at times. If they're trying to input the pass to the high post or the baseline, I was smaller so I could duck down. I remember in that Dayton game getting into the passing lanes and intercepting the ball."

The result was not a surprise to Jerardi, who was joined on press row for this game by *Philadelphia Daily News* columnist Rich Hofmann as the media contingent continued to grow.

"I was already convinced they weren't losing," Jerardi said. "It was just a question of how they were going to win the games."

Opponents, like Waleskowski, recognized the same thing as Jerardi, that the Hawks had so many options. Everything started with Nelson, and St. Joe's went from there.

"Jameer read situations extremely well, he had a fantastic handle, and he could shoot the ball," said Waleskowski, who had 20 points and 10 rebounds against the Hawks. "He was shorter, but he was strong. He didn't get tired. You couldn't wear the kid out. He just kept coming and was super under control the way he moved, the way he controlled his body. You couldn't just focus on Jameer because if you did, it was like, 'That's fine, shut me down, but I'm going to have everyone else kill you guys.' And they would. Just multiple heads to that snake.

"You have Delonte West, who was super shifty and can shoot. You have Pat Carroll throwing daggers. You had a couple of bigs that did a very effective job just scoring off dump-offs. They had really good role players that knew their role, accepted their role, and played their role extremely well."

Waleskowski also played his role well. His big game against the Hawks was typical of his career, as he finished with 1,515 points and 1,092 rebounds to earn a spot in Dayton's Hall of Fame. He went on to play nine seasons professionally overseas and, in 2007–08, teamed with Carroll in Spain.

"I was glad to be on a team with a sharpshooter like him," Waleskowski, who today is a financial advisor for Callahan Financial Management Group in Dayton, said. "I was like, 'I hated how good you guys were. It was super tough.'" In reply, according to Waleskowski, Carroll echoed those remarks exactly.

"It was nice to finally be teammates after doing so many battles," Waleskowski said.

Teaming up with Waleskowski would come later for Carroll. For now, he and the Hawks could catch their breaths and take a moment to read the feature story in *Sports Illustrated* after yet another impressive performance. But they couldn't relax for very long. Another challenging opponent was headed to the Fieldhouse in just three days. Rhode Island didn't have the pedigree of Dayton, but the Rams were tough, physical, and always gave St. Joe's a problem. If the players started to struggle against Rhode Island, they could look over toward the home bench. There, a student inside of a feathered costume would be flapping his arms from the moment the game started until it ended, embodying the spirt of the school's mantra that *The Hawk Will Never Die.*

CHAPTER 27

Game 22: The Hawk Will Never Die

Saturday, February 14, 2004
Alumni Memorial Fieldhouse, Philadelphia
Rhode Island at No. 3 Saint Joseph's

Inside of the Fieldhouse's cramped home locker room approaching noon on Saturday, February 14, 2004, Phil Martelli gathered the Hawks for final preparations and words of encouragement for their 22nd game of the 2003–04 season. The rollicking Fieldhouse crowd outside of the locker room was already loud, overflowing, and excited to see another magical performance. Inside of the locker room, Martelli was all business as usual. The coach knew Rhode Island presented a different and real challenge. Martelli harped on the need to match the Rams' tough, physical style; reminded his players that Rhode Island handed St. Joe's one of its seven losses in the previous season; and pointed out again the importance of cutting off the driving lanes of Dawan Robinson, the talented, prolific scorer out of Philadelphia's Martin Luther King High School. When Martelli finished, the coach turned his game face toward the door and told Chris Bertolino they were ready.

Bertolino does not appear on the official 2003–04 Saint Joseph's University men's basketball roster. But Bertolino was an integral and essential member of the program and, like Jameer Nelson, Delonte West, and the others, was on a full athletic scholarship. Already attired in a feathered costume up to his neck, Bertolino took a deep breath, slid the beaked adornment over his head, and raised both of his arms high over his shoulders in a flapping manner for the first of approximately 3,500 times over the next two and a half hours. Bertolino pushed the door ajar as band director Tim Laushey orchestrated a stirring rendition of "When the Saints Go Marching In," with students singing in reverberating unison the revised lyrics of, "When the Hawks Come Flying In." With pregame adrenalin rushing through Nelson, West, and the rest of the players who were lined up single file behind him, Bertolino opened the door fully. Everyone was now ready. And The Hawk led them out.

After serving for two seasons as a team manager, Bertolino successfully wrote a letter and completed an interview to be named The Hawk for the 2003–04 season.

"Holy cow, I'm going to have the opportunity to represent the school and be part of something special," Bertolino said of his reaction when Martelli informed him he would be The Hawk. "I look back on it with pride and gratitude."

Bertolino continued a long line of mascots to represent the Hawks. The school's nickname was born in 1929 when Saint Joseph's student John Gallagher responded to yearbook editor Charlie Dunn's contest request to name the school's athletics teams. Inspired by St. Joe's football team's passing attack, Gallagher submitted "Hawks" as his entrant. It beat out Grenadiers, which was an ode to World War I soldiers who tossed hand grenades. By 1940, St. Joe's had disbanded its football team, but the nickname stuck. It was a good name, but undergraduate Jim Brennan thought there could be more school spirit behind it. So, in 1954, Brennan proposed that the school ought to have a mascot to go along with the nickname. Everyone agreed, and the student government organization raised $120 for a hawk costume, which debuted with Brennan inside of it at the Palestra on December 3, 1955.

The Hawk was born.

Beginning with Brennan, every Hawk mascot has flapped the wings without stop during games, including Bertolino, who was the 27th student to wear the costume. Since the costume was updated to add a beaked head, the flapping has begun from the moment the head of the costume went on until it was removed in the locker room after the game. This dedication to nonstop flapping spurred the school's motto, *The Hawk Will Never Die.*

It is a motto, yes. But it is so much more. It motivates St. Joe's athletes and becomes a way of life for students and graduates.

"That's totally real, I'm telling you right now," Chuck Sack, The Hawk mascot from 1991–93, said of the motto. "I've lived it in so many different ways. It's attitude. It's a mindset. It's a frame by which everyone wants to look at stuff, through persistence, determination, grit, and the passion that goes into wanting to be successful."

Sack, as the team's academic advisor, saw it infused in the 2003–04 Hawks.

"They never wanted to stop playing with each other," Sack said. "And that attitude is part of this mindset of *The Hawk Will Never Die.* They're not going to stop being there for each other."

Opponents also recognized the importance of The Hawk and the motto. Bill Avington recalls hearing a story about No. 17-ranked Xavier practicing the night before its contest against St. Joe's at the Fieldhouse on February 8, 1997. Xavier's coach at that time, Skip Prosser, gathered the team at the center circle, where the school's logo was painted.

"This hawk means something here," Prosser told his players, according to Avington. "They play for this, and you better come ready."

If Xavier was ready, the Hawks were more ready the next day, as St. Joe's pulled off a 79-65 upset.

Bobby Gallagher was behind the bench for that game as a student manager for Martelli's squad. It was Gallagher's grandfather, John, who had coined the Hawks nickname. Bobby Gallagher fell in love with the team from a young age and wanted to be inside The Hawk costume from the first time he saw it.

"I saw The Hawk lead the team on the court, and at that point I just became enamored," Gallagher said. "I was watching The Hawk most of the game."

He got involved with the men's basketball program as a sophomore in 1995 as a manager and studied Brian Kearns as much as Martelli or any of the players. Kearns was The Hawk mascot from 1994 to 1996.

"I just watched everything Brian did," Gallagher said. "In the back of my mind, I'm like, 'I know I'm going to do that.'"

Gallagher completed the formal application and interview process prior to 1996–97, and it went well. The committee decided that Glenn "Trip" Whittaker would serve as The Hawk that season, and Bobby Gallagher would take over during his senior year in 1997–98. Gallagher was elated.

"I will be eternally grateful to St. Joe's, in general, but specifically to Coach Martelli and Mr. DiJulia," he said. "Without their blessing, I don't get that opportunity. It's a big honor."

Gallagher understood the importance and tradition of The Hawk.

"It's our unique identifier," he said. "It's what makes us St. Joe's. It's epic. Of course I'm biased, but it's the greatest tradition in college sports. It's amazing. It's absolutely amazing."

As with every Hawk mascot before and after him, Gallagher knew he played a huge role in *The Hawk Will Never Die* mantra by continuously flapping the wings of the costume from the moment its head went on until taken off. The physically demanding yet inspiring requirement was tested for Gallagher immediately. The Hawk not only performs at basketball games but also is requested by alumni at major events, like weddings and funerals. It was at a backyard wedding in the summer of 1997 that Gallagher made his debut as The Hawk mascot, producing one in a long line of memorable tales involving The Hawk.

"This guy brings me in the house, shows me the backyard, brings me upstairs and says, 'Do you think you'll be able to climb out this window? I'll have the DJ play 'When the Saints Go Marching In.' When you hear the music, jump down there on the deck,'" Gallagher said.

Gallagher looked down at the eight-foot drop, thought about it, and in his 21-year-old cocksure voice said, "Sure."

"I'm like, 'That's a great idea. Absolutely, I can do that,'" he said. "Then I hear his wife come upstairs and say, 'Do not do that. That's ridiculous. The kid is going to get hurt. It's a liability.' He looks at me, and I give him the nod like, 'No problem, man. I'll do it.'"

In this case, listening to the wife would have been smarter, if not as memorable. With the wedding party in place, the DJ cued the music. Gallagher, feeling euphoric in his first official appearance as The Hawk, placed the mascot's head over his own and raised his arms in excited elation that quickly turned to terror.

"I jump and my right foot gets caught in the gutter," Gallagher said. "I'm literally hanging upside down for about three seconds and then fall right on my head."

His health and job requirement flashed through his mind in an instant.

"I'm lying flat on my back for a split second," he said. "I was fine. I pop up and just start flapping as fast as I can."

It would not be the first time Gallagher's requirement to flap at all times was tested. On February 3, 1998, the Hawks were at Rhode Island when Gallagher was flapping as St. Joe's huddled during a timeout. The Rams mascot snuck behind Gallagher with an inner tube. The opposing mascot planned to prevent Gallagher from raising his arms by having the inner tube secured tightly around The Hawk. The plan backfired when the tube got caught on the beak. In the struggle to get the tube off, the Rams mascot ripped Gallagher's beaked costume head off.

Stunned and irate, Gallagher, his face showing for all to see, charged the Rams mascot. Afterward, as he calmed down, Gallagher wasn't worried about any possible repercussions from Saint Joseph's; rather, he hoped that in his rage he had remembered to keep on flapping.

"I was so nervous because I didn't want to get in trouble, and the main thing was, 'Did I keep flapping the whole time?'" Gallagher said. "I honestly blacked out. We got back to the hotel and, lo and behold, *SportsCenter* showed the Hawks–Rams incident. Everyone is laughing. I'm just staring at myself. And thank God I kept flapping."

***

It was Bertolino's turn to flap nonstop against Rhode Island on Valentine's Day in 2004 at the Fieldhouse. There would be no issues for Bertolino having to fight off the Rams mascot, and he didn't nearly pass out like in the fourth game of the season when an ice vest was strapped too tightly to his chest. In contrast, the Hawks players had their hands full with the Rams. Rhode Island was tall and strong and just the type of team that could give St. Joe's problems.

"We just had a bunch of guys that played hard," Robinson said. "We didn't have the most talented team on paper, but we were dogs and we played together. Rebounding and defense were really, really lockdown. That kept us in a lot of games. We were a hard-nosed team."

Robinson was in the midst of a breakout season. He had dedicated himself in the offseason to improving his already strong game, and it would result in a career year in 2003–04 that ended with him leading the Rams in scoring and raising his three-point shooting from 26.3 percent in the previous season to 40.3. He also came to the Fieldhouse with extra motivation, as he did in every game against a Philadelphia school, after not being recruited by any of the city's six Division I colleges despite a sensational high school career in the Philadelphia Public League.

"I didn't even get a letter from any of the Philadelphia schools, and I took that personally," he said.

Years later, he acknowledged that he might have been too hyped for the matchup and probably tried too hard. That and Tyrone Barley was nipping at his heels. Barley's assignment, as on most nights, was to guard the opposing team's top scorer whenever he entered the contest. Barley knew he wasn't going to score a ton of points but figured his team would be successful if whatever he contributed offensively was more than the opposing team's leading scorer.

Barley hounded Robinson all game, halting the athletically gifted and speedy 6-foot-3 guard's path to the basket, contesting every shot with ferocious intensity, and just making his every dribble or movement an incredible challenge. By game's end, Robinson had managed just six points, 11 shy of his season average, and missed 11 of 13 field goal attempts. Barley, meantime, chipped in 14 points to help the Hawks improve to 22-0 overall and 11-0 in the Atlantic 10 with a 73-59 victory.

"I just wanted to play good for my family and friends, and I think I put too much pressure on myself and they did a good job," Robinson said. "They scouted me really well. They knew I was having a good season. Barley was on me. They made it tough on me. They cut off my lanes when I was attacking the basket. I didn't get any open shots, and the shots that I did get, they just didn't fall for me. It was a rough game. I didn't feel any nervousness or anything like that but had the extra motivation to play well in front of my friends and family, and sometimes that doesn't go the right way."

Robinson would go on to a successful, 12-year professional career overseas that included winning three championships. Today, he runs a skill development academy, called Life of Hoops, in Rhode Island for aspiring ballers. In all of his experiences in basketball, Barley ranks near the top of Robinson's list of premier defenders.

"They had some dogs on their squad," Robinson said. "Barley was one of the best defenders I've ever played against."

Barley's performance against Robinson left Martelli glowing afterward. Otherwise, the coach was furious. Part of that, likely, was a motivational tool to keep the Hawks on their toes, and part of it, in fact, was the Rams' rebounding dominance. The physical Rams grabbed 48 rebounds to St. Joe's 26, and Martelli knew the Hawks would be facing similarly physical teams later in the season and couldn't afford another slipup like that.

With Bertolino finally resting his shoulders afterward in the locker room with the sweaty, beaked mascot head on a bench next to him, Martelli shared his displeasure with the players.

"When people would dig at our Achilles' heel, it was always about our rebounding and our size," Martelli said. "So, getting wiped out like that on the glass, that was a concern because teams were bigger than us. It was not acceptable to lose a battle on the glass like that."

Quietly, Bertolino undressed from The Hawk costume, and the players changed out of their uniforms and into street clothes. They had won another game, but the celebration was subdued because of the rebounding discrepancy. Though it wouldn't be said aloud by anyone inside the program, everyone knew there wouldn't be a similar problem in the Hawks' next game, at Fordham on February 18. Fordham wasn't very good, and St. Joe's already had defeated them by 44 points once this season. Martelli wouldn't let the Hawks look past them, though. He was going to do everything he could to keep the Hawks rolling. And athletic director Don DiJulia would be supporting him every step of the way.

CHAPTER 28

Game 23: DiJulia's Steady Leadership

Wednesday, February 18, 2004
Rose Hill Gym, Bronx, New York
No. 2 Saint Joseph's at Fordham

Two days after defeating Rhode Island at home, Saint Joseph's awoke to the heady news that the school had risen a spot to No. 2 in the Associated Press Top 25 poll. Only fellow undefeated Stanford stood between the Hawks and the No. 1 ranking in the country. St. Joe's had gotten as high as No. 2 once before, on December 21, 1965. Don DiJulia remembers those Hawks well. A season after serving in a reserve role as a player for coach Jack Ramsay's famed 1964–65 team, DiJulia supported the 1965–66 squad as a dedicated fan who didn't miss a game.

Supporting St. Joe's was typical for DiJulia, the 1967 St. Joe's graduate who has advocated for the university in one role or another for most of his life. In 2003–04, DiJulia was in his second stint as the school's athletic director. He was out of the spotlight but central to the success of the program. During the hectic season, DiJulia used his experience, connections, and people skills to calmly guide the Hawks through the firestorm.

"I was amazed at his tentacles," Phil Martelli said. "He touched all these aspects of it without being flustered."

Always grateful for the opportunity DiJulia gave him to live out his dream as St. Joe's head coach, Martelli has the ultimate respect for DiJulia.

"I think I always knew that he wanted me to have a shot at the job," Martelli said. "I always appreciated that and never wanted to put him in an awkward position. I knew that he had this remarkable, remarkable, remarkable humility. So humble. He loved the school. Loved it. He was very much at least an older brother to me if not a father figure. I have great appreciation for his spirituality and his love of family."

DiJulia's reach extended well beyond Martelli and St. Joe's.

"He had respect from our opponents, from all facets of the NCAA, the league, and the institutions," Martelli said.

St. Bonaventure women's basketball coach Jim Crowley is among those who holds DiJulia in high regard.

"In all of my years being in this league, St. Joe's is my favorite place to go," Crowley said. "To me there's never been a better example of the right way to do it than Don. He's a special man. His influence wasn't just on that campus, without question."

When the outspoken Martelli had missteps, such as for criticizing officials or incidents like with Mary Palmer at St. Bonaventure, he was disappointed for letting down DiJulia.

"[DiJulia's example] needed to be emulated," Martelli said. "And when I did lose it, I felt badly for him. When I screwed up, I knew I screwed up."

When that happened, DiJulia had just the right words and recommended actions for Martelli.

"Don deserves so much credit," said Father Timothy Lannon, who was St. Joe's president in 2003–04. "He has this presence so much that he's revered and very, very special to all of us. He encouraged the coaches and the players. He is just a fine, fine person. Anything Don said, I appreciated. I think the world of him. Even his encouragement of me as president, and I think that's one of Don's greatest gifts. He was a huge factor [in the success] in the way he supported the players and their well-being. He's a holy man."

DiJulia also had the admiration of the athletics staff.

"Don was awesome as an administrator," athletic trainer Bill Lukasiewicz said. "He was just good to everybody and tried to always put the person first. My wife and young kids would come to games, and they were just made to feel welcome."

The weight of DiJulia's respect across campus was especially helpful in 2003–04 because the athletic director had to knock on the president's door during the season to help with the rising costs of basketball.

"Winning is expensive with the extra time demands, the staffing needed, and all of the extra precautions to handle crowds," DiJulia said. He went to Lannon and asked if he could reasonably spend as needed. "'We're OK, right?'" DiJulia asked. "'We have to do what we have to do.' It was, 'Absolutely.' That was a community understanding. We can't stop now."

Much like the players on the court, the school banded together on all of the off-the-court logistics to make everything work and work well.

"Sometimes this is said, but I don't think you can overstate its importance, there was great alignment in that university," said national college basketball reporter Andy Katz, who covered the 2003–04 Hawks for ESPN. "Everyone was on board. They didn't have a lot. They sort of did what they could with what they had in their tiny little gym and their offices under the stairs. But they had full support."

Joe Lunardi sensed the brewing storm in early January. Lunardi wore several hats for the university in 2003–04, working in public relations and as the Hawks' radio analyst. He also was a budding national star as ESPN's resident bracketologist who predicted with uncanny accuracy the NCAA tournament field. Helped by the advent of social media, Lunardi's role with ESPN and his stardom have exploded today. In early January 2004, Lunardi was crunching numbers for his brackets and saw a track to an undefeated season and No. 1 seed in the NCAA tournament for St. Joe's. Soon after, he crossed paths with Lannon.

"How about our Hawks?'" Lunardi remembered Lannon saying. "I said, 'If my numbers are telling the truth, we are so not ready for what's coming.'"

Lannon responded immediately, bringing all facets of the university together for a coordinated plan that would handle the day-to-day logistics and help promote the basketball program and the school.

"Our whole thing was really to take advantage of the season with our alums, our friends, our parents, and past parents," Lannon said. "We tried to counsel together a plan that rode on the tails of the success of the men's basketball program. The team and Phil Martelli and the coaches deserve all of the credit. They were generating so much spirit and pride on the part of St. Joe's people, and we wanted to take advantage of that."

Lannon's committee included members of athletics, communications, alumni relations, fundraising, and admissions departments.

"I still have a binder with the playbook," Lunardi said.

The effects of the success in 2003–04 were being felt on campus in the moment and for many, many years later. Admissions applications rose so high so fast that St. Joe's scrambled in the short term to accommodate undergraduates with housing.

"They couldn't keep up," Atlantic 10 commissioner Linda Bruno said. "It was a nice problem to have. It really does show you that college sports is a very real thing."

When Lannon eventually left St. Joe's in 2011 to become president at his alma mater Creighton, a St. Joe's press release announced that $139 million in capital campaign money had been raised during his tenure. The school purchased 38 acres across City Avenue of what formerly was Episcopal Academy that would become the expanded Maguire Campus, named after 1958 St. Joe's graduate James Maguire. The school's endowment doubled under Lannon's term, student housing was upgraded, and facilities were renovated. The most notable of those renovations was to the Fieldhouse, which was rebuilt into 4,200-seat Hagan Arena and opened for the 2009–10 season. Hagan Arena, named for 1985 graduate Michael J. Hagan, included sorely needed upgrades to locker rooms, office spaces, and player lounges as part of the new Jack Ramsay Basketball Center.

Throughout his tenure, Lannon was a fervent supporter of the basketball program. His stewardship of St. Joe's was strong, and he also acknowledged the impact basketball had on the university during his eight years as president.

"I really enjoy college basketball, I love it," Lannon said. "I see what it can do for a university community. The spirit of the university was just breathtaking. The city was really behind us and very excited about it."

The enthusiasm on campus started early in 2003–04. Before the season even began, students were willing to do just about anything for coveted tickets, even if it meant shaving their heads.

Ryan Darrenkamp, a junior food marketing major from Lancaster, Pennsylvania, knew he had to do just that in order to win a Phil Martelli lookalike contest held at a pep rally prior to the season.

"Only two of us shaved our heads," Darrenkamp said. "The rest of them either thought they looked like Martelli or had a pillow in their shirt or something."

Darrenkamp and the other suddenly bald student each were awarded a prize for the lengths to which they went to imitate the Hawks coach. They could choose either a student season ticket package or a road trip with the team. Since Darrenkamp already had season tickets, it was an easy decision to select the road trip. And what an experience it would be. He boarded a bus with the Hawks and rode up to New York for the 23rd game of the 2003–04 season, against Fordham at Rose Hill Gym on Wednesday, February 18, 2004.

"I remember it being so awkward as a shy kid with all of these people I idolized," Darrenkamp said.

At the pregame dinner, Darrenkamp ate at a table with Tyrone Barley, Jameer Nelson, and Delonte West. Barley wondered how Darrenkamp got the invite.

"I told him I shaved my head to look like the coach, and he got a laugh out of it," Darrenkamp said.

The next day, Darrenkamp, his hair fully grown back in by now, sat at the end of St. Joe's bench inside of jam-packed Rose Hill Gym. He watched as the Hawks overcame a slow start with a 16-2 first-half run that pushed their lead to 37-21 at the intermission. St. Joe's overwhelmed Fordham early in the second half and led by as many as 33 points after halftime. That was more than enough of a lead for Martelli to get Nelson, West, and other starters some extra rest. Nelson, who had a team-high 18 points along with nine assists in 30 minutes, ended up sitting right next to Darrenkamp.

"The whole team shifted down to let him go to the end of the bench, so I sat beside him in the last 10 minutes," Darrenkamp said, adding that he made small talk with Nelson. "It was pretty cool."

When the final horn sounded, Nelson, Darrenkamp, and the Hawks rose from their seats after a 72-54 victory that improved St. Joe's to 23-0 overall and 12-0 in the Atlantic 10. Then, they all tried to make their way back to the visiting locker room.

"You know what was cool that night? Jameer and I stayed on the court to be interviewed and when I turned and looked to the path to the locker room, there were so many people on the court that I couldn't see the path," Martelli said. "Fordham was always a good crowd for us anyway but trying to get to the locker room was extraordinary."

On his way there, Martelli greeted good friend and UConn women's basketball coach Geno Auriemma, who took a car service down from Storrs to support his pal from their days working together on the boys' basketball staff at Bishop Kenrick High School. "He might've said something to me like, 'You might win them all. Celebrate them all,'" Martelli said.

When Martelli and Nelson finally made it back to the locker room, Darrenkamp was there to hear the coach's postgame message to the players, which included congratulations to Nelson and Barley for winning their 91st career game, breaking the school's record for career victories for a senior class. Nelson later asked Darrenkamp to bring his signed shoes to a young fan who had greeted the Hawks star in the packed postgame crowd.

"The kid was so pumped to see Jameer," Darrenkamp said. "When I delivered the shoes to him, the kid was almost in tears."

It had been an incredible experience for Darrenkamp and a really good one for St. Joe's. As happy as Martelli and the Hawks felt afterward, the victory came with a loss. As he was going up for a rebound during the contest, Dave Mallon heard a pop behind his foot. Mallon had been heartbroken when he had to sit and watch the first seven contests due to a stress fracture in his right foot, and he sensed quickly that he would be sidelined again. As it turned out, Mallon would miss the final four regular-season games with an Achilles' injury.

"It was frustrating to sit there and say, 'Alright, you guys go play and win games,'" Mallon said. "'I have to sit out because I'm not going to be able to contribute.' It hurts. I'm missing games that I want to be out there playing. My body is holding me back."

As much as he would've liked to have played through it, Mallon knew that wouldn't be smart.

"If I'm out there and can't keep in front of my guy, I'm a disservice to everything they're working for," he said. "I always wanted to provide some positive contribution. I didn't ever want to be a reason we fail a game. Let me get to the point where I can get back out there and bring something to the table."

On the bus ride home, Mallon iced his foot and thought about how quickly he could return. Darrenkamp tried to process the whirlwind of the last couple of days. Martelli turned his attention to the Hawks' next game. It was another matchup against Temple, and the coach was running his own special Temple formula and practice plans for the matchup zone through his head. Only this time, the Owls would give the Hawks some added incentive. Martelli's formula and offensive scheme against the zone were proven, but after what Mark Macon said in the game's lead-up, Jameer Nelson and Delonte West had all of the preparation and motivation they would need.

CHAPTER 29

Game 24: Nelson and West Answer Macon with Their Games

Saturday, February 21, 2004
The Palestra, Philadelphia
Temple at No. 2 Saint Joseph's

Any conversation about the best players in Philadelphia college basketball history most certainly will include Temple great Mark Macon. And any debate over the best teams in Philadelphia college basketball history most certainly will include Macon's great 1987–88 Owls.

Macon came to Philadelphia from Saginaw, Michigan, and he immediately made a historic impact on the Big 5. A 6-foot-4 guard who could score inside and outside and take opponents out of their games with strong defense, Macon averaged 20.7 points, 5.6 rebounds, 2.8 assists, and 2.2 steals over his marvelous four-year career. With 2,609 points, he is the Owls' all-time leading scorer, and his 281 steals rank third on the school's list. After four consecutive All–Atlantic 10 first-team honors, Macon was picked No. 8 overall in the 1991 NBA draft and would play six seasons with the Denver Nuggets and Detroit Pistons.

Macon's brilliance as a freshman in 1987–88 helped the Owls rise to No. 1 in the Associated Press poll, finishing 32-2 overall and 18-0 in the A-10. Temple just missed reaching the Final Four, losing 63-53 to Duke in the NCAA Elite Eight. That arguably was coach John Chaney's best Temple team, and it was loaded with talent. Alongside shooting guard Macon was point guard Howard Evans, who averaged 8.6 assists while setting a single-season school record of 294 assists; Mike Vreeswyk was a deadly outside shooter who averaged 16.6 points; Tim Perry was a near double-double every contest, with 14.5 points and 8.0 rebounds per game; and 6-foot-10, 260-pound Ramón Rivas was the key cog in the middle of Chaney's matchup zone who contributed 6.8 points and 7.1 rebounds.

There is no denying both the greatness of Macon and the 1987–88 Owls. In the lead-up to Temple's rematch against Saint Joseph's on Saturday, February 21, 2004, however, Macon publicly went a little further when comparing himself and the Owls to the Hawks.

In his first season as an assistant coach for Chaney, the 33-year-old Macon said in a television interview the week of the game that Jameer Nelson was no better than Evans, and not only was Macon himself better than Delonte West but he could prove it with two weeks to get in game shape.[43] Macon went on to say that the Owls' 1987–88 team was better than the 2003–04 Hawks at every position and singled out the guard spot.[44]

Needless to say, Macon's comments did not go over well at St. Joe's when they got back to Nelson, West, and the Hawks.

"Mark made a big mistake," Phil Martelli said.

St. Joe's coach was schooling his players once again on his formula to beat the Owls and rehearsing the offensive concepts to thwart the matchup zone that had led to six victories in the last eight matchups against Temple. The recent success for the Hawks versus the Owls came after Martelli had started his coaching career with 10 consecutive defeats to Chaney's teams. But nothing Martelli said at Friday's practice the day before the game would be as impactful as what Macon had said on television.

"It was someone that I looked up to, the name, the career, Philly, all that stuff," Nelson said of Macon. "I looked up to this dude, and he's talking shit about us. And we're trying to make it. It wasn't warranted. He's years removed from the game, and we're trying to get where he got, a high-level college player, professional level."

Later on, Macon and Nelson would make peace over the comments. At the Palestra, in St. Joe's 24th game of the 2003–04 season, however, Nelson and West were singularly focused on answering Macon's comments with their games.

"Yo man, don't wake up a sleeping giant," Nelson said.

On offense, Nelson and West carved up the Owls. It didn't matter what defense Temple was playing, including Chaney's shocking switch at times to man-to-man defense after the Hawks had shredded the matchup zone with a school-record 20 field goals from three-point range in an 83-71 victory in the first meeting of the season, at the Liacouras Center on January 31. After each made basket, Nelson and West turned to Macon and woofed at him.

"I never saw anything like it," Martelli said. "I never saw Jameer so out of character."

Defensively, West took turns with Tyrone Barley putting the clamps on Owls leading scorer David Hawkins, who entered averaging 24.4 points. After Hawkins had torched the Hawks in the first contest with 36 points in defeat, West and Barley pestered him into missing 16 of 21 field goals, including six of seven from three-point range, in the second meeting. St. Joe's limited Hawkins to 13 points this time.

There was nothing the Owls could do, and Macon could only watch from the bench.

Temple entered on a five-game winning streak, but the Hawks shut down any thought of an upset by stretching an 18-point halftime advantage to 52-30 with 14:09 remaining. When it finally ended and the Hawks had secured a 76-53 victory to improve to 24-0 overall and 13-0 in the A-10, Nelson and West had put up huge numbers. Nelson had 18 points, a season-high nine rebounds, and four assists, while West contributed a game-high 20 points along with seven rebounds and seven assists.

As he subbed out for the final time, Nelson had a message for Macon.

"Jameer came off the court and said, 'Go get your stuff,'" Martelli said.

Dick Jerardi also remembers Nelson challenging Macon afterward. Later, Jerardi asked Chaney about the comments.

"[Chaney] said, 'You gotta know when your time is up,'" Jerardi said. "It's a great line."

While West and Nelson clearly were motivated by Macon, Owls assistant coach Dan Leibovitz also pointed out the fact that St. Joe's was elite and Temple, which would finish with a 15-14 record and miss the NCAA tournament for the third straight year after making it in 17 of the 18 previous seasons, was not on the Hawks' level.

"We were just not ready for that, not ready to beat that team," Leibovitz said.

Was Macon better than West? Were the 1987–88 Owls better than the 2003–04 Hawks? Was Evans better than Nelson?

On the last question, it's doubtful that anyone, including Evans, would think that. But the first two questions certainly are debatable, and Temple supporters likely would say yes to both.

Could a 33-year-old Macon beat a 20-year-old West?

It's highly unlikely that Macon, even in game shape, would have defeated West one-on-one with any consistency, though it's not far-fetched to think Macon could've given West a tough game—even with 13 years in age difference.

The biggest error in the comments, besides the erroneous Evans versus Nelson comparison, wasn't necessarily that Macon made them but that he did so right before the game when saying that would only add to the Hawks' motivation to win.

"The Temple–St. Joe's thing was intense," Martelli said. "[Macon's comments] just added fuel to it."

The rivalry continued to be one-sided, as the Hawks won their seventh contest in nine games against the Owls. St. Joe's did it again by picking apart the zone—when Chaney *was* utilizing his trademark defense. West, Nelson, Pat Carroll, and Chet Stachitas once again found holes in the zone from the outside and buried three-point shots when open. The four players made 10 of 16 jumpers from beyond the arc this time to complete a deadly two-game barrage from the outside against the Owls in which the quartet made 30 of 49 (61.2 percent) three-pointers.

Leibovitz was particularly impressed with the transformation of West's long-range game, remembering when the Hawks sharpshooter had missed 15 of 17 attempts from three-point range as a freshman during the 2001–02 season.

"He was a complete non-threat on the perimeter against our zone," Leibovitz said of West's freshman season. "You fast-forward and he was absolute deadeye. It was a stark difference in the way you had to defend him. Changing somebody's shot is one of the hardest things in coaching because no matter how much you work on it, the first thing they go out and do is play pickup in the summer and when push comes to shove, they're going to revert back to the way they shoot. It takes someone to really commit. That's an unbelievable thing, and I give Matt [Brady] and Delonte a lot of credit for that."

Leibovitz continued to be impressed with Nelson's game, particularly with how much fun the Hawks point guard appeared to be having on the court.

"There are some players that play the game with joy," Leibovitz said. "Magic Johnson is the ultimate for me. In the heat of competition, he would smile. I watched Tyrese Maxey through his time at Kentucky and now with the Sixers, and he smiles. It doesn't mean he doesn't take the game seriously, but he enjoys it that much that he can smile. And Jameer, as much of a killer as he was on the floor, I perceived that he was someone who played the game with joy, who loved to make his teammates look good, who loved to make the extra pass, who loved to make a shot or a finish that he had been working on."

Nelson and West put it all out there for Leibovitz and everyone to see at the Palestra, where Jack Scheuer scribbled "corners" on a colleague's notepad in reference to the announced sellout crowd of 8,722 that probably was even larger. The victory was significant for more than just keeping alive the Hawks' undefeated season, as it marked St. Joe's second consecutive 4-0 record and outright Big 5 title. It was St. Joe's eighth perfect mark in the Big 5, though the first five occurred between the inaugural season of 1955–56 and 1965–66 when St. Joe's also did it for the second time in consecutive seasons. Following 2003–04, it would be another 20 seasons before the Hawks would claim another outright Big 5 title when they won the inaugural Big 5 Classic on December 2, 2023, with a 74-65 victory over Temple that resulted in St. Joe's getting a banner raised to the rafters of the 76ers' home arena in South Philadelphia.

In 2003–04, St. Joe's was looking to raise a banner that said "National Champs." With Macon, Temple, and the Big 5 in the rearview mirror, the Hawks turned their attention to a two-game road trip that would make or break their undefeated regular-season quest. Both would be rematches of home victories, first at UMass and then another matchup against tough, physical Rhode Island. This time, there would be more than just the coaches, players, and The Hawk included in the traveling party. The attention had gotten so enormous for Nelson, in particular, and the Hawks, in general, that Don DiJulia and Martelli brought a security consultant on board. And St. Joe's would need Dan Kropp's help on this trip.

CHAPTER 30

Game 25: Hawks Sign Security to Control Autographs

Wednesday, February 25, 2004
Mullins Center, Amherst, Massachusetts
No. 2 Saint Joseph's at UMass

Ever since Jameer Nelson appeared on the cover of *Sports Illustrated,* the adulation for Saint Joseph's just kept getting greater and greater as the winning continued without a loss. Phil Martelli's practices always were open to anyone who wanted to attend. Suddenly, it wasn't just family and friends and hoop heads taking in the sessions but also professional autograph seekers looking to make a buck, including one who parked in front of the Fieldhouse with a pickup truck full of basketballs waiting for players to sign after practice.

"We called public safety and had him escorted out," Don DiJulia said.

Martelli wanted the players to experience the moment, to sign autographs as best as they could, and to enjoy their status as one of the top teams in the country. But the demand just got to be overwhelming for the Hawks.

Two days after the *SI* cover hit newsstands, St. Joe's issued a press release saying that players would only sign items sent in that benefited charity and would do so on just two dates, February 20 and March 5. Still, the autograph hounds didn't relent, especially in seeking out Nelson.

"Jameer started to be followed to class," said Alicia Lange, who was the coordinator of academic services for student-athletes in 2003–04. "He would come to my office and be like, 'I can't go to class.' I would call the professor and say, 'Jameer is here. I'm going to send him after class.'"

Dan Kropp heard Martelli talking about the large crowds around the Hawks during an interview on a sports radio station. Kropp, a 1984 St. Joe's graduate, had recently started a security consulting business and thought he might be able to lend his alma mater a hand. On the way home from another business appointment, he stopped in to the school's public safety office and knocked on the door of director Al Hall.

"I asked Al, 'Have you thought about executive protection?'" Kropp recalled. "He said, 'I don't think there's an appetite for it.'"

Kropp left Hall his business card and headed for home, only to be interrupted by a phone call during his car ride.

"Before I got home, he called me and said, 'You walked out of my office and Don DiJulia walked in,'" Kropp said of Hall's message. "'You probably passed him in the hallway. Don came in and said, 'Al, we need help, what do you suggest?''"

Hall asked Kropp if he could meet with DiJulia and Martelli the following day. At the meeting, the athletic director and coach asked the security expert what he could provide.

"You don't need someone in uniform, you don't need a big guy with muscles," Kropp said. "You need a guy with a suit who looks like he can be a member of your staff who could simply walk up to a friendly person, touch someone gently and say, 'The players have to get on the bus. I'm sorry but they can't sign any more autographs.' You just need a little bit of crowd control."

Martelli, who wanted to downplay the appearance of security, liked what Kropp offered.

"Phil said, 'Well, we play Temple tomorrow at the Palestra. Can you be there?'" Kropp remembered.

Kropp had an unannounced meeting with Hall on Thursday, talked to DiJulia and Martelli on Friday, and was in the Palestra locker room before the Hawks raced past Mark Macon and Temple on Saturday.

"Phil said, 'This is Dan. He's going to be with us the rest of the season,'" Kropp said of the locker-room greeting with the players. "'He's going to give us a hand here.' It was no big introduction, just go about your business. I didn't wear security credentials. I wore a media credential or an assistant coach credential. Phil didn't want to appear big-time. He really low-keyed it. He wanted the practices to be open, he wanted the players to sign autographs, he wanted to be accessible, and never wanted to be standoffish. I was sort of an ambassador."

Kropp helped the Hawks off the bus and into the Mullins Center for their 25th game of the season, against UMass on Wednesday, February 25, 2004. Surprisingly, the security consultant would have less to do than expected, as there was an announced crowd of 5,912, which was about 3,500 shy of capacity. After playing in front of full houses and surrounded by throngs of people everywhere they went, especially in the last few weeks, Martelli noticed the difference immediately.

"There was nobody there," Martelli said. "From Cal [on December 20] on, it was like a circus, a traveling, tented circus everywhere we went. And we went there and there was nobody there."

Maybe due in part to the subdued atmosphere, the Hawks came out sluggish against UMass. Maybe it also had something to do with the 92-67 home rout of the

Minutemen just 35 days prior. UMass coach Steve Lappas certainly was wondering how the Minutemen could win the rematch.

"I went up to Steve in his office before the game, and I remember him saying to me, 'How do you beat these guys?'" Dick Jerardi said. "As if, 'I know I have no chance here.'"

To his players, though, Lappas preached confidence.

"There isn't a coach in America who doesn't go into every game thinking, 'If we do these things, we could win the game,'" Lappas said. "And that was our approach always."

Things started out well for UMass, as the hosts took a 13-9 lead. Sensing that the Hawks were a step slow, Martelli quickly summoned Tyrone Barley into the game. St. Joe's super sub immediately knew the Hawks needed some instant offense, and he hit a pair of jumpers that would put St. Joe's ahead for good. He continued to bring energy and his defensive prowess, helping the Hawks to a 10-point lead at the half that reached 22 points early in the second half.

"His preparation, his practice habits, his willingness that summer to not just be labeled a defensive player, it was fierce," Martelli said of Barley.

Throughout Martelli's career, there were certain players who had to be starters. Others, like Barley and Terrell Myers, a three-point ace on Martelli's early St. Joe's teams, were just fine coming off the bench when they knew their role and could expect a reasonable amount of minutes. Those types of players were extremely important to winning, something Lappas experienced at Villanova, where he coached from 1992 to 2001.

"The best thing about good bench guys is knowing their role," said Lappas, mentioning former Villanova standouts Alvin Williams and Zeffy Penn as two of the best he has had. "And it helps if a good bench guy has versatility, can guard a couple of different positions, can play outside, play a little inside."

Barley had it all and even would mix it up down low when asked despite being a bit undersized for that role at 6-foot-1. With Barley providing the spark, the rest of the Hawks got in gear. Nelson netted 17 of his 19 points in the first half and finished with eight assists, while Delonte West led everyone with 23 points to go with seven rebounds and four assists. Barley ended up hitting all four of his three-point tries for 12 points, Pat Carroll also drained four long-range shots on his way to 14 points, and the Hawks rolled to an 83-58 victory that improved them to 25-0 overall and 14-0 in the Atlantic 10.

While the crowd in the stands was underwhelming, Martelli was swarmed afterward.

"I always had my little private audience with Phil after these games," said St. Joe's graduate Joe Sullivan of the *Boston Globe*, who attended most every Hawks game in New England. "I would get great insight after those games. I checked in with Phil's dad. I had a little routine that was great fun."

But not after this UMass contest.

"I go out to do my usual after the game, and I couldn't get near him," Sullivan said. "The press conference was huge and so many people wanted to talk to him and just shake his hand, people I'd never seen at these games before, and I just gave up. I didn't even talk to him after that game. It was an impossible task."

The Hawks would be met by a similar crush of people the following day when Martelli took them to Springfield College for practice in preparation for their next matchup, at Rhode Island on Saturday, February 28. Springfield's Blake Arena is about two miles from the Naismith Basketball Hall of Fame.

"We went there because it was like, 'This is where we should go,'" Martelli said.

When word got out on campus that Nelson and the Hawks were practicing there, students started showing up with copies of *Sports Illustrated*, basketballs, and other items to be signed. Martelli welcomed them all.

"School security came to me and said, 'Can the students come in?'" Martelli recalled. "I said, 'They can come in, they can watch. I don't change. It's an open practice.' So, the students came in and were lined up all the way around the court."

Kropp took it from there.

"I walked over," Kropp said, "and said, 'Here's what we're going to do. Our bus is outside. I'm going to ask everyone to line up against the wall. One by one the players will walk past you and whatever is in your hand, they will sign it. And if you stay where you belong, you'll get every player. But if you crowd them, we're leaving.' The players signed every autograph. No crowding. No problem."

Just as Martelli had hoped, the Hawks remained accessible but with some structure, organization, and control thanks to Kropp. At Rhode Island, however, Kropp would not have the luxury of being as friendly. The Rams students had some sinister plans in the works. On the court, Rhode Island's players wouldn't be too kind, either. Both the Hawks' security consultant and St. Joe's players would need to use all of their skill and experience to overcome a pair of tough tests.

CHAPTER 31

Game 26: West Keeps Perfect Ride Going

Saturday, February 28, 2004
Ryan Center, Kingston, Rhode Island
No. 2 Saint Joseph's at Rhode Island

Each summer, bicyclists compete in the world's most prestigious race in the Tour de France. Traditionally, the final stage of the race finishes on the Champs-Élysées in Paris with essentially a ceremonial ride. (The 2024 race did not end in Paris due to the Summer Olympics in the city.) The race's winner is decided, for all intents and purposes, in the penultimate stage. Similarly, Saint Joseph's quest for an undefeated regular season would be determined in its 26th game of 2003–04, at Rhode Island on Saturday, February 28, 2004.

In fact, the Hawks would have one more game left to complete college basketball's first perfect regular season since UNLV in 1990–91. But that was a home contest the following week against a St. Bonaventure team that had been decimated by a scandal that had rocked the university the year before. Basically, there would be a ceremonial final victory for St. Joe's. But the Hawks had to get there first. Beating tough, physical Rhode Island again would not be easy, and everyone knew it.

"They just played with an edge and physicality," Dwayne Jones said. "They thought that was their way to get us out of our game, getting physical, hitting us, nothing easy in the paint, trying to attack the glass. That was always a challenge for us in the frontcourt. And they put a lot of pressure on us defensively with how their guards played. It was always a physical matchup."

St. Joe's had traveled to Rhode Island the previous season and lost 58-57.

"Rhode Island was one of those teams we struggled with, especially playing at Rhode Island," Pat Carroll said. "It was a super tough environment."

In spite of the noon start, a sellout crowd of 7,616 at the Ryan Center was loud and ready from the opening tip.

"That building doesn't get loud that often, it just doesn't," said Mark Blaudschun, a national college basketball writer for the *Boston Globe* for 25 years who covered the game that day. "It's a nice place, a really nice building. But that one was like a tournament game, and I think the crowd sensed blood."

The pregame attention couldn't have been greater for a regular-season contest. ESPN and its biggest college basketball star, Dick Vitale, were there to broadcast the game to a national audience. All eyes were on the Hawks.

"This thing was bigger than a game now," Phil Martelli said. "Not that people were rooting for us to get knocked off, but people were really, really, really paying attention."

The Rams always got up for games against St. Joe's, and the situation and atmosphere brought their focus to another level.

"Every game we played against them was a big game," said Dawan Robinson, the Philadelphia native who was Rhode Island's leading scorer in 2003–04. "But I would say everybody was following their undefeated season. It was all over ESPN; it was everywhere. So that did give us some extra motivation. We did want to break that streak."

Rhode Island's players weren't the only ones eager to wreak havoc on the Hawks. The school's students came ready to do some damage of their own. Perhaps inspired by the Rams mascot's attempt to stop Bobby Gallagher from flapping The Hawk's wings in 1998, the Rhode Island student section was full of inner tubes prior to tipoff. Chris Bertolino was inside of The Hawk costume during the 2003–04 season and took notice of the crowd. Luckily for Bertolino and St. Joe's, Dan Kropp was on-site. The recently hired security consultant had been smiling at everyone to this point while keeping crowds and autograph seekers under control. Now, though, Kropp wouldn't be so friendly.

"There was an entire student section swinging bicycle tire inner tubes in their hands," Kropp said. "I was like, 'What the hell is going on?' Somebody said someone [previously] put bicycle inner tubes over The Hawk to get him to stop flapping."

Kropp then went right to the school's on-site security.

"I said, 'You know what they want to do, I know what they want to do,'" he said. "I'll tell you what, 'You wouldn't let them rush the court and attack Jameer Nelson. This guy [Bertolino] is not a bird; he is a student. I'm telling you right now, 'If someone touches The Hawk, he's going to jail.'"

"No one touched him," Kropp said.

"He always had my back," Bertolino said.

Kropp had solved one problem for the Hawks. But they had another big problem inside the lines of the 94-by-50-foot court that the security consultant couldn't address.

St. Joe's players were having all kinds of trouble. They couldn't hit from close range. They couldn't hit from long range. They were missing free throws. The game-changing run that always came didn't this time. Nelson was off the mark. Usually, someone else would step up and fill the role when another player was misfiring, but it just wasn't happening.

"It was just never right," Dick Jerardi said. "They never looked right. They could never get comfortable. I remember a couple of times in the second half that Jameer would come over near me. We often would make eye contact during games. He was just shaking his head like, 'What is happening here?' They were just off. It's amazing they weren't off more often."

The Rams were physically imposing their will and, as much as they tried, St. Joe's struggled to come up with answers.

"I just remember it being ugly," Jerardi said. "That was kind of their style. They just beat up teams."

When Rhode Island's Dustin Hellenga made one of two free throws with 1:22 remaining, the Rams had a 55-53 lead.

"The crowd was going crazy," Blaudschun said. "They're ready to storm the court."

The Rams got the ball back with a chance to pad the lead and put the students and the frenzied fans on even more of an edge. But the Hawks caused a turnover by forcing a rare five-second violation on a Rhode Island inbounds play.

"When does that happen? Force a five-second call?" said Joe Sullivan, who was there as per usual for a New England game. "It speaks to their speed, and they're also a great defensive team."

Martelli called timeout to set up a play. Maybe on another day, he would've just let Nelson do his thing, but the Hawks star was off his game for one of the rare times in his career. The play Martelli designed had options for a three-pointer for either Nelson, Carroll, or Delonte West. Just before they rushed back onto the court, assistant coach Matt Brady pulled Carroll and West aside.

"I grabbed Pat and Delonte and said, 'Look, this ball is coming to one of you two guys,'" Brady said. "Be ready. Step up and make the shot."

Brady had complete confidence in both shooters. He had helped transform West from an afterthought for opposing players guarding the perimeter during his freshman season, when he was two of 17 on three-pointers, into a legitimate long-range threat. West had taken Brady's advice and worked tirelessly by himself in the gym, sometimes sleeping in the locker room so he would have time to get up more shots. Carroll didn't require much help with form but received needed positive reinforcement from Brady and the coaches, especially assistant Mark Bass. As good as both were, almost nothing was falling for the Hawks on this day. However, Martelli had a good vibe when he saw the Rams line up defensively.

"They played us zone," Martelli said. "We had practiced the day before against the zone, and we were really clicking. I remember saying to one of the coaches, 'If they play the zone, we're in good shape.'"

The play design worked perfectly. Just as Brady said it would, the ball came to West. He raised up a little to the right of the top of the key and, just like he had countless times all alone in the Fieldhouse and often in the wee hours of the morning, West calmly drained the three-pointer.

"Monster shot," Martelli said.

With 59.9 seconds to play, St. Joe's led 56-55.

"There was so much noise and when they got the lead someone turned on a muffler switch," Blaudschun said.

The game was not over, though. After Rhode Island missed two shots on its ensuing possession, West went to the free throw line. He'd already had a rare miss earlier in the contest that broke his school-record streak of 37 consecutive made free throws. He missed another on this possession, and St. Joe's was clinging to a 57-55 lead with 19 seconds left after West converted one of two free throws.

Rhode Island quickly hustled into its offensive set and got the ball to Robinson. He misfired, but the Rams, who hammered St. Joe's on the glass for the second straight contest, got the offensive rebound. The ball landed in the hands of Steve Mello, who unleashed a three-point attempt. It was the second time in the season the ball was in the air just before the buzzer with a chance for an opponent to win, following a similar situation in the Hawks' 59-57 victory at Cal on December 20.

Mello's shot was off the mark. Somehow, some way, St. Joe's had pulled it out.

"My memory says they should have lost," Blaudschun said. "The teams that stand out are the teams that know they're going to win. By then, that team didn't think it was going to lose no matter the situation they were in."

The Hawks had won despite one of their worst offensive performances of the season, making just 35.8 percent from the field, including only 23.1 percent from the arc. Both would end up being the second-worst percentages of the season. St. Joe's also badly lost the rebounding battle, 44-29, to the physical Rams.

Unlike last time when Martelli was miffed by St. Joe's performance against Rhode Island, the Hawks coach had nothing but praise for his team in spite of the unusually poor statistical offensive performance.

"It was pride because of how hard we had to fight," Martelli said.

Martelli exhaled a sigh of satisfaction.

"It wasn't relief," he said. "I didn't want to fall short because then everyone would say, 'See, you couldn't win on the road. How good can they be?' Not relief but justification that I knew how good we were."

West finished with 19 points, two shy of Nelson's game-high 21 points in which he needed 20 field goal attempts and seven free throw tries to get there. West's final three points will be remembered forever by St. Joe's supporters. His three-pointer set the Hawks up for a perfect regular season.

"The biggest memory is, 'Thank you Delonte,'" Carroll said. "Walking out of that game, it was like everything we had worked for and we knew we were so close to could have fallen apart. Of course, it comes down to more than one shot. But if Delonte doesn't hit that shot, there's no special story. It's a great season, but there's no special story."

The players and coaches showered West with congratulations in the locker room afterward. It could have been Nelson, or Carroll, or anyone else. They all would have been happy for one another.

"Nobody on that team cared who took the last shot," Brady said. "Nobody was seeking to be the hero. They only cared about getting out of Kingston with a win at the University of Rhode Island."

St. Joe's had done just that, but barely. Everyone knew that there would be no similar trouble in four days when the Hawks hosted St. Bonaventure in their final regular-season game of the 2003–04 season. The game would be the hottest ticket in town. Television stations were competing over the rights to carry the contest. Elaborate planning would go into what surely was going to be a memorable victory celebration. But there was a big question that first needed to be answered: Where would the game be played?

CHAPTER 32

Game 27: A Perfect Regular Season

Tuesday, March 2, 2004
Alumni Memorial Fieldhouse, Philadelphia
St. Bonaventure at No. 2 Saint Joseph's

After barely defeating Rhode Island on Delonte West's clutch, late three-pointer, Saint Joseph's needed just one more victory to complete a perfect regular season. The Hawks would be hosting St. Bonaventure at nine o'clock on Tuesday, March 2, 2004. But where would the game be played? Originally, the contest was scheduled for the Fieldhouse. But in the weeks leading up to it, Don DiJulia was in talks with the Palestra and the home of the NBA's 76ers to possibly move the game from their 3,200-seat on-campus gym to either of the larger venues. The demand, everyone knew, would be there. Undoubtedly, St. Joe's would easily sell out the 8,722-seat Palestra as it already had done several times during the season. And if every one of the 20,000-plus seats in the 76ers' arena wasn't filled, it certainly would be close.

Moving the game from the Fieldhouse not only would accommodate more fans, but it would be a huge payday for St. Joe's. The school operated on a shoestring budget relative to the big-time programs to which it now was being compared and could have used every extra dollar. But this decision wouldn't be about money. DiJulia and Phil Martelli agreed that Jameer Nelson and Tyrone Barley, the Hawks' two senior captains, should decide on the venue for their final home game. DiJulia met Nelson and Barley on the Fieldhouse court when the players returned from Rhode Island.

"I went to Jameer and Tyrone," DiJulia began saying.

And then DiJulia paused. Unlike the outspoken Martelli, who wears his emotions on his sleeve, DiJulia is reserved and epitomizes a calm demeanor. This time, though, the Hawks' longtime athletic director and former St. Joe's student whose passion for the university likely is unmatched was struggling to unleash the words in his typically reserved manner.

Choking back tears, DiJulia continued. "Two captains. I want to ask you where"—and DiJulia paused again, trying to collect himself—"They're standing there and they look at each other"—tears are now gathering in DiJulia's eyes—"Jameer turned to me and said"—DiJulia is now fully emotional and crying—"'We started our career here. Let's keep it here.'"

Now composed, DiJulia finished his thought. "Done deal. People were saying, 'Oh yeah, go for the money.' No. This."

The Fieldhouse had meant so much to Nelson that he didn't think of playing anywhere else when DiJulia consulted him and Barley.

"It's a special moment. I got chills now as you were talking about it," Nelson said, recalling the conversation. "The simplicity of that school and that gym. It's up on you. Small. Quaint. The one thing about it is people cared. All the people who traveled all over the place, who traveled throughout my career, they deserved that game to be at the Fieldhouse. I'm making the best decision for my team, for the program, and for the fans. And I think we made the right decision. It just made it more organic and genuine doing it at the Fieldhouse."

Once Nelson and Barley made their choice, DiJulia sprang into action. There were precious few hours to prepare, and there was a mountain of coordination to do.

"OK, case closed. Now we really have to get ready," DiJulia said.

***

Linda Bruno also had work to do. The Atlantic 10 commissioner fielded a call from ESPN, which wanted to broadcast the historic contest. The league had a TV deal with ESPN for several games, but the network didn't select the Hawks' final regular-season game as part of its package when making its schedule the previous summer. The TV rights were held by Comcast, which planned to televise the game in the Philadelphia market. But any chance to get on national television was a boon for the A-10, so Bruno started working the phones.

"I just couldn't see past an ESPN opportunity," Bruno said. "I worked something out. I think Comcast is still mad at me. I said, 'Can we do a coexist?'"

By that, Bruno meant that she asked Comcast if ESPN also could televise the game, a rare setup in which competing networks would both offer their own feed to viewers. In return, Bruno would provide Comcast with some additional gratis games the following season as part of its A-10 contract. Comcast agreed to the dual-broadcast arrangement. It also helped Bruno that Comcast is headquartered in Philadelphia, knew the St. Joe's story, and was being a good community citizen.

"I'm sure they weren't thrilled," Bruno said. "They also understood because they were in Philly. That worked for me a little bit."

So, the venue was set. And now there would be two TV networks broadcasting the game. That meant two sets of announcers. Two statisticians. Two TV crew workers. All of them would need media credentials. Press row at the Fieldhouse already was tight. Now, it would get even tighter.

"If there was one day that was extremely overwhelming, it was that day," said St. Joe's sports information director Marie Wozniak, who had to figure out how to accommodate the additional TV broadcast in addition to the countless requests from other electronic and print media outlets.

"Just berserk," said Phil Denne, a 1996 St. Joe's graduate who assisted Wozniak that season. "There's just not the space to account for all of the different media. It was absolutely insane with people and requests."

***

And there was the ticket demand. Martelli made light of the situation two days before the contest when he delivered a talk at a mother/son Communion breakfast at his high school alma mater, St. Joseph's Prep.

"I remember talking about my love of the Prep, what my mother thought of the Prep, but said, 'To be honest with you, that's all fluff. I'm really here to ask, 'Does anybody have two tickets to the St. Joe's game Tuesday night?'" Martelli joked.

Brian O'Connell had a pair of tickets, but he wasn't selling. O'Connell and his father, Bill, a 1971 St. Joe's graduate, would be seated in Section 104, Row FF, Seats 12 and 13, just as they were for every game at the Fieldhouse that season. And O'Connell was elated the game was there.

"That was the right move," he said of Nelson and Barley's decision. "That's their home court. That's where the game should be. The atmosphere at the Palestra is absolutely second to none, but if we're going to make history, we should do it on our court."

Dean Bozman wasn't as lucky as O'Connell. A 1994 St. Joe's graduate, Bozman describes himself as a "passionate" Hawks fan, though friends and family say the adjective is more like "obsessed." He often brought large groups to St. Joe's contests but didn't have tickets for the final game and struck out in getting them despite trying every way imaginable. Bozman's father, also named Dean, knew how important being there was for his son and wouldn't let him miss it.

"My dad knew I wanted to go to the game bad," Bozman said. "He said, 'We're going to go. We're going to head up to the Fieldhouse. We'll get tickets.'"

The Bozmans scalped a pair of tickets for $300 but almost didn't make it inside.

"I got through security real easy, but my dad had a little bit of a hang-up," Bozman said. "When he finally got through, I asked him what was going on. He said, 'Well, they were asking me where I got the ticket, and I told them we knew someone and got the ticket that way.'"

The following day, Bozman realized why his dad got held up in the line.

"My dad's ticket was actually a fake," he said. "Someone had taken a real ticket [from another game] and printed a fake front and glued it over top of it. I still have it."

Nevertheless, the Bozmans were inside.

***

Outside, the scene was like nothing anyone had ever seen before at St. Joe's. People were everywhere. Police on horseback were keeping control. Television trucks from every local station and many national ones parked wherever they could. Just a throng of people everywhere. All wanting to be part of history.

"It was just insanity on campus," Denne said. "Just nuts."

And Brendan Prunty, a St. Joe's sophomore in 2003–04, was enjoying every second of it. Prunty's residence at Flanagan Hall was so close to the Fieldhouse that he heard the squeaking of players' sneakers during practices when the windows were open. On a white bedsheet in front of their residence, Prunty and his buddies spray-painted the following: "THANK YOU JAMEER" in red letters, with "#14" to the left and "GO SJU!" in black capital letters at the bottom.

"We waited for the TV trucks to show up, and we unfurled the banner," Prunty said. "Every TV truck came over."

Mike Jensen covered college basketball in the city for the *Philadelphia Inquirer* from 1988 until retiring in 2023. There had been many big games, but what Jensen witnessed outside of the Fieldhouse that night was unlike anything he'd ever seen before.

"Craziest college basketball scene I've ever been at live," Jensen said. "You're talking about students forging tickets, students in the bathroom hours and hours ahead standing on toilets trying not to get noticed."

DiJulia tapped on Martelli's office door before tipoff and beckoned the coach outside. A stickler for his routines, Martelli didn't want to divert from his norm. But DiJulia convinced him to come and have a look even though the coach never looked at crowds before games.

"Never can I remember this happening any other time," Martelli said. "Don said, 'You have to see this scene.' I said, 'I'm good. I just want to coach the game.' Don [again] said, 'You have to see this scene.' We went to the second floor of the Fieldhouse and looked out. I saw the horses and the line of people just wanting to get in all the way down the street."

The people that did make it inside were squeezed in like sardines. Many, like the Bozmans, had nowhere to sit, so they just stood at the very top of the Fieldhouse. Others without a seat just plopped down in the aisles. There were no aisles this night.

"You could barely move," O'Connell said. "People were everywhere. It was just beyond packed. It was like the old saying, 'Thank God the fire marshal wasn't there.'"

Well, actually, he was. The Philadelphia fire marshal was in attendance with his 10-year-old son. DiJulia helped him to his seats.

"I asked someone to move from the lower area so he could sit where he wouldn't see all of the people standing upstairs," DiJulia said.

The atmosphere was basically indescribable for anyone who wasn't there.

Jameer Nelson takes the court for the season-opening game against Gonzaga at Madison Square Garden on November 14, 2003. St. Joe's set a Coaches vs. Cancer record by selling 4,100 tickets, which was more than the school's entire undergraduate enrollment of 3,850. (Greg Carroccio/Sideline Photos)

In the sixth game of the season on December 9, 2003, Phil Martelli thought the game against Boston College at the Palestra was over before it even started when he saw BC enter the gym with luggage after apparently checking out of their hotel. "They're thinking about their flight. They ain't thinking about this competition. I knew that it was over then," Martelli said. (Greg Carroccio/Sideline Photos)

Delonte West hit five three-pointers when St. Joe's set a school and Atlantic 10 record with 20 three-pointers in an 83-71 win at Temple on January 31, 2004. The Owls' Keith Butler is contesting West's shot without leaving his feet, as Temple Hall of Fame coach John Chaney never wanted to foul long-range shooters. (Greg Carroccio/Sideline Photos)

Saint Joseph's defeated rival Villanova 74-67 at the Pavilion on February 2, 2004, providing coach Jay Wright and the Wildcats an example that helped to turn them into a national powerhouse. "They came in very mature, very businesslike, no yelling at the crowd, no trash talking. Nothing. Just business," Wright said. (Greg Carroccio/Sideline Photos)

In a "corners" game at the Palestra, named as such by sportswriter Jack Scheuer because every one of the 8,722 seats, including those in the four corners of the gym, was full, the Hawks defeated La Salle 89-63 to improve to 20-0 on February 7, 2004. They won despite La Salle assistant coach John Gallagher's intimate knowledge of St. Joe's and well-prepared scouting report. (Greg Carroccio/Sideline Photos)

Dayton's Keith Waleskowski shoots a free throw in front of a jam-packed student section at the Fieldhouse on February 11, 2004. "It's packed, it's loud, everybody is just on top of you," Waleskowski said. Both teams entered 9-0 in the Atlantic 10, but the Hawks prevailed 81-67 to improve to 21-0 overall and 10-0 in the A-10. (Greg Carroccio/Sideline Photos)

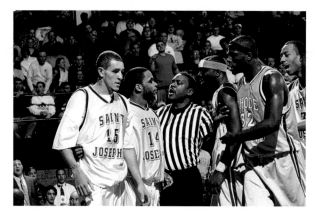

Rhode Island's Dawan Robinson and Jamaal Wise (32) jaw with Jameer Nelson and Delonte West during the Hawks' 73-59 win at the Fieldhouse on February 14, 2004. "They just played with an edge and physicality. They thought that was their way to get us out of our game," Dwayne Jones said. (Greg Carroccio/Sideline Photos)

Tyrone Barley; Jameer Nelson; and The Hawk, Chris Bertolino, are honored on Senior Night prior to St. Joe's 82-50 win over St. Bonaventure at the Fieldhouse on March 2, 2004. The victory clinched a 27-0 regular season. (Greg Carroccio/Sideline Photos)

Jameer Nelson cuts down the net after the Hawks defeated St. Bonaventure to finish 27-0 in the regular season. Nelson and Tyrone Barley chose to play the game at the Fieldhouse, the Hawks' on-campus home, rather than at the Palestra or at the home of the Philadelphia 76ers. (Greg Carroccio/Sideline Photos)

Jameer Nelson consoles Delonte West after Phil Martelli removed his starting backcourt with four minutes remaining against Xavier in the Atlantic 10 quarterfinals on March 11, 2004. The ultracompetitive West just didn't accept or understand it when Martelli took him out of the game, which the Hawks would lose 87-67 for their first defeat of the season. (Greg Carroccio/Sideline Photos)

Saint Joseph's (left to right) Caitlin Ryan, the director of basketball operations, and players Brian Jesiolowski, John Bryant, Delonte West, and Dwayne Lee celebrate after CBS's announcement that the Hawks had received a No. 1 seed into the NCAA tournament on March 14, 2004. (Greg Carroccio/Sideline Photos)

Neil Hartman interviews Jameer Nelson on Selection Sunday. Hartman's *Hangin' with the Hawks* gave Comcast SportsNet viewers a behind-the-scenes look at St. Joe's. (Greg Carroccio/Sideline Photos)

A large-screen television at the Fieldhouse shows Saint Joseph's as a No. 1 seed in the NCAA tournament, along with power conference programs Kentucky, Duke, and Stanford. (Greg Carroccio/Sideline Photos)

After CBS analyst Billy Packer rattled off nine schools he thought were more deserving of a No. 1 seed than Saint Joseph's, Phil Martelli grabbed a microphone and told the Fieldhouse crowd and a swarm of reporters that Packer could "kiss [his] ass." (Greg Carroccio/Sideline Photos)

Phil Martelli and Bob Knight each had complimentary words for the other's team. "We knew we had to play with an intensity and fierceness and be that tough to beat them," Martelli said. Dave Mallon hit a key three-pointer during a game-changing first-half St. Joe's run, and the Hawks advanced to the Sweet 16 with a 70-65 victory, just as Joe Lunardi predicted, on March 20, 2004. (Greg Carroccio/ Sideline Photos)

Chris Paul was 42 days shy of his 19th birthday when his Wake Forest team met St. Joe's in the Sweet 16 at the Meadowlands on March 25, 2004. Tyrone Barley, usually tasked with marking the opposing team's top scorer, defended the future Hall of Famer for most of the game. Paul finished with 13 points on two of six shooting while Barley had 14 points. (Greg Carroccio/Sideline Photos)

CBS's Jim Nantz (left) and Billy Packer interview Phil Martelli after Saint Joseph's 84-80 win over Wake Forest. To his credit, Packer did not hold back in praising the Hawks while broadcasting their two games at the Meadowlands despite his criticism of St. Joe's on Selection Sunday. (Greg Carroccio/ Sideline Photos)

Oklahoma State's John Lucas III prepares to shoot a game-winning three-pointer after a broken play in which Pat Carroll barely missed a steal and Tyrone Barley barely missed a block. The shot with 6.9 seconds left gave the Cowboys a 64-62 advantage, which was the eventual final score in the Elite Eight game on March 27, 2004. (Greg Carroccio/Sideline Photos)

Phil Martelli consoles Jameer Nelson after Nelson's game-tying attempt against Oklahoma State from 18 feet with 2.8 seconds left came up short. (Greg Carroccio/Sideline Photos)

"You didn't feel like you were going to a basketball game," O'Connell said. "You felt like you were going to this huge event and there just happened to be a basketball game played that night, too."

***

Both Martelli and Nelson had struggled all day in the buildup to the final home game of the season.

"I remember fighting myself to stay in my routine," an emotional Martelli recalled. "I had a routine. A certain time of the day I said my prayers, I changed, I never went around people. There were people on campus all day shooting shows, and I just wanted to stay with my routine."

That would prove impossible because nothing in Martelli's routine called for scripting how he would substitute players in order to get Nelson out of the game at just the right time for one, final Fieldhouse ovation by the Hawks faithful. St. Joe's already had defeated the Bonnies 114-63 on January 24 in Olean, New York. No one ever doubted the outcome for the rematch beforehand. Martelli knew the Hawks were going to win and spent as much time planning how to properly handle the victory as anything else.

"I don't mean this disrespectfully, but they didn't have a chance," Martelli said. "Joe Lunardi came into my little office, and I said, 'Joe, I feel really bad, but I've scripted out when I want to sub these guys.'" Martelli also helped to orchestrate the postgame celebration in which the Hawks would celebrate with cake and by cutting down the nets. The school also wanted to retire Nelson's No. 14 jersey that night, but Nelson declined and wanted to wait until after the season. The Hawks point guard was in no rush to end the season, but he was looking forward to getting through the final regular-season contest.

"I honestly couldn't wait to get it over with," Nelson said. "I want to go through the moment, and I don't want to rush it. But I was like antsy. I had nervous energy throughout the day. I tell people all the time, and they think I'm joking, but I've never been nervous before a game, during a game, anything. But that game I was antsy. I was ready for it to be over."

Part of that was the intense spotlight the Hawks were under, and part of it, likely, was the fact that this game was so different from any other. Winning was almost a guarantee, so focusing your mind as competitors normally do was challenging. Even Martelli, who hadn't let the Hawks get ahead of themselves all season and preached the importance of each game, let his guard down in the pregame pep talk. And the players actually appreciated the approach.

"Martelli kept us so focused on one game at a time," Pat Carroll said. "That's a challenging thing to do. You start looking at the bigger picture, but he kept us so locked in on who's our next opponent, one game at a time, we're not thinking about the win streak. But going into the St. Bonaventure game, it was like, 'You know what, let's look at the big picture here.' We knew we were going to win the game, and you take it all in."

Chet Stachitas also remembers the coach's message.

"It's almost like an unwritten rule of coaching that you don't get complacent, almost an, 'Any Given Sunday' mentality," Stachitas said. "But he was up-front and said, 'Guys, there's no way we're losing this game.' It was such a different approach than all season. Obviously, we went through our usual practice leading up to a game routines. But I almost appreciated that he was like, 'Guys, there's no way Tyrone and Jameer are going to lose on their Senior Night with the chance to go undefeated. It's almost a foregone conclusion. Let's just make sure it happens. Let's put it away early.'"

***

And the Hawks wasted little time following their coach's message. St. Joe's led by 20 points at the half. Nelson shook off his antsy jitters and had a magnificent floor game. He was playing so well that Bernard Blunt's career St. Joe's scoring record was in sight. That was not part of Martelli's script because Nelson entered needing 30 points to tie Blunt's mark of 1,985 points. When Martelli finally removed Nelson after he had scored 25 points, to go along with eight rebounds and six assists in 31 minutes, coming up five points shy of tying the record, the Hawks coach got booed by fans eager to see more history on this already historic night.

"I was in shock. I was getting booed at home," Martelli joked.

West added 15 points, five rebounds, and three assists. Stachitas netted a season-high 16 points in just 20 minutes.

"I just remember knocking down shots, and I think I was fairly open on a lot of them," Stachitas said.

John Bryant also had a big night, grabbing a season-high 10 rebounds in 19 minutes.

"At that moment, they caught our best," Bryant said of the Bonnies.

With the rout on, Martelli emptied his bench as he'd planned. It gave walk-on Brian Jesiolowski a chance to make his own lasting memory. Jesiolowski had worked hard to get himself in shape to push the Hawks in practice just as Martelli had asked. When he wasn't loaning West his car, Jesiolowski did his best in late-night one-on-one sessions with West to give him a game. He had given so much of himself to the program, and he brought that unselfish mentality into games whenever he got into contests, passing up shots to set up his teammates. So, he still was looking for his first career points when Martelli pointed at him to enter the contest with four minutes remaining. Not only would Jesiolowski score his first-ever basket, but he did so with a highlight-reel play that had his phone buzzing later.

"Dwayne Lee passed the ball ahead of me on a fast break, and I did a spin move," Jesiolowski said of the setup to his only career field goal. "[Later] I have all of these calls and text messages from friends. 'Yo, you better turn on *SportsCenter*.' I watch the Top Ten, and I'm number three on the Top Ten. It was a surreal moment."

It was a night full of surreal moments. When it was finally over, St. Joe's had won 82-50 to improve to 27-0 overall and 16-0 in the A-10.

A perfect regular season. An unforgettable night.

"You just knew it was going to be a special night, and it lived up to every part," Bill Avington, a 1994 St. Joe's graduate, said. "You say to yourself, 'I'm glad I saw this. I'm glad I'm here.'"

Dean Bozman felt the same way.

"My dad knew I desperately wanted to go, and he wanted to make that happen for me," Bozman said. "He's not here anymore, and it's something I'll always remember. To have a chance to experience that and with my dad, I know that's a once-in-a-lifetime thing."

The Hawks also soaked in the moment.

"You knew you did something special," assistant coach Mark Bass said. "It was like, 'Wow guys, we really accomplished something here. We really did.'"

"You kind of pinch yourself," Carroll said. "Like, 'Holy crap, did this really happen? We just went undefeated?' Unbelievable."

Dick Jerardi had called Martelli after the opening game and said he wasn't sure the Hawks would lose another game. By midseason, Jerardi had become convinced that they wouldn't lose. Now, he would get a keepsake from the historic season. After filing his story for the *Philadelphia Daily News*, Jerardi ambled back toward the home locker room. Inside, Nelson and a few players were still there, still soaking in the moment. An appreciative Nelson previously had thanked Jerardi for a feature story on him, and the Hawks guard had something else for the veteran, grizzled reporter.

"He handed me a piece of the net, which I still have," Jerardi said. "That's just who he was. You never thought for one minute he was the star player. He was just good people who happened to be an extraordinary player."

By now, the Fieldhouse had quieted. The noise and excitement of that night, though, would live on forever in the hearts, minds, and souls of O'Connell, Bozman, and every other fan in attendance. Of course, the Hawks coaches and players would never forget it, either. But their celebration would not be endless. There was still more season to play. More games to win.

A national championship was no longer a pipe dream. It was a real possibility. First, though, the Hawks would be heading to Dayton, Ohio, for the Atlantic 10 Conference Championship before competing in the NCAA tournament. No doubt, the attention on the Hawks would be even greater, if that was even possible. That would be no problem for Martelli, who was comfortable in the spotlight. The coach had done a marvelous job all season with media demands, and this would be no different. However, between the final whistle of the St. Bonaventure game and the opening one in the A-10 tournament, there were a couple of things that, with the benefit of hindsight, Martelli would have done differently.

One other thing happened before St. Joe's played its next game. The Hawks and their fans would be celebrating another historic moment for the school. Four days after the win over St. Bonaventure, Stanford lost its final regular-season game. Now, there was just one undefeated team in the country. Saint Joseph's, the little Catholic school whose home games were played in a gym smaller than those at some high schools and whose players were bypassed by every so-called power conference team, was now the No. 1 team in the country.

CHAPTER 33

Game 28: First "X" in the Loss Column

Thursday, March 11, 2004
University of Dayton Arena, Dayton, Ohio
Xavier vs. No. 1 Saint Joseph's, Atlantic 10 tournament quarterfinals

Four days after Saint Joseph's completed the first perfect regular season in college basketball in 12 years, Phil Martelli was relaxing in his suburban Philadelphia den watching on television as Washington hosted No. 1-ranked Stanford, which was the only other unbeaten team in the country. But it wouldn't last. The Huskies defeated Stanford 75-62. Now, the Hawks were the sole NCAA Division I team without a loss. Martelli knew exactly what that meant. He called out to his wife, Judy, and said, "We gotta get out of here. We just became the number one team in the country."

The Martellis drove to a neighborhood restaurant, where the crowd recognized the coach and had seen the Stanford result as well. "People there were clapping for me," Martelli said.

In two days, it would become official. St. Joe's was a unanimous choice as the No. 1 team in the ESPN/*USA Today* coaches' poll, garnering all 31 first-place votes. And they were No. 1 in the Associated Press media poll, getting 67 of 72 first-place votes. John Bryant was on the trainer's table at Monday's practice still trying to process the news. "I said, 'Coach, I can't believe that I'm a starter on the number one team in the country,'" Bryant said.

Linda Bruno wanted to make sure Martelli and the Hawks had a keepsake from the school's first-ever No. 1 ranking. Bruno, the Atlantic 10 commissioner, bought a copy of *USA Today*, had it framed, and brought it to Martelli's office.

"It was just mind-boggling," Bruno said of the No. 1 ranking. "This can't go away. Phil needs something permanent. I remember bringing it to get framed and the guy said, 'This is great. Who are you bringing it to?' I told him and he said, 'Oh my God, I don't follow sports, but I know this.' That was interesting because you have to do something extraordinary for non-sports people to really know what's going on."

Bruno took the framed memento to Martelli's tiny office in the Fieldhouse.

"I just said, 'I wanted you to have this,'" Bruno said as the two shared a teary embrace. "The entire season was very emotional. It was a great feeling. It really was."

The Hawks had brought joy to Philadelphia and to Saint Joseph's, which was finally able to shed its perennial underdog status as the undeniable best team in the country.

"To see that, proud is probably the biggest descriptive," Dr. Michael McCormick, a 1994 St. Joe's graduate who had continued a long line of family Hawks, said of the ranking. "This is pretty damn cool."

The No. 1 ranking would mean even more attention now. And Don DiJulia figured security consultant Dan Kropp would need some assistance at the Atlantic 10 Conference Championship that was being contested at the University of Dayton Arena in Ohio, where the top-seeded Hawks had a bye into the quarterfinals. As was always the case at St. Joe's, it was all hands on deck. So, that's how David Leach, St. Joe's director of recreation, ended up being Jameer Nelson's personal bodyguard.

"I told Don that I'm available for any role that was needed," Leach said. "Don said, 'Great!' A day or two before travel plans were being made for the A-10 tournament, he goes, 'You're on security detail for Jameer.'"

With the crush of fans who awaited the undefeated and No. 1-ranked team in the country in Ohio, DiJulia thought Leach could help Kropp.

"Not because of fear but because of density," DiJulia said of the rationale for adding Leach. "That was another new element everyone had to deal with."

Once out in Ohio, the Hawks practiced at a small Christian school near Dayton, where large crowds awaited an opportunity to watch St. Joe's and get Nelson's autograph.

"I couldn't believe that no matter where we were going for shootarounds or wherever it was, Jameer would have a million people," Leach said. "Our job was to make sure there was order and to cut off [autographs] so Jameer didn't have to. We could've gone into the next morning with all of the people."

While the post-practice autograph session went smoothly, thanks to Leach and Kropp's help, the on-court session did not.

***

Martelli's team was perfect to this point in the season. If his coaching wasn't perfect as well, Martelli's leadership was close to it. Other than the shouting incident with Mary Palmer at St. Bonaventure, Martelli had flawlessly led the Hawks through the regular season. He had stressed the importance of focusing on each game and not the undefeated record, had muted postgame celebrations by calling out areas for improvement, and had gotten in front of the anticipated media attention early to help alleviate pressure on his players.

Looking back more than 20 years later with the benefit of hindsight, though, Martelli would have changed a couple of things between the final whistle of the St. Bonaventure contest and the opening whistle of the A-10 tournament.

In his euphoric excitement in the postgame celebration after defeating the Bonnies to complete a 27-0 regular season, Martelli addressed the overflow Fieldhouse crowd by letting them know that the season was not over and that the Hawks still had nine games left, a reference to reaching—and, not said but understood, winning—the finals of both the A-10 tournament and the NCAA tournament.[45] Six days later, in the school's press release announcing the No. 1 ranking, Martelli said the team's focus wouldn't be on the ranking but bringing home a trophy from the A-10 tournament.[46]

All season long, except for the pregame pep talk against overmatched St. Bonaventure in the final regular-season game, Martelli had drilled into his players the importance of focusing only on the next game, keeping the big picture out of view. It had worked, well, perfectly. Now, though, he was projecting into the future beyond just the next game.

"I regretted that because it put the prize out there and not right here," Martelli said. "And every game was the prize. I got ahead of myself."

The coach also had agonized over how to prepare his team for the conference tournament. The Hawks didn't know their opening-game opponent, only that it would be the winner of Xavier and St. Bonaventure. In previously similar situations, Martelli would spend a day of practice preparing for each of the potential opponents. As always, he wanted to make sure his preparation was thorough. He had learned the importance of attention to detail in practice from Cathy Rush after coaching his first high school season. So, Martelli stuck to his plan and devoted a day of practice to Xavier and another day of practice to St. Bonaventure. Ultimately, Xavier would come a game away from reaching the Final Four, so preparing for the seven-win Bonnies would seem rather unnecessary looking back. At the time, though, the Musketeers were a beatable, 10-loss team that had seemingly underachieved. Still, if he had a do-over, Martelli would scrap the preparation for St. Bonaventure and use the extra day to get even more ready for the Musketeers.

"I should've rolled the dice on Xavier," he said.

For whatever reason, whether their focus wasn't squarely on the game at hand, whether there wasn't enough time to prep for Xavier, or whether it was something else entirely, the Hawks were just not right in the pre-tournament practice in Ohio.

"It wasn't sharp," Martelli said.

And it would carry over into the A-10 quarterfinals at noon on Thursday, March 11, 2004. The opponent was indeed Xavier, which had easily ousted St. Bonaventure 90-64 in the opening round. The Musketeers were still smarting from their 81-73 home loss to the Hawks on January 17 when Delonte West grabbed national headlines by making all 12 of his field goals, including three three-pointers, and every one of his six free throws.

Dick Jerardi had an almost prescient feel for the Hawks that season. He shared with *Philadelphia Daily News* readers in the preseason just how good the Hawks would be, pushed aside naysayers like ESPN's Digger Phelps publicly in print, brushed off comparisons by Bruiser Flint and Mark Macon of their teams to St. Joe's in 2003–04, and told Martelli after the opening contest that the Hawks might not lose again before becoming convinced of it in midseason. As he was watching Villanova compete in the Big East tournament on television in his Dayton hotel room the night before the St. Joe's–Xavier A-10 contest, Jerardi felt like there was something amiss.

"I had a bad feeling about the game the next day," he said. "Something was wrong. Xavier had underachieved. Xavier was the second-best team in the league. I just remember having a bizarre, weird feeling about that game."

Joe Cabrey was just thinking about seeing another victory. The 1974 St. Joe's graduate had attended each of the previous 27 contests and left every one of them with the same victorious feeling. He and some friends hustled out to Dayton to make the opening tip, arriving just in the nick of time.

"We dropped our bags off at the hotel without checking in and walked to the arena," Cabrey said.

But Cabrey never would check into that hotel. There would be no need. The Hawks would be going home after just one game.

***

Xavier came out quickly and started making shots. The Musketeers' senior trio of Romain Sato, Lionel Chalmers, and Anthony Myles seemingly couldn't miss. Xavier was grabbing every rebound. St. Joe's, playing for the first time in school history as the No. 1 team in the country and after an eight-day layoff, looked out of sync and overmatched.

"It got crazy in a hurry," Jerardi said. "I mean, that game was over fast."

Dave Mallon was excited to return to the lineup after missing the final four regular-season games due to an Achilles' injury. It tore at Mallon's core to be sidelined and not be a part of the special season. Mallon's return would have to wait a little longer, as he had a blister during warm-ups. Trainer Bill Lukasiewicz took him back to the locker room to quickly remedy it before returning in the opening minutes. Lukasiewicz did a double take at the scoreboard once back on the sidelines.

"We went back to deal with it and, by the time we came out, we were getting smacked," Lukasiewicz said. "I couldn't believe it."

Martelli vividly remembers a play early in the contest in which Sato rejected a West shot as a sign that this might not be St. Joe's day.

"It was very, very early," he said of the block. "Delonte had been perfect against them at Xavier. I was like, 'Ah, this is a different thing.' We were never in the game."

The Musketeers entered halftime ahead by 22 points. Still, everyone figured the Hawks had a run in them like they had been doing all season. Not only didn't a St. Joe's run come after the halftime break, but Xavier kept making shots and went on its own run. Eventually, the Musketeers' advantage reached an unfathomable 37 points in the second half.

"Nobody could believe it," Cabrey said.

"It was just like, 'What is going on here?'" Jerardi said. "It was just nuts."

As the lead remained in the high double digits in the waning minutes, Martelli thought there was no point in keeping his star backcourt in the contest, electing to save their legs for the NCAA tournament. He pulled Nelson and West with four minutes remaining. No one has seen a competitive drive the likes of West's before or since at St. Joe's. As Mallon had found out early in his Hawks career, there was nothing casual about pickup games when playing alongside West and there were no water breaks after losing. Drills in practices were not merely drills but opportunities to win for West. Even when playing casual table games in Ralph Maresco's basement, West took winning seriously.

So, West just didn't accept or understand it when Martelli took him out of the game.

"Oh my God, he said, 'Give me 30 seconds and I'll go back and we'll win the game,'" Martelli recalled. "I said, 'It's not going to be today.'"

West appeared as if he were going to turn around, head back to the scorer's table, and check himself back into the contest when Nelson intervened.

"Jameer got up and said, 'Coach, I got him,'" Martelli said.

The scene was captured perfectly by photographer Greg Carroccio, a St. Joe's student in 2003–04 who chronicled the season and today shoots Philadelphia college basketball and other sports as the owner of Sideline Photos. West is staring out onto the court with a shocked, disbelieving look while Nelson empathetically has his left arm draped over West's left shoulder and right arm grasping on West's right biceps muscle. It is a beautiful image of a caring teammate. West would continue to need support afterward in the postgame locker room.

"There was no talking to him," Martelli said of West. "That was his thing. There was winning or nothing else."

There would be no winning on this day for St. Joe's. When the final whistle blew, Xavier celebrated an 87-67 victory after an unbelievable performance. As a team, the Musketeers shot an astonishing 71.1 percent from the field. The trio of Sato (24 points), Chalmers (23), and Myles (19) were, incredibly, even better, as they made 73.5 percent of their shots. Xavier crushed the Hawks in rebounding with an astounding 43-18 advantage. After all the Hawks had done, the result and the way it happened were hard to comprehend.

"That was the first time that it didn't matter what we did," Dwayne Jones said. "I remember us almost being shell-shocked, like, 'Wow, we tried everything.' I give them credit."

Later, when all of the games had been played for the season, the defeat would not appear so bad in retrospect, though the lopsided nature of the loss remains surprising. Xavier likely would not even have made the NCAA tournament with a loss to St. Joe's in the A-10 quarterfinals. Afterward, the Musketeers ran off an amazing streak, first beating George Washington in the semifinals and then host Dayton in the A-10 title game. The Musketeers then topped Louisville, Mississippi State, and Texas in the NCAA tournament before losing a nail-biter, 66-63, to Duke in the Elite Eight.

Being defeated by a team that would finish the season four points away from a Final Four is nothing to be ashamed about. That perspective was not available in the moment. The Hawks and their fans were just bummed.

***

Cabrey and his traveling party dejectedly walked back to the hotel, picked up their bags, and headed home.

"It was very somber," he said.

Maresco was used to the feeling of losing to Xavier. He had finally felt the joy of victory the day after the Hawks ate dinner at his house when West was perfect in the win at Cintas Center. Maresco left University of Dayton Arena once again getting razzed from all of the locals.

"There were a ton of Xavier fans, neighbors, church people, whatever, and I must've run into all of them after the game," Maresco said. "Boy, did I get abused. I went into a funk for probably 48 hours after that. I couldn't even drive home. I was distraught."

Inside the locker room, West was despondent. The rest of the players and Martelli were disappointed. St. Joe's certainly would not be No. 1 in the country when the new Top 25 polls came out in four days. But the Hawks were able to quickly pick their heads up and look forward.

"It wasn't devastation because we knew we were going to the NCAA tournament," Martelli said.

Some even thought that a loss before the NCAAs might be beneficial to take some pressure off the Hawks, though Martelli didn't believe that. "I didn't feel relief," he said. "The whole cliché is nonsense. You can learn from winning."

During his postgame interview with Nelson, Jerardi asked the Hawks star if he remembered losing an important playoff game during his senior year in high school. Nelson's Chester Clippers were defeated by Coatesville in the PIAA District 1 Class

AAAA title game before recovering to win the Pennsylvania state title when Nelson netted a team-high 19 points in a 73-48 win over Uniontown.

"The A-10 [title] would've been nice, but this isn't the goal," Jerardi said.

St. Joe's radio play-by-play announcer Tom McCarthy left Dayton earlier than expected and headed back to spring training to call Phillies preseason games. Foremost on his mind as he traveled to the airport was how the defeat would be received around the country.

"I was disappointed for the guys because I wondered what society would think of them," McCarthy said.

St. Joe's would find out in just three days when the NCAA selection committee revealed its seedings for the field of 64 NCAA tournament. The loss to Xavier, and the way in which the Hawks were defeated, opened the door for criticism from analysts who thought St. Joe's was nothing more than a nice story and not really a team worthy of either its lofty ranking or a No. 1 seed in the NCAA tournament nor one that could realistically compete with the big boys.

Martelli soon would tell one of those analysts just what he thought about that in a reaction that would make national headlines. For now, though, the coach was focused on just one thing and one thing only: He would not get ahead of himself again. The Hawks' minds would be on the next game, the next opponent. And to hammer that point home, the coach started from scratch when they resumed practice after returning to Philadelphia. The NCAA tournament was up next. St. Joe's would be ready for its first game. And the Hawks and their supporters gathered at a crowded Fieldhouse on Selection Sunday to find out just who their opponent would be.

CHAPTER 34

A No. 1 Seed and Controversy

Sunday, March 14, 2004
Alumni Memorial Fieldhouse, Philadelphia
Selection Sunday

Saint Joseph's returned home to Philadelphia two days earlier than expected after, shockingly, getting blown out by Xavier in its first game of the Atlantic 10 Conference tournament. The downsides were many, foremost among them that there would not be an A-10 title for the Hawks in any of Jameer Nelson's historically memorable four seasons. Also, St. Joe's lost the chance to become the eighth team in college basketball history to finish the entire season undefeated and the first since Indiana went 32-0 in 1975–76. Finally, the Hawks would now have to fend off the naysayers, many of whom were waiting for their first loss like hungry predators ready to pounce because of their belief that only teams in so-called power conferences deserve the admiration, attention, and accolades being directed at St. Joe's.

But there was at least one positive of the defeat. The Hawks' early arrival back in Philadelphia meant Phil Martelli had two extra days to practice. And Martelli would not repeat what happened after St. Joe's final regular-season win against St. Bonaventure when he got ahead of himself. The focus would be on the present and the next game and the next opponent. Nothing more. And Martelli had just the perfect idea for how to drive that point home and ensure a mental reset following the Xavier blowout.

Unlike out in Dayton while preparing for the A-10 tournament, the Hawks' first practice after returning home was sharp. Martelli saw on the practice court what he had become accustomed to witnessing that season. There was no need for Nelson to address the team when Martelli brought the Hawks together for a post-practice cheer. Previously, after an uncharacteristically poor practice, Nelson had challenged the players to practice as if their spots in the lineup were on the line just like he was doing, no matter the number of preseason honors being directed at him. That was the type of leadership Nelson brought to the Hawks every day. After this practice, though, he might have only offered congratulations on a job well done. Martelli did the speaking afterward.

"You know what we just did?" Martelli asked the players. "This was our first practice. It went pretty well, didn't it? So, we're just starting over."

Martelli had pulled out his detailed notes and replayed the entire practice from the opening session of the 2003–04 season to the minute. It was a way for the Hawks to put Xavier behind them and also to signal the need to get back to the singular, one-game-at-a-time focus that had benefited St. Joe's all season. The following session, using Martelli's exact plan for the second practice of the season, also went well. Both Martelli and the players felt St. Joe's was back.[47]

As good as the two post-Atlantic 10 practices were, in fitting fashion for St. Joe's, they were not held on their own court because the Fieldhouse was not available. The Hawks loaded in vans to work out at neighboring Drexel on the first day and at Philadelphia College of Osteopathic Medicine (PCOM) on the second.

"That was the beauty of what was done," said Martelli, referencing more odds the Hawks had to overcome.

The Fieldhouse already had been booked for an event for accepted students on the first day of practice. St. Joe's couldn't practice there on the second day because crews were readying its on-campus home court for the second watch party of the season, following the closed captioning broadcast of the game at Villanova. This one was for Selection Sunday, and the Hawks and their supporters would gather to find out whom they would be playing in the NCAA tournament and what effect, if any, their first defeat would have on their seeding.

***

To reinforce the renewed, one-game-at-a-time focus, many players wore to the Selection Sunday watch party a Saint Joseph's T-shirt that said on the back: "Let's Win the Next Game." Jameer Nelson didn't have on a T-shirt; rather, continuing the love he'd shown to a distraught Delonte West in the final minutes on the bench versus Xavier, Nelson was sporting a No. 15 West jersey. All of the Hawks and hundreds of their fans gathered at the Fieldhouse in advance of CBS's selection show in which the NCAA tournament field would be unveiled at six o'clock on Sunday, March 14, 2004.

Since their loss three days earlier, there had been much debate in print and on television over whether the Hawks deserved a No. 1 seed. St. Joe's was 27-1 and had the best Rating Percentage Index (RPI) in the country. RPI is no longer used today as a metric for the selection committee to evaluate potential NCAA tournament teams, but it was an important factor in 2004. When the graphic flashed on the large screen, along with an announcement from CBS's Greg Gumbel, that St. Joe's was the No. 1 seed in the East Rutherford region, the Fieldhouse erupted. Athletic director Don DiJulia shed tears, and the players reacted with joyful, priceless smiles that were captured for eternity by photographer Greg Carroccio.

Joining the Hawks as top seeds were Stanford, Kentucky, and Duke, all of which are from power conferences, with the latter two among the preeminent programs in college basketball. St. Joe's, playing as a No. 1 seed for the first time in its 17 NCAA tournament appearances, would meet No. 16 Liberty in the opening round on Thursday in Buffalo.

David Leach watched along with everyone else. Leach, who would be taking a few days off later in the week from his job as St. Joe's director of recreation to continue in his new role on security detail for Nelson, was struck by the magnitude and significance of the top seed.

"It dawned on me at that point, like, 'Holy shit, we're in this tiny shoebox of a gym on national TV,'" he said. "Oh my God, this is tiny St. Joe's. Look at this place. This is the Fieldhouse. It seats 3,200 people. This is St. Joe's Fieldhouse. And we're a number one seed right up there with these tremendously storied programs. It was like, 'Wow, we're a small school right there with all of these giants.'"

Father Timothy Lannon, in his first year as the school's president, was on hand. He was thrilled for St. Joe's and everyone involved with the basketball program.

"I remember saying how proud I am of the success of the team and our coaches," Lannon said. "Not only are our basketball players great student-athletes, but they're great ambassadors for the university. That's what I really appreciate, how they handled themselves so well and how impressive they are."

Bill Avington was there as well. A 1994 St. Joe's graduate, Avington pushed aside his fandom after being contracted by the Associated Press to write a story chronicling the Hawks' reaction to their seeding. As he worked the room for interviews with the players and coaches alongside a large media contingent, a scene he described as chaotic, Avington thought about the enormity of the accomplishment and noted the reactions of the excited players.

"The number one seed was really symbolic of how far they'd come," Avington said. "There was a lot of jubilation and excitement. They were happy they got this honor. Little St. Joe's who nobody really knew much about, here they are at the pinnacle of college basketball. They were a number one seed. That couldn't be taken away."

No, but Billy Packer would try.

***

Packer was CBS's No. 1 college basketball analyst and had been for a long time. As the Associated Press reported in a story announcing Packer's passing on January 27, 2023, he also was viewed as a controversial figure in the sport.[48] Packer would spark more controversy when asked what he thought of the Hawks getting a No. 1 seed by rattling off the names of nine other schools he thought were more deserving.[49]

"I think it was just wrong to do that with kids," said longtime college basketball reporter Dick "Hoops" Weiss, who was writing for the *New York Daily News* at the time. "They had worked hard all year."

Jim Nantz, who was CBS's lead college basketball announcer and Packer's partner on many of the analyst's 34 Final Fours, said that Packer's opinion was not intended as a personal slight at the Hawks.

"Billy relished wearing the black hat," Nantz said. "He never shied away from playing the role of contrarian. His beef with St. Joe's had more to do with teams he felt were 'mid-majors' getting as much or more respect than schools from conferences like the Big Ten and ACC. It was never personal with Billy. It was a good debate. He would often say he could debate anyone on any subject matter—tell me which side you want to represent and I will take the other."

However it was meant, Martelli took it personally.

"He felt that his players were being slighted," Ray Parrillo said.

With microphone in hand addressing the large Fieldhouse crowd, and with television cameras and reporters surrounding him, Martelli responded to the CBS analyst by saying, "Billy Packer can kiss my ass."

"I was just like, 'I'm not having this,'" Martelli said. "You're not disrespecting this team. And we're hurt because we lost that [Xavier] game, but we were back on track saying what are we going to do to beat Liberty. So, for somebody outside who hadn't experienced this team, I wasn't having it. I just was not having it."

Martelli's comment would draw national headlines. At St. Joe's, it elicited cheers from fans.

"Phil was rightly defensive about his team and the run they had," Avington said.

The university wasn't as thrilled with the comment. Martelli had to issue a formal apology to school officials.

The coach's directive toward Packer would only brighten the already intense spotlight on the Hawks. The notoriety would not only be good for Saint Joseph's but also the A-10. It had been a successful year on and off the court for the league, as the Hawks were one of four A-10 entrants into the NCAA tournament, joining conference champ Xavier and fellow at-large selections Richmond and Dayton. And the Hawks' claw grip on local and national headlines boosted the league's cachet.

"It was an amazing season," then-Atlantic 10 commissioner Linda Bruno said. "The amount of attention the Atlantic 10 got changes the rest of the league's stature. We had other years [with great attention], but St. Joe's was different because the small, Catholic school thing is real. That is something you have to really appreciate.

"It's mind-boggling a little bit that so many people who aren't sports fans caught that. The other thing is the sports world caught it. Everyone jumped on board and embraced what was happening."

St. Joe's success paid dividends for the league not just in 2003–04 but also going forward.

"If one of us is good, all of us are good," Bruno said. "It certainly helped in the next round of negotiations with ESPN. There's nothing like winning as a bargaining chip. It's hard to even put into words now that I'm trying to."

Like when she brought a framed copy of the No. 1 ranking to Martelli's office, Bruno and the Hawks coach got emotional again when she called to congratulate him on the No. 1 seed.

"All I could think about was that it would mean so much to these kids for them to be a one seed," she said.

With all of the prognosticating, if not the controversy, about the NCAA seeding behind them, the Hawks began preparation for Liberty. St. Joe's was aiming to become the first A-10 team since UMass in 1996 to reach the Final Four. But neither Martelli nor the players nor anyone close to the program made mention of that—definitely not publicly and probably not privately. After learning from Xavier, they were now back to focusing solely on the next game. A No. 1 seed had never lost to a No. 16, and Martelli was going to take no shortcuts in order to continue that trend. And the coach had a little wrinkle in his game plan prepared for the opening matchup to help ensure it.

CHAPTER 35

Game 29: Hawks Douse
Flames in NCAA Opener

Thursday, March 18, 2004
KeyBank Center, Buffalo
NCAA First Round: No. 1 Saint Joseph's vs. No. 16 Liberty

When No. 1-seeded Saint Joseph's arrived in Buffalo for the NCAA tournament, snowy conditions greeted the Hawks and the rest of the competitors. But St. Joe's wasn't concerned about the weather. The Hawks weren't thinking about who they might play in the second round, or the possible opponents a pair of wins might bring. The only thing on their collective minds was playing Liberty in the opening round at 2:45 p.m. at the KeyBank Center on Thursday, March 18, 2004.

At Wednesday's pregame press conference, Phil Martelli told the large media gathering that St. Joe's focus was only on their next 40 minutes of basketball.[50] The Hawks coach had learned his lesson after the St. Bonaventure win to end the regular season and wouldn't repeat it. St. Joe's had been practicing well ever since returning to Philadelphia after the blowout loss to Xavier in the Atlantic 10 tournament and continued to train well in Buffalo. Martelli was not taking the Flames lightly. A No. 16 seed had never beaten a No. 1 seed, and St. Joe's coach prepared to keep it that way.

"I vividly remember our preparation," he said. "We took no shortcuts."

Martelli wasn't nervous about making history as the first top-seeded team to lose to a No. 16; rather, he was wary of the fact that the next defeat meant the season would be over.

"Not 16 against one, but the next loss was the last time this group would play," he said. "And you just didn't want it to end."

Glenn Farello also was in Buffalo and wasn't worried. Farello coached Delonte West at Eleanor Roosevelt High School, and he was there to support his star pupil. Farello had no doubt that West would deliver a strong performance.

"I just knew in big moments he'd bring it," he said. "So, I had a sense of ease."

Randy Dunton was not feeling at ease. Dunton was in his second season as Liberty's head coach after serving as a Flames assistant for the previous 12 seasons with a one-year stint, in 1997–98, as the school's interim head coach. Though Liberty was a member of the Big South Conference, squarely a mid-major league, Dunton had competed against plenty of stars. That included 14 players in 2003–04 who would later lace up their shoes in the NBA.

The Big South is a one-bid league, with everything coming down to the end-of-season conference tournament for the lone NCAA representative awarded to the conference tournament champ. Dunton's philosophy in order to get ready for the league's postseason tournament was to play as tough of a nonconference schedule as possible to harden his team for league play. In 2003–04, the Flames scheduled Duke, Arizona, Iowa State, and Seton Hall. Duke, alone, had six future NBA players on its roster, including JJ Redick and Luol Deng. Arizona had Andre Iguodala and four other future NBA pros. Iowa State and Seton Hall, similarly, had NBA players.

Dunton had seen great players before turning on the tape to scout the Hawks. But, in preparing for St. Joe's, Liberty's coach never had seen a player quite like Jameer Nelson.

"I just thought Jameer was impeccable," Dunton said. "We played a lot of good players over the years, but I really felt like Jameer Nelson was the best player we'd ever prepared for. His ballhandling skills were way beyond what typically was going on in college at that time, more like what is going on today, with all of these workout gurus and six different crossovers.

"He had a nasty pullback. He would attack you, then pull back. He had the uncanny ability to go either way. He could cross you and go, or he could attack back to the same side. Our scouting report on him was to try to keep your [jersey] numbers in front of him."

Dunton knew it wouldn't be easy, but the Flames had played top talent and top teams. So, he didn't think his players would be intimidated. They also were riding into the NCAA tournament with a wave of confidence after a brilliant performance in the Big South title game in which they routed High Point 89-44.

"What I remember about that game is everything is clicking," Dunton said. "The kids were great. It was a really fun day for us."

Dunton got stuck sitting on the scorer's table for 15 minutes after the final whistle when students rushed the court.

"There was not a place to move," he said. "It was a great celebration. And then you wake up the next day and say, 'OK, you have to play the number one team in the nation.'"

And when he saw what happened on Selection Sunday after the seedings were announced, Dunton knew that beating the Hawks would be even tougher than he first thought.

"I think there was a motivational edge with getting criticized about being number one," Dunton said. "We weren't happy with Billy Packer that he got them more motivated. The last thing you need to do when you got a caged lion is not feed him for a week."

The Hawks, and Nelson in particular, came out like they hadn't been fed for a year. They also had a little wrinkle for Liberty.

***

All season, Martelli had started games by playing a full-court, man-to-man defense. In January, in the 17th game of the season, St. Bonaventure season ticket holder Mary Palmer got upset at Martelli's strategy because she thought it was bad sportsmanship when the Hawks' defense overwhelmed the Bonnies. But it was the same "55 Press" defense the coach used in every game. Martelli's yelling response to Palmer, reportedly calling her a "nitwit" and a "moron," drew national headlines. He publicly apologized to Palmer and took it a step further by inviting her as his personal guest to Buffalo for the NCAA tournament.

Martelli explained that he hadn't used the Hawks' trapping defense, called "55 On," against the Bonnies. But with Palmer sitting courtside once again, this time St. Joe's coach *did* go to a trapping defense when the opening whistle blew. And Dunton was not expecting it.

"They came out and trapped us a little bit, which we hadn't seen them do in the half-court as much," Dunton said. "And it was unsettling to our guys. You think, 'Are they going to come into that game and make adjustments? Or do they think talent-wise they'll beat Liberty?' And they did come in with some adjustments, and I said, 'Wow, I've got a little more respect for Martelli now.'"

Besides the Hawks' defensive scheme, there was the problem of Nelson. Martelli had cornered the Hawks' star point guard in the locker room before the contest and told him that these are the games great players live for. Nelson, smarting for a week since losing to Xavier the previous Thursday and even more after Packer's Selection Sunday barbs, was locked in. He scored all nine St. Joe's points as the Hawks started the game on a 9-1 run.

Dunton's game plan to keep defenders' numbers in front of Nelson was not working.

"He's the best individual talent of trying to take away his strengths, the inability of taking away any of his strengths, that I coached against," Dunton said. "We wanted to make him shoot over you, and he just came out and made shots. There are just some nights where you just realize how good of a player somebody is."

The trapping defense continued to constrain Liberty's offense, and Nelson continued to light up the Flames' defense. Very quickly, St. Joe's had taken a 17-point lead.

"They punched us pretty hard right in the mouth. Boom. Bang," Dunton said. "It took us a while to find our footing. Once we got down 17, we actually played pretty good the rest of the way."

By then, the margin was too great for Liberty to overcome. The Hawks were up by 20 points at the half, and they kept alive the winless streak for No. 16 seeds against No. 1's by beating Liberty, 82-63. St. Joe's trapping defense forced 26 Flames turnovers. Nelson finished a magnificent game with 33 points to pass 2,000 for his career, becoming the first player in school history to reach that mark. He also had four assists, three rebounds, and three steals.

"We're glad we got to play them, but unfortunately, like I said back then, we found out how good Jameer Nelson was that day," Dunton said.

St. Joe's also got a strong contribution, as Farello predicted, from Delonte West, who had 18 points, nine rebounds, five assists, and two steals. And John Bryant, motivated by the opportunity to play against a Division I team from his home state of Virginia that did not recruit him, chipped in with eight points, seven rebounds, and two blocks in 23 minutes. Two of those points came on a dunk that would be immortalized in 'One Shining Moment,' the highly anticipated post-tournament highlight reel that airs at the conclusion of the NCAA championship game.

"This was the first challenge, and why not beat a team from my home state?" Bryant said. "They passed on me type of thing. These are the things you tell yourself in your main character movie moment. I think I probably had a little groove going. I'm not used to scoring and having that many rebounds. I do remember my dunks in that game that I now show my players to this day. I put it on my scouting reports."

It was an all-around great opening performance by the Hawks and led by a sensational game from Nelson.

"I think that St. Joe's team was more athletic and bigger and stronger than people realize," Dunton said. "This was not somebody that someone could sit there and say they didn't belong. You have two NBA players and some other really quality kids. But Jameer, mm-mm-mm, he was something."

With their opening-game victory behind them, the Hawks finally could turn their attention to their next opponent. Eighth-seeded Texas Tech defeated No. 9 Charlotte to set up a second-round matchup between the Red Raiders and St. Joe's on Saturday evening in Buffalo. Texas Tech was big, strong, and physical like Rhode Island, which always gave the Hawks trouble, but even more talented. The Red Raiders also were coached by a legend. Martelli knew he'd have to have St. Joe's prepared because Bob Knight certainly would have Texas Tech ready.

CHAPTER 36

Game 30: A Matchup with a Coaching Legend

Saturday, March 20, 2004
KeyBank Center, Buffalo
NCAA Second Round: No. 1 Saint Joseph's vs. No. 8 Texas Tech

After an awe-inspiring performance against Randy Dunton and Liberty, Jameer Nelson returned to the Hawks' Buffalo hotel to unwind. St. Joe's would be back on the court in less than 48 hours, but Nelson wasn't thinking about that. He was just taking in the moment, enjoying being surrounded by family, friends, and St. Joe's supporters.

"Everybody was there, and we're in the hotel lobby. I'm sitting and resting, but I'm enjoying it," Nelson said. "My friends and family are on the dance floor. It was surreal. You can't explain that feeling, the joy of people going through the whole year. You kind of saw it there after that game in Buffalo."

Saint Joseph's isn't a large school by any means, but it's a tight-knit community. Hawks fans, like Joe Cabrey, traveled with them every step of the way. As the winning continued, the bandwagon just got bigger and bigger. Against Liberty, Nelson felt the fans' large presence inside the arena.

"The energy in the building, it was generated by our fans, by our school," Nelson said. "You look at TV, you watch basketball growing up, you see all of these great schools with the camaraderie, the togetherness. We had that. Even throughout the year, there were busloads of people going everywhere we went."

Father Timothy Lannon made the trip to Buffalo, flying on the team plane and staying in the team hotel. Only in his first year as the school's president, Lannon immediately felt the unique passion of alumni.

"I loved it when we were in the NCAA tournament," Lannon said.

The Jesuit priest celebrated Mass with the large St. Joe's community who made the trip to Buffalo.

"The mob of people was unbelievable," Lannon said. "It was like, 'Oh my God, here we are gathered to give thanks to God and praise to the team.' It was just an expression of the terrific spirit of St. Joe's and the love that people have for the university. That's one of the things I love about St. Joe's, how deeply people love the university."

Greg McDermott was among the Hawks fans at the Mass said by Lannon. A 1987 St. Joe's graduate, McDermott capitalized on the program's success by launching a website that sold Hawks gear. He started The Hawk Store in part because of the lack of availability of St. Joe's merchandise and because of the demand he knew there was. McDermott stuffed his minivan with merchandise, and drove through a snowstorm to reach the Buffalo hotel in plenty of time to watch the games. He set up shop inside Room 712 of the team hotel for anyone who wanted a Nelson jersey, a St. Joe's hat, or a Hawks sweatshirt.

"This is pre-internet," McDermott said. "There's no Fanatics, there's no nothing. We were shipping out 25 to 30 orders per night. I was Fanatics before Fanatics."

McDermott's St. Joe's swag was showing up all over Buffalo. The town was awash in crimson and gray. Others might have been wearing T-shirts featuring the words, "Jameeracle on 54th Street," a reference to Nelson and St. Joe's location at the intersection of 54th Street and City Avenue. The T-shirts were the brainchild of fraternity brothers Steve Del Fra and Frank Garafalo, and they helped pay for books and, well, beer.

"It was pretty cool, man," Garafalo said. "We were able to do a lot for the fraternity. And there was a sense of community it created in our organization."

That same sense of community could be felt in Buffalo.

"We took over the city," Cabrey said. "There were Hawks everywhere."

After the opening-round victory, Cabrey's traveling party went to dinner on Friday at the Buffalo Chophouse. Their bill totaled around $1,600. When the check arrived, however, there was nothing to pay. A gentleman seated at an adjacent table covered the tab.

"He said, 'I hope you guys enjoy your time in our city,'" Cabrey said. "'It has been phenomenal watching your team play. It's my treat. And good luck tomorrow.' We were stunned. Who in the world would've expected something like that to happen? Extremely cool."

Cabrey and his friends paid the act of kindness forward. They found a suite that was available for Saturday's second-round game against Texas Tech and used the money they saved on dinner to reserve it. They then gave their original tickets, which were located just rows behind the Hawks bench, to some St. Joe's students who had traveled to Buffalo without tickets but hoped to land some.

"It was just an incredibly happy experience," Cabrey said.

Everyone attending Lannon's Mass, buying wares from McDermott, and touring around Buffalo like Cabrey hoped to continue the joyride against the Red Raiders. There were a few issues facing the Hawks, though, first among them a certain Robert Montgomery Knight.

***

Like John Chaney, Bob Knight was a living legend in 2003–04. Knight was in his third season at the helm at Texas Tech after leading Indiana to three national titles, including a 32-0 season in 1975–76, 11 Big Ten crowns, and five Final Fours. He is one of few coaches who have led teams to an NCAA title, NIT championship, and Olympic gold medal. When he completed his Hall of Fame career, Knight retired with 902 victories. The demanding coach's teams played a tough, disciplined style, and Knight cast an intimidating presence on the sidelines, in locker rooms, and at press conferences.

It was not St. Joe's versus Bob Knight. It was St. Joe's versus Texas Tech. But Knight clearly had everyone's attention—the Hawks, their fans, the media, and all of college basketball—in the lead-up to the matchup at 5:30 p.m. on Saturday, March 20, 2004.

Martelli, who'd never met Knight prior to the game, was touched by Texas Tech's coach's complimentary words in the pregame press conference. Doing a 180-degree turn from Billy Packer's critical comments, Knight praised the Hawks and credited them with a remarkable achievement of going undefeated in the regular season.[51] It's not surprising that Knight would laud the Hawks, considering how much of a stickler he was for team basketball. But, Martelli knew, Knight wouldn't be Mr. Nice Guy a day later when the referee threw the ball up in the air with both teams' seasons on the line.

Martelli had been similarly impressed watching the Red Raiders.

"You know they're great because they're all where they should be," Martelli said. "His man-to-man defense was like the Temple zone. This is what the tournament is supposed to be about. You're supposed to play a better team each round. We knew we had to play with an intensity and fierceness and be that tough to beat them. They weren't better than us, but they could've been tougher than us."

Martelli shook hands with Knight prior to the contest. It seemed as if the Red Raiders coach got the attention of all of the Hawks and everyone in attendance.

"There isn't probably a more well-known coach," Dave Mallon said. "It's not a person but becomes an aura or a figure."

"Coach Knight was a legend at that point, finishing up his career," Pat Carroll said.

Hawks assistant coach Mark Bass looked toward the opposing bench and thought about his own journey from McCorristin High School just outside the border of his hometown of Trenton, New Jersey, to a successful playing career at St. Joe's, and now a spot on Martelli's staff with Knight on the other sideline.

"You're playing against Bob Knight, a Hall of Fame coach," Bass said. "As a young coach myself, you're in awe. You watch Bob Knight when he's at Indiana, you know how great of a coach he is. So, in my eyes, it's like, 'OK, I made it. I'm going against Bob Knight.'"

Joe Lunardi could just hear the likes of Packer, Digger Phelps, and other St. Joe's detractors and what they might say afterward.

"This is when they get their comeuppance," Lunardi, predicting detractors' words, said. "They're playing a real school from a real league with Bob Knight."

Lunardi, the longtime Hawks radio analyst and ESPN bracketologist, didn't share that sentiment.

"I would always write a score on the other side of my card and not show it until after the game," Lunardi said. "I wrote, 'Hawks 70, Red Raiders 65.'"

Lunardi's radio partner, Tom McCarthy, had some concern about Knight, but then he looked at the bigger picture.

"I worried about Bob Knight," McCarthy said. "But then I realized these guys are way better than Bob Knight's Texas Tech team."

It sure didn't look that way, though, when the game started.

***

As Ray Parrillo reported in the *Philadelphia Inquirer*, Texas Tech raced out to a 21-12 lead. It had been just two games since the shocking blowout loss to Xavier in the opening round of the Atlantic 10 tournament. That game had started similarly to this one, and St. Joe's never got back into that contest. It got so bad that the Hawks trailed Xavier by as many as 37 points at one point in the second half, and Martelli didn't even bother to keep Nelson or Delonte West on the court in the final minutes. The run that everyone expected that the Hawks had shown all season never came against Xavier.

It would come against Texas Tech, though. And the Hawks would get a lift from an unlikely source.

Dave Mallon was thrilled to be back in uniform for the third straight game after missing four consecutive contests to end the regular season due to an Achilles' injury. Mallon had started the season by sitting out the first seven games with a stress fracture in his right foot. In other years, Mallon probably would've redshirted the season, gotten healthy, and come back at 100 percent the following year. But Mallon didn't want to miss this special season. He couldn't. Every second on the sidelines pained him. But he was healthy enough now to be back as an option for Martelli. And, now, here he was, in the NCAA tournament in Buffalo just two years after he and a group of high school buddies were in the last row of the same arena watching the NCAA tournament and dreaming of one day being there themselves.

"We all sat there talking to each other and saying, 'How cool would it be to play on that stage?'" Mallon said.

The stage was, in fact, now Mallon's. He was just a 25-minute drive from the gym at East Aurora High School, where he averaged 21 points, 11 rebounds, and 7.3 blocks as a senior in 2001–02. His family, friends, and anyone who'd ever helped him in basketball were in attendance. And they would all witness a moment that neither they nor Mallon will ever forget.

With the Hawks still trailing, Martelli signaled for Mallon to enter the contest. Although he was an outstanding scorer in high school, Mallon's role on the Hawks was as a backup big man who set screens and did any and all of the dirty work down low that wouldn't show up in the box score but is vitally important to winning. He had no expectations of doing much more than that when he checked into the game.

"I remember saying to myself as I inbounded the ball, 'Alright Dave, you're cold coming in here. Just get a few touches, get a feel for the game, and just do your thing out here,'" Mallon recalled.

But, much like when Nelson summoned a surprised Chet Stachitas to shoot immediately upon entering against Drexel in the seventh game of the season at the Palestra, Mallon would find himself with no time to merely settle into the contest. On the Hawks' first offensive possession with him in the game, the ball found Mallon open from the outside. He instinctively shot the three-pointer and drained it. The next time down the court, he dived on the floor for a loose ball, which ended up in Tyrone Barley's hands for a layup. Next, he found West with a swing pass in the corner for a three-pointer.

Just as quickly as it all happened, a stunned Mallon was subbed out.

"It was almost like this moment was made for me," Mallon said. "It didn't feel real. I was expecting to get some blood flowing, get out there, and set some screens. I kind of looked around and said, 'What the hell just happened?'"

Knight and the Red Raiders might have been thinking the same thing. This wouldn't be Xavier all over again for St. Joe's. The Hawks used a 24-2 run to turn a 21-12 deficit into a 36-23 advantage. However, no one expected a Knight team to wilt, and the Red Raiders didn't. Texas Tech whittled St. Joe's advantage down to five points at halftime, and the game remained close throughout the second half. It wasn't until Nelson's three-pointer from the top of the key with 23.1 seconds left that gave the Hawks a four-point lead that St. Joe's could begin to exhale.

When it was over, the final score was just as Lunardi had predicted.

Hawks 70, Red Raiders 65.

Nelson completed a brilliant two-game showing in Buffalo with 24 points. Against Liberty and Texas Tech, he made 20 of 39 (51.3 percent) field goals, including seven of 17 (41.2) three-pointers, and 10 of 11 (90.9) free throws. West added 15 points, eight assists, and seven rebounds against Texas Tech, while Carroll chipped in with 14 points. St. Joe's defense was menacing, finishing with a season-high 15 steals.

"I remember going into the locker room, and we were just celebrating," Carroll said. "People were chanting, 'SWEET 16! SWEET 16!' It was just a surreal, powerful moment, like, 'We're going to the freakin' Sweet 16 at St. Joe's. Holy shit, here we are. We made it.' It was just an unbelievable ride."

Mallon, after all of the injuries and the disappointment at having to watch 11 games in street clothes, also was euphoric in the locker room afterward. He had played just six minutes and finished with just those three points, along with an assist, but it had been a huge three-pointer right on the court where he had dreamed of playing just two years prior.

"That was my basketball moment," he said. "This was the one."

A local sportswriter, Allen Wilson of the *Buffalo News*, gave Mallon a hearty embrace in the locker room.

"Everyone was looking around like, 'Who the hell is this?' You would've thought I scored 40 in that game the way Allen was treating me," said Mallon, who appreciated the gesture. "It was something."

Martelli was thrilled with the Hawks' performance, especially their toughness, and humbled by Knight's words in the handshake line in which the legendary coach said the Hawks are a good example of how to play the game.[52] The Hawks returned to their hotel, said goodbye to their supporters, and returned home. There were more practices to have and at least one more game to play. Up next, St. Joe's would be traveling up the New Jersey Turnpike to play Wake Forest in the Sweet 16 at the Meadowlands in East Rutherford, New Jersey. That was the same Wake Forest in which Billy Packer had played. And Packer would now get a firsthand look at the Hawks. CBS assigned its announcing crew for the game as follows: Play-by-play, Jim Nantz. Analyst, Billy Packer.

CHAPTER 37

Game 31: Paul, Packer, and Wake Forest

Thursday, March 25, 2004
Meadowlands, East Rutherford, New Jersey
NCAA Sweet 16: No. 1 Saint Joseph's vs. No. 4 Wake Forest

On Selection Sunday, Billy Packer rattled off nine teams from so-called power conferences that he thought were more deserving of a No. 1 seed than Saint Joseph's. Eleven days later, in a delicious bit of irony, Packer was courtside as CBS's analyst for the network's broadcast of the Hawks' NCAA Sweet 16 contest at the Meadowlands in East Rutherford, New Jersey. As if the subplot needed more fuel added to the fire, St. Joe's opponent was Packer's alma mater, Wake Forest.

"When we were going up there, I remember laughing and saying, 'Of course they would assign him to this regional,'" St. Joe's coach Phil Martelli said. "He had an opinion, I had an opinion, and I voiced my opinion."

Martelli's opinion drew national headlines when he said, "Billy Packer can kiss my ass." However, the coach was all smiles when he met up with Packer during St. Joe's practice at the Meadowlands on Wednesday, March 24, 2004, the day before the top-seeded Hawks faced off against No. 4-seeded Wake Forest. Packer was endorsing a frozen pizza company, and Martelli joked that he had helped increase the broadcaster's celebrity and advertising power.

"Yo, I really helped your career. Everybody in the country knows you. You now owe me," Martelli recalls of the conversation. "That was it."

Jim Nantz, CBS's lead broadcaster and Packer's longtime partner, also remembers the meeting as rather anticlimactic.

"I recall Billy and Coach Martelli shaking hands at practice," Nantz said. "It was all civilized and friendly."

The Packer versus Martelli story was an intriguing, amusing angle. But the Hawks had more important, more serious matters on which to focus.

Wake Forest was led by a freshman point guard who was as close in talent to Jameer Nelson as Martelli had seen in any player. He knew the Hawks would have their hands full trying to guard Chris Paul.

***

Paul was 42 days shy of his 19th birthday on March 25, 2004, when St. Joe's and Wake Forest met for a 9:57 p.m. tipoff. There was no doubt that he had already made his mark on the college game, as Paul would be named the Atlantic Coast Conference Rookie of the Year and tabbed by several national publications as the national freshman of the year after the season.[53]

"Phil said, 'Wait until you see this guard from Wake Forest; he's like Jameer,'" St. Joe's athletic director Don DiJulia said. "I said, 'Get out.'"

Paul, of course, would go on to become one of the greatest point guards in basketball history.

A certain Hall of Famer, Paul entered the 2024–25 NBA season, his 20th in the league, ranked second in both career assists and steals with 11,894 and 2,614, respectively. Only John Stockton and Jason Kidd were ahead of him in both categories. Paul has won two Olympic gold medals (2008 and 2012), made 12 NBA All-Star teams, and is a former MVP, Rookie of the Year, and nine-team selection to the NBA All-Defensive Team.

In 2003–04, Paul was a superbly talented freshman with lots of potential.

"If you would've said, 'Chris Paul is going to be this unbelievable NBA player,' I would've said, 'Yeah, maybe,'" Mike Skrocki, a senior guard at Richmond in 2003–04, said.

One thing was certain: The Hawks would be facing a player similar to the one they saw in practice every day.

Skrocki has the unique perspective of having matched up against both Paul and Nelson during the 2003–04 season. Paul had 17 points, eight assists, and five steals to help the Demon Deacons defeat Richmond 81-66 on December 6, 2003. Skrocki was impressed. Like Nelson, who had 32 points, six steals, and five rebounds in the Hawks' 71-60 win at Richmond on January 6, 2004, Paul did whatever his team needed him to do.

"They were both great point guards," Skrocki said. "Both had the uncanny ability to know when to score and when to defer to others. That's kind of an art a point guard has to have. I'm sure Chris Paul could have, and I know Jameer could because he did it to us, but they both can go off and score 30 every night if they want to. But it's not going to reflect in wins because they're going to lose some of their teammates, and teams are going to focus on them. They just had that ability to know, 'Here's where I have to go and score. Here's where I have to get so-and-so involved. Here's where I have to drive and kick.' They had a good way to manage the game, but also know when it's their turn to take over."

It's no surprise that Skrocki, as Martelli and many others would, noticed the on-court similarities between the players because Paul had patterned parts of his own game by watching Nelson while still in high school.

"I was a fan of Jameer," Paul said in an interview inside the Golden State Warriors' locker room before a game against the 76ers during the 2023–24 NBA season. "He was so strong and so smooth and change of direction and all that. I had just been watching him the year before."

Just like the Hawks' win over Texas Tech wasn't St. Joe's versus Bob Knight, this wouldn't be Jameer Nelson versus Chris Paul. It would be St. Joe's versus Wake Forest. But, still, everyone was looking forward to the highly anticipated showdown between the Hawks' stellar senior point guard and the Demon Deacons' freshman phenom point guard. In spite of its 29-1 record, there also were many who still doubted that St. Joe's could hang with an Atlantic Coast Conference team.

"Going into Wake Forest, understanding they were an ACC team, there were a lot of doubters," John Bryant said. "We were an unproven Atlantic 10 school going against the ACC and Chris Paul, who we knew was good. There were a lot of doubters that didn't think we were going to be able to beat them."

Everyone on the Hawks knew it would be a challenge.

"They had Chris Paul," Dwayne Jones said. "They also had a big guy that I had to match up against named Eric Williams. That was a tough battle for me. It was a tough matchup."

The Hawks weren't the only ones with great respect for their opponent entering the contest. Paul also knew it wouldn't be easy.

"Really good team," Paul said. "You could tell how connected they were. We knew that everybody had been talking about Jameer and Delonte."

While both teams were good, Martelli was supremely confident before tipoff. Thanks to Neil Hartman, Martelli's exact words have been preserved for history. Hartman, then a sportscaster for Comcast SportsNet, chronicled St. Joe's every move with inside access granted to him by Martelli for the popular series, *Hangin' with the Hawks*. Hartman showed Comcast SportsNet's viewers a behind-the-scenes look at St. Joe's, beginning with the Atlantic 10 tournament. Martelli allowed Hartman, cameraman Jerry Hines, and producer Matt Howley to go wherever the Hawks went.

"It was just such a magical time," Hartman said. "And it was not something a lot of people were doing. It was so unique."

For the NCAA tournament, due to the organization's restrictions, neither Hartman nor his crew could go into the locker room when it was off-limits to the media. So, a St. Joe's student team manager shot footage from inside the locker room and shared it with Comcast SportsNet. As shown on *Hangin' with the Hawks*, Martelli made sure to send St. Joe's out to the court with a final message that they were the best team taking the floor on this night.[54]

And the coach marveled at what he saw when the opening whistle blew—from both sides.

"My God, that game was really high-level," he said.

Both teams were playing well and making shots. Pat Carroll knew it was going to be a good night for him in the opening minutes.

"One of my first shots, it might have been a corner three, I remember Jameer flipped one back to me early on and I hit a deep three on the wing," Carroll said. "When that went in, it was like, 'Alright, you know what, I feel good. It's going to be a good night here. Alright, this is going to be a good one.'"

And it sure was for Carroll, as he would finish with 17 points while making five of seven shots from three-point range.

But the Demon Deacons had plenty of firepower of their own, including Justin Gray (23 points) and Williams (19 points). And, of course, Paul was running their show.

Everyone knew just who would be guarding Paul. And it didn't matter to Tyrone Barley how many accolades Wake Forest's sensational freshman had received.

"I remember this highly touted freshman that we were playing against," Barley said. "I didn't know him or anything, just the scouting report, that this guy is the real deal. But, to me, it didn't matter who the other person was. I felt like I'm going to play as hard as I can and try to make it as tough as possible."

Barley hounded Paul for every one of the 2,040 seconds the St. Joe's shutdown defender was on the court.

"I remember Tyrone just D'ing up, dogging Chris Paul the entire game," Carroll said. "And there was a moment where he turned his back to him, and he was guarding him backwards as Chris Paul was bringing the ball up the court. I'm like, 'What the hell is he doing?' But you knew Tyrone was in the zone. I'm sure [Paul] didn't see too many defenders like Tyrone. That memory definitely sticks out."

Barley always had prided himself on defense, even enjoying stopping opponents in All-Star games. He knew he wasn't going to score a ton of points, so he made it his mission to keep whomever he was guarding to fewer points than his own. When the final whistle blew and the points were tallied, the box score looked like this:

Barley, Tyrone, 13 points

Paul, Chris, 12 points

Paul had managed just six field goal attempts, making two. He did contribute eight assists. Meantime, Barley made four of six three-pointers.

Even with Barley's lockdown defense and Carroll's three-point shooting, St. Joe's would need everything it had to defeat the Demon Deacons, especially with Jones and Bryant battling foul trouble in the second half. Wake Forest cut into the Hawks' 10-point second-half advantage and made it a nail-biter in the final minute, in part because St. Joe's struggled at the free throw line all game (14 of 23, 60.9 percent). It wasn't until Chet Stachitas followed a Nelson miss on a running layup attempt with a putback layup with 33 seconds left that the realization that the Hawks would be advancing to the Elite Eight became apparent.

The final score was St. Joe's 84, Wake Forest 80.

"To score that many points and to need to score that many points was sensational," Martelli said.

The Hawks had proven to Packer and to everyone else that they belonged with the big boys. Nantz remembers Packer calling a fair game and praising St. Joe's afterward.

"Of course, Billy helped take Wake Forest to the Final Four 40 years earlier. Not that you could ever detect the slightest hint of favoritism in any of his calls," Nantz said. "The fans always thought he had favorites. But he truly never did. North Carolina fans didn't like him because they thought he was pro-Duke. Duke fans thought he was pro-Carolina. Wake Forest thought he should be kinder on the air to his own university. And then nationally everyone believed he was on the take for the ACC. None of these were true. But when St. Joe's beat the Demon Deacons, I thought Billy's respect for the Hawks went way up."

St. Joe's showed they also could contend with a future superstar.

"They beat Chris Paul, and it was not an upset," said Mike Jensen of the *Philadelphia Inquirer*. "It wasn't the Chris Paul that came to be an NBA All-Star, but he was really good."

So were West and Nelson. Each scored 24 points and had strong all-around games. Nelson added seven assists, three rebounds, and three steals, becoming the school's all-time steals leader by passing Jeffrey Clark's career mark of 250. West contributed four rebounds and three assists. Both played all 40 minutes.

"That was a great matchup," St. Joe's assistant Mark Bass said. "Chris Paul had all of the hype. He was a great guard. It came down to the end, and we were fortunate to pull it out."

Though disappointed with the defeat, Paul had fond memories of the game and playing in the Sweet 16 when he looked back more than 20 years later.

"I used to talk about it to Jameer every now and then when we became competitors in the league," Paul said. "That's something I'll never forget. Nothing like it. The energy behind it, the way the school got behind us. It was an amazing time, and I'm forever grateful for those memories."

While Paul and the Demon Deacons were headed home, St. Joe's was eager to make more memories. Up next would be Oklahoma State, which had defeated Pitt 63-51 in the earlier game on Thursday night. Playing in the late game meant that Martelli, with Hartman trying to stay awake nearby, would be up all night preparing for the tough, physical Cowboys. Now was no time to sleep. A trip to the Final Four was on the line.

CHAPTER 38

Game 32: A Shot at the Final Four

Saturday, March 27, 2004
Meadowlands, East Rutherford, New Jersey
NCAA Elite Eight: No. 1 Saint Joseph's vs. No. 2 Oklahoma State

Saint Joseph's players exited the court in pure exhilaration after defeating Chris Paul and Wake Forest to advance to the NCAA Elite Eight. But the Hawks would have practically zero time to celebrate the victory. Because St. Joe's played the second game of Thursday night's doubleheader, the contest didn't end until after midnight. The Hawks returned to their hotel at 1:40 in the morning and shuffled off to bed shortly after Phil Martelli addressed them at 2:30 a.m.

Martelli had only briefly glimpsed at their next opponent, second-seeded Oklahoma State, which defeated Pitt 63-51 in the opening game on Thursday night. But the Hawks coach sent his players to bed with a message that the Cowboys were the toughest opponent he'd seen in two years.[55] While his players were trying to catch up on sleep, Martelli's night was just beginning; he headed to a conference room to start his film study of Oklahoma State. Assistants Mark Bass, Matt Brady, and Monté Ross also were there. In addition, Dick Jerardi of the *Philadelphia Daily News*, and Neil Hartman, cameraman Jerry Hines, and producer Matt Howley of *Hangin' with the Hawks* were in the room, too, trying to stay awake to chronicle this part of the current No. 1 sports story in Philadelphia and all of college basketball.

The fact that Martelli invited reporters into an all-night film session before an NCAA Elite Eight game tells you everything you need to know about how accommodating he was to the media. However, Hartman sensed that this was a rare time where the coach needed some distance. Certainly, a lack of sleep could have caused irritability, but it also was what Martelli saw on film that had him on edge.

"It wasn't just that they were good, it was their physical nature," Martelli said. "And this was the team that could get us. They had size and physicality like Rhode Island and Xavier and another level up. Our guys didn't look like their guys, so we had to play our skill game."

"It was a bad kind of matchup," Jerardi said. "You'd rather have a team that wants to run up and down the court."

As the hours ticked by and the morning sunlight began to shine through, everyone was exhausted. But Hartman noticed a sense of calm starting to return to the affable Martelli.

"This is the fascinating part, overnight he started getting more at ease because he realized, 'We can play with these guys. We can beat these guys,'" Hartman said. "And the one thing I felt Phil is so good at is making players believe. He would do that really well. And the players had a sense of confidence because of Phil's confidence."

Martelli knew it wouldn't be easy, but he was convinced the Hawks could win if they imposed their style on Oklahoma State and not the other way around. He took a one-hour nap at 8:15 on Friday morning, and then spent two hours developing a game plan. At 11:30 a.m., Martelli met with the players for 45 minutes to review film and reveal the plan. He stressed to the Hawks the need to play their game and made the Cowboys' physicality clear.[56]

"They were on a different weightlifting program than we were," Chet Stachitas joked.

Following the film session, the Hawks did not return to their rooms for a nap; rather, they boarded a bus for the Meadowlands. St. Joe's arrived back at the arena about 12 hours after leaving it, this time for press conferences and a public practice session. When finished, the Hawks headed to the New Jersey Nets' facility, where they would conduct an actual practice, as the NCAA-mandated one was more of a made-for-cameras event.

Hindsight is always 20/20, but Martelli would not have sent his players on the court at the Meadowlands if he had a do-over, saving their legs and energy for his late-afternoon practice and the following evening's game.

"Retrospectively, I wish I would've done a pause," he said. "Do the interviews, but we won't take our practice time."

Jerardi, who had his finger on the pulse of the Hawks all season, sensed a fatigue starting to overtake St. Joe's.

"You could see it maybe the last eight games or so, it was starting to wear on them," he said. "When you're playing all of those guard minutes, which is what they were, they are harder minutes than big man minutes and you wear out a little bit."

And playing the second game on Thursday, he said, didn't help matters.

"It was brutal," Jerardi said. "I stayed up the whole night watching tape with Phil and the coaches. I was exhausted, and I wasn't playing any basketball. To me, the No. 1 seed should have the preference of the early game. They still don't do this. TV decides all that stuff. I knew from covering Final Fours that the team that plays the early game [in the semifinals] has an advantage. No question."

The good news for St. Joe's was tipoff time was 7:05 p.m. on Saturday, March 27, 2004. So, the Hawks would have some time to put their legs up before playing for a spot in the Final Four.

The Final Four? Marie Wozniak couldn't believe it. The magnitude of that possibility finally hit St. Joe's sports information director when she stepped foot on the court many hours before tipoff on Saturday.

"There was hardly anyone around, and I was just kind of looking around the arena and all of a sudden it hit me, 'Holy crap, we could be going to the Final Four,'" Wozniak said. "It just overtook me for a second."

Hours later, inside the Hawks' locker room, as viewers would eventually see on *Hangin' with the Hawks*, Martelli imbued his players with a level of confidence that had them thinking there was no way they could lose.[57] No matter the size and strength of Oklahoma State, St. Joe's would play its game. The Hawks planned to impose their will on the brawny Cowboys.

***

However, the game did not start as the Hawks wanted. Nelson's opening jumper, a three-point attempt, was on target but short. The Hawks would miss their next three shots and found themselves in an early hole.

Maybe the critics were right. Maybe the Hawks couldn't match up with the likes of Joey Graham, a chiseled 6-foot-7, 225-pound forward; or Ivan McFarlin, a menacing 6-foot-8, 240-pound center; or Tony Allen, a gifted 6-foot-4, 213-pound wing; or the athletic John Lucas III, at 5-foot-11 more comparable in size to the Hawks but also tremendously talented. All four players would go on to NBA careers. McFarlin would have a brief stint in the league; Lucas and Graham would combine for 619 games; and Allen would have a standout pro career, making the NBA All-Defensive Team in six of his 14 seasons and winning a title with the Celtics in 2008.

Maybe those four were just too strong and too good. Or maybe not.

***

Dwayne Jones's dunk on a brilliant pass from Delonte West finally got St. Joe's on the board after going the first 3:41 without a point. Then, the Hawks started showing everyone the type of basketball that led them to an undefeated regular season and made them the biggest story in the sport in 2003–04. The ball moved from one player's hands to another with speed and fluidity until finding the player who had the best shot. Jameer Nelson was getting wherever he wanted on the floor, finding teammates, stepping back for shots, and carving up the Cowboys. Billy Packer, the Hawks' biggest critic on Selection Sunday, suddenly was their biggest fan. To his credit, Packer held nothing back in his praise of St. Joe's. After Nelson drew three defenders on a drive and perfectly set up West for a wide-open three-pointer with a deft pass, Packer told television viewers that Nelson had as good of a basketball IQ as any player he'd seen in a long time.

And then there was St. Joe's defense. The Hawks made the big, strong Cowboys look like a grade-school team at times, torturing them with pressure defense that caused one turnover after another. And it only turned up infinite notches when Tyrone Barley entered the contest for the first time with 13:50 left in the half. Shortly after, Barley got right up in Allen's face, captured wonderfully by CBS's cameras. It was the second straight possession of Oklahoma State turnovers, both caused by Barley, first when he came from the weak side to take a charge and then when his pressure defense frustrated Allen into throwing the ball away. Packer and CBS lead announcer Jim Nantz marveled at Barley's defense, with the analyst saying St. Joe's guard had gotten into the Cowboys' heads.

The outsized, outmuscled Hawks were manhandling Oklahoma State. They scored their final points of the half on an unbelievable play by Nelson, who stole a pass at midcourt and blindly—except, apparently, to him—threw the ball over his shoulder perfectly into the hands of Barley for an easy layup. It had been absolute dominance by the Hawks. They forced nine Cowboys turnovers that led to 16 points while committing just two turnovers themselves. The Cowboys' size and strength advantage did not materialize, as Oklahoma State grabbed just four offensive rebounds to St. Joe's one. The Cowboys, hounded by Hawks perimeter defenders, missed all eight of their three-point tries.

And, yet, when the teams entered the locker room, the scoreboard said only this: Saint Joseph's 33, Oklahoma State 27.

***

St. Joe's had taken its unique style to Oklahoma State in dominant fashion. But the Hawks were just not making the shots they normally would drain from the outside and led by only six points because they missed 13 of 16 tries from long range. One of the misses was a block by Allen, but most were open shots that St. Joe's just didn't convert. Nelson's first try was right on target but short, a sign of things to come. The Hawks star was one for five from long range in the opening half, and three of the misses were right on target but short, giving credence to the notion of tired legs. But Pat Carroll's shots were not short. His beautiful lefty stroke looked as flawless as ever but somehow most of his tries would not fall. Carroll missed five of six from beyond the arc in the opening 20 minutes, and three of those shots improbably went in and rimmed out.

In spite of shooting 18.8 percent from the arc, St. Joe's was in complete control of the game. The Hawks would just need to play another 20 minutes like this and, by law of averages with a few more shots falling, they would be headed to San Antonio for the Final Four.

There was no overconfidence, but there was nothing about the first half that made any Hawks supporters think that they couldn't beat Oklahoma State.

"Don [DiJulia] gave me a look of both amazement and terror all at once," Joe Lunardi said of their halftime meetup. "I'm like, 'Can you believe it? Maybe 20 more minutes?' He's like, 'How do we airlift the whole Fieldhouse to San Antonio if it happens?'"

Martelli, as viewers would later see on Comcast SportsNet, was not focused on the missed shots when he addressed St. Joe's in the halftime locker room. He praised the Hawks for how everyone contributed in the opening half and encouraged each one to focus on making a small contribution that would lead to bigger things.[58] St. Joe's just needed to keep doing what it was doing.

But the Hawks couldn't continue their outstanding play at the outset of the second half.

***

St. Joe's added carelessness on offense to its continued misfiring. Oklahoma State, meantime, finally started to take advantage of the size mismatch. The Hawks opened the second half with two turnovers and three missed field goals on their first five possessions, and the Cowboys erased their halftime deficit with an 8-0 run that made it 35-33 OSU. Nelson finally ended the drought with a layup that tied that game at 35. But Carroll hit the back iron on a three, Nelson missed a layup and then another, and West was short on a jumper.

When Graham drained a short baseline jumper from the right side, it was 41-35 OSU with 15:05 left. The Cowboys had scored 14 of 16 points to start the second half, making six of eight field goals and both of their two three-point tries. St. Joe's was one of eight overall from the field and zero of two from the arc. But the Hawks still had hope, especially with Barley about to enter the contest for the first time in the second half. He checked in with 14:53 remaining after West converted the first of two made free throws, the second of which made it 41-37. Almost immediately after Barley's return, the Hawks got their mojo back.

***

Nelson and West nailed consecutive three-pointers to draw St. Joe's even at 43 with 12:43 left, and the partisan St. Joe's crowd erupted. From there, it was just a back-and-forth duel between two teams giving all they had.

There was Graham throwing down an emphatic dunk for a three-point play. There was Nelson answering with a between-the-legs dribbling sequence followed by a step-back three-pointer that would leave basketball purists grasping for superlatives. There was Lucas showing moxie and fortitude to overcome a hellish start by finding his long and midrange game. There was Carroll having the mental strength and courage to push aside any thoughts of the eight misses—five of which, inconceivably, went in and out—in his first nine three-point tries to bury a game-tying long-range shot from the left wing with a defender right in his face after a breathtaking skip pass across the court from Nelson. There was West orchestrating a Tchaikovsky-like spin move that was a work of art, like his jaw-dropping charcoal of Martelli, uncanny watercolor replica of Georgia O'Keeffe, or the untold pencil drawings in his sketchbook, and finishing with a perfect fadeaway jumper in the corner just like he'd practiced in countless solo midnight sessions at the Fieldhouse. There was Graham, again, somehow muscling past three Hawks defenders for a layup that tied the contest.

Back and forth they went, like two boxers trading haymakers, giving all of their hearts and souls and every ounce of their fibers into the effort. It was beautiful to watch, if not easy for either team's supporters. The game was tied at 59 heading into the final minute. Everyone was on edge. It was anyone's game now. Neither team was wilting. Then, Lucas got free for a 13-foot fadeaway that put the Cowboys ahead 61-59 with 41.9 seconds to play.

***

Nelson hustled up the court. When Carroll set a high screen, both defenders converged on Nelson leaving Carroll wide open. Nelson tossed him the ball. There were just over 30 seconds on the clock. The Hawks were down by two points. Carroll had been in a similar situation in the NCAA tournament. A year earlier, in the seventh-seeded Hawks' 65-63 overtime loss to No. 10 Auburn in the first round, Carroll not only missed a potential game-winning three-pointer with 2.6 seconds left but shot an airball.

This attempt would be from the exact same spot on the floor, and Carroll was ready for it.

"It's the shot you dream of at the park or in your driveway," Carroll said of the Auburn miss. "You count down '3-2-1,' and I airballed that shot in my first, and thinking at the moment, maybe my only NCAA game of my life. It doesn't get any lower than that as a player. But having that mindset that I knew if I ever had that opportunity again, I wanted to take that shot. I was going to embrace it. I've already been at the bottom. I can't get any worse than airballing a buzzer shot in the NCAA tournament. So, there is only one way to go: up."

Carroll's mindset and preparation paid off, as he swished the three-pointer this time to give the Hawks a 62-61 lead with 29.9 seconds left. Bass, who had spent innumerable hours sharing his secrets to help Carroll learn how to find openings to shoot, as well as rebounding for him and providing positive reinforcement, proudly watched from the bench.

"It was just like all of the hard work paid off for that moment," Bass said. "That's what you geared yourself up for. That's what we prepared for. He was ready for the moment. It goes to the growth of the person of missing that [Auburn] shot and having the heart to take that [Oklahoma State] shot without thinking about it and not going back to say, 'I missed this shot a year ago.' But saying, 'That's in the past. I'm not worrying about that. I practiced this shot. This is my shot. I know if I get another opportunity, I'm going to take it and make it.' And that's what he did."

Carroll's three-pointer sent the crowd into an absolute frenzy. Oklahoma State was without any timeouts. St. Joe's was ahead by a point and one defensive stop away from going to the Final Four.

"It flashed in my head for"—Martelli snapped his fingers—"that long that we're going to the Final Four," Martelli said.

The coach quickly had to turn his focus back to defense, but Hawks fans let the thought linger longer.

"When he hits that shot, people were like, 'Oh my God!'" said Brendan Prunty, who was among those in a frenzy in the crowd. "We knew it, but nobody allowed themselves to think we're going to the Final Four [until then]. There was a shock like, 'Woah, we're going to do this!'"

Joe Cabrey had been to every Hawks game that season and was looking forward to continuing the joyride.

"It was like, 'Alright, we're about to go to San Antonio,'" he said.

Bill Avington was trying to do a quick mileage calculation in his head.

"I remember thinking, 'How am I going to get to San Antonio? How long of a drive is it?'" Avington said.

But the Cowboys still had one more possession. What would transpire next still is unbelievable watching it today.

***

Lucas dribbled the ball upcourt guarded by Barley. Carroll was marking Graham. When Graham set a high screen, they switched. But Lucas, with Carroll now guarding him, retreated all the way back to the center circle. Time was wasting away. Lucas took five left-handed dribbles to the left wing. Then, with 13.3 seconds left, Lucas surprisingly passed it back to Graham, neither a ball handler nor a shooter, who was now nearly 30 feet from the basket. As Graham tried to dribble, he slipped and lost control of the ball. Carroll, seeing this, left Lucas and instinctively dived forward for the loose ball. He came within a fingertip of a steal that likely would've ended the game, but Graham grabbed the ball.

Now, an open Lucas shifted two sidesaddle steps to his left, got into a shooting position, and accepted the pass from Graham. Barley sprinted over to contest the three-point attempt and lunged forward, his left hand just inches away from the ball. But Lucas somehow got the shot off. He had missed nine of 11 tries from three-point range to that point. None of those would matter. This one went off the back iron and rolled smoothly through hoop. A three-pointer. It was good. The Cowboys led 64-62. It was a stunning turn of events.

"The whole thing was crazy," Jerardi said. "They had no timeouts. They had no idea what was going on. They were in total panic mode. It was just really, really unlucky."

It is almost inconceivable that the play was a success for the Cowboys.

First, the loose ball had to elude a diving Carroll.

"It was just an immediate reaction," Carroll said. "I saw the ball and it was like, 'If I tip the ball, we're going to the Final Four.' There was no thought. It was just an instant reaction. Looking back on it, I'm like, 'Shit, if I just stayed back and played defense, maybe it would've been a different result.'"

Carroll had repeated something similar after the game, but two things ring true: First, there's no telling what would've happened if he stayed with Lucas. The Cowboys still could have scored. Second, his coaches believe it was the right play.

"I saw exactly what Pat was going to do," Martelli said. "It was going to be one of the most extraordinary plays in that whole year. He was going to push the ball down the floor and the clock was going to run out. He couldn't get his hand there. It was the right play. I never even thought about he didn't make the right play."

"That's what you're taught all your life," Bass said. "That ball is on the floor. I'm going to get that loose ball. He's just a fingernail away."

After the near steal, there still was the near block by Barley. It's hard to believe, based on replays, that the ball didn't connect with the fingers of Barley's left hand.

"I mean, I jumped my highest," Barley said. "I put every ounce of effort into it. I really did put it all in that jump, and I tried to stretch out as far as I can. People say it was close."

After the near steal and the near block, the ball still needed to go in. To his credit, Lucas had recovered from a horrid start in which he was shaky with the ball and badly misfiring from the outside to play a second half that was much more indicative of his talent. Still, no one would've been surprised, based on his game that day, if the shot was off. It wasn't.

"It was a clutch shot," Barley said.

***

The game wasn't over, though. The Hawks had time. And they had Jameer Nelson.

Nelson caught the inbounds pass from Carroll underneath Saint Joseph's basket in stride and ready to sprint up the court. There were precious 6.9 seconds showing on the game clock.

Nelson shot a quick glance toward the Hawks bench. Martelli never thought for even a second to call timeout. Carroll's pass, like the go-ahead three-point shot he had just drained from the top of the key exactly 23 seconds earlier, was perfect. Nelson caught it at head level and burst toward half-court with one left dribble, then another left dribble, and then one with his right hand.

Now, 5.0 seconds showed on the clock.

Nelson broke past midcourt, dribbled hard to his left once and then again. Now, a mere 3.9 seconds showed on the clock with Nelson at the three-point line. Carroll was to Nelson's right and a bit behind him, ready and willing to shoot. Barley was farther to the right, West way to the left, Jones in the middle. All had scored key buckets that season and could again.

Really, though, there was never a doubt that this would be Nelson's shot.

Oklahoma State's Daniel Bobik had the unenviable task of guarding Nelson. At 6-foot-6, Bobik had seven inches on Nelson. Bobik braced himself for Nelson's speed and retreated, but, paying due respect to his outside game, also stayed close enough to contest a jump shot. Nelson thought about trying a game-winning three-pointer but instead drove hard toward the foul line, forcing Bobik to his heels.

Now, 2.8 seconds showed on the clock.

Bobik had to know he was in deep trouble. Seeing that Nelson was not going to continue his forward motion toward the basket, Bobik moved from his heels to his toes. It was too late.

Nelson, settling on a game-tying two-point attempt, stopped on a dime, drove his right foot hard into the hardwood, sprang off of both feet high into the air, fading just so slightly backward, and cupped his right wrist on the ball ready to launch. Bobik lunged with his left hand and forced every single inch of his 6-foot-6 frame toward the ball. But he couldn't reach it.

Nelson had broken free from yet another defender yet again.

It was Nelson's time to make a little more magic. He released a high-arcing shot. It was from 18 feet away. Everything went quiet. Everyone stopped. Everyone held their breaths. And looked up at the basket.

The ball was right on line. But, just like his first shot of the game, it was short. Final: Oklahoma State 64, St. Joe's 62.

With Cowboys celebrating joyously behind him and television cameras racing toward him, Nelson collapsed to the floor, lay on his back, then sat up, dejectedly resting both arms on his knees, clasping his left fingers over his right fingers, and stared out into nowhere in complete disbelief. The Hawks' dream of a Final Four had ended. Their incredible, inspiring season was over, leaving immense hurt for what they didn't accomplish and immense hope for all that they did.

CHAPTER 39

Hurt and Hope

With Oklahoma State celebrating wildly in the background, Jameer Nelson slowly rose to his feet, his head staring down at the floor, both hands planted on his knees. Phil Martelli placed his left arm around Nelson's back, and the two men who will be forever linked quietly headed to the Hawks' locker room. The hurt was deep. The emotions were raw.

The Hawks never believed they could lose. Now, their season was over. More painfully, their magical ride together as teammates in the 2003–04 season had come to an abrupt end.

"Losing wasn't even in our thought process," Tyrone Barley said. "So much weight fell on us because we never thought it was possible. We play hard, we play our own brand, we thought we could beat anybody."

All season long, it had been about the next game. And, now, there wouldn't be another game.

For maybe the only time in his career, Martelli restricted media access afterward. Neil Hartman and his *Hangin' with the Hawks* crew were not permitted in the locker room for a behind-the-scenes look. Martelli kept the doors closed to everyone until he felt his players were emotionally ready to handle interviews. Even when the locker room finally opened, the hurt was palpable.

"I've been in empty rooms that made more noise than that locker room," said Mike Jensen, who covered the game for the *Philadelphia Inquirer*.

"Just the hurt, man," Mark Bass said of the reaction to the defeat. "It hurt to the point where you cry in the locker room. You cry when you get back to the hotel. It really was painful."

The agonizing feeling of the locker room was experienced everywhere in the arena, on St. Joe's campus, and throughout the city of Philadelphia. Grown men and women were in tears, and others were doing everything they could do to hold them back.

David Leach, St. Joe's director of recreation turned security detail for Nelson, couldn't restrain his emotions.

"I just remember standing outside of the locker room and being a grown dad of two young girls dripping tears after the game," he said. "It was an emotional roller coaster."

Trip McClatchy, a 1979 graduate who today won't relocate in retirement because it would take him away from attending Hawks games, had the same experience in the stands.

"There were tears in my eyes," McClatchy said. "My son was seven and said it was the first time he ever saw me cry. We drove home from the Meadowlands, and I did not speak the entire drive. I didn't utter a word. I was just devastated."

Linda Bruno didn't cry, but it took everything the Atlantic 10 commissioner had to hold tears in.

"If you're in the business long enough, especially at the conference level, you're programmed to be very stoic," Bruno said. "I had to get myself together really quick. [A-10 public relations director] Ray Cella was sitting next to me and goes, 'Don't you dare cry.'"

St. Joe's sports information director Marie Wozniak understood Bruno's predicament.

"I try not to let losses affect me. A person in my job shouldn't," Wozniak said. "I was not crying, but it was genuinely the saddest I've ever been after a game because I knew what it would have meant to the school, to the program, and everything. Just to see the guys crying broke my heart."

Tom McCarthy, the Hawks' first-year radio play-by-play announcer, had to console his then-young children, Patrick and Tommy, on the way home.

"They were so vested in it," McCarthy said. "They cried the whole time home. For me, it was a game. It was important, obviously. For them, it was their whole year. Their responses stood out to me."

Brendan Prunty and his "Wild, Wild West" student fan club didn't cry. They were just stunned. Too stunned even to speak.

"I never felt sicker," Prunty said. "No, that didn't just happen. We were going to the Final Four. We were going to San Antonio. It's 96 minutes from the Meadowlands to campus. No one said a word. When we pulled into Flanagan Hall, everyone was like, 'Alright, see ya.'"

Andy Schwartz, the young reporter covering the team for Comcast SportsNet, could relate.

"When it was over, it was a gut punch," he said. "I still remember driving home and being like, 'It sucks.' And turning into a fan when you're not supposed to because you can't help it."

Ray Parrillo, the Hawks' beat writer for the *Philadelphia Inquirer* who had chronicled them every step of the way, closed his laptop after filing his wrap-up story and was met by grief.

"I just sat there and thought, 'It's not going to get any better for me in this job,'" Parrillo said. "It was depressing in the sense that I'm never going to have it this good the rest of my career, and I never did. It was a great job, but I never covered anything that was as fun."

Andy Katz, covering the game for ESPN, had empathy when he noticed Martelli and his wife, Judy, huddled in a side room afterward.

"You knew at that moment that this might be the only time in his career that he would be this close to a Final Four," Katz said. "I remember feeling so bad for him because the chances of something like this are so slim at a school like St. Joe's. And it was right there, literally right there."

It had all happened so suddenly.

"It was just like within seconds, the game was lost and the magic was over," Father Timothy Lannon, St. Joe's president, said.

"In a second, you went from the pinnacle of joy to the feeling of being gutted, just absolutely gutted," said Chuck Sack, St. Joe's academic advisor in 2003–04. "You're sitting in silence. Here was this tangible, joyful identity that is still alive and full of magic and then to have it just fall short or ripped out of your hands. You're stunned."

Sack joined hundreds of St. Joe's supporters back at the team hotel. There, fans greeted the players by changing the words of the "LET'S! GO! SAINT! JOE'S!" chant to "THANK! YOU! SAINT! JOE'S!"

"You fluctuated on a continuum of deep, deep pain and deep reverence for what you just experienced," Sack said.

"It was just incredible," Joe Cabrey, who attended every Hawks game in the 2003–04 season, said of the support at the hotel. "For a second, it didn't matter that they lost. We just had something really special and might not ever see it again."

Phil Denne, Wozniak's assistant, had pumped his fist under the press row table after Pat Carroll's late, three-point shot. Like everyone else affiliated with St. Joe's, Denne was disappointed but had an appreciation for what he'd witnessed in that game and all season.

"You're just right there," Denne said. "Nothing you can do. It wasn't a bad call. Sometimes that's just the way it goes. It's a bummer, but it was the biggest thrill of my professional career to be part of that experience all the way through. It was not to be. But it was a great ride and great people."

The players left the hotel the night of the game, electing to return to Philadelphia as soon as possible. Martelli woke up on Sunday morning and attended Mass, where he was greeted by people in tears.

"If you're sad that it's over, it must've been really cool when it was happening," Martelli said.

Indeed, it had been a special season and a special team.

***

From the first day of practice, the players bonded in a way that could be felt but is hard to describe.

"When your energy comes together with other people's energy and you form a bond like that, it creates something amazing," Brian Jesiolowski, the senior walk-on, said. "It's chemistry. When people have that chemistry, it creates amazing things. It can get you further than skill and talent ever could in some instances. It's wild."

"It was the right group of people, and the personalities were right," Dave Mallon said. "It's something that's tough to describe. It was a feeling you got all year long. We have a good group to do something here."

The players' togetherness was apparent to everyone who watched them play.

"When they stepped on the court, they all had fun together and it exuded through the entire community," said Alicia Lange, who was St. Joe's coordinator of academic services for student-athletes. "They just liked each other. They just liked playing with each other."

"It was the perfect mix of talent, experience, heart, guts, and just that 'it' factor that every winning team needs," Schwartz said.

"They had a culture centered around being willing to work hard and centered around love," Sack said. "I think that was their magic ingredient, that they all loved each other."

There also was a deep belief in themselves.

"They knew how to win," said Lynn Greer, the former Temple guard and Nelson's good friend. "They weren't scared of anyone. They just had a tough group that really played together."

The Hawks inspired people in a tangible and spiritual way.

"They brought so much joy to people here at St. Joe's and in many, many places around the country," athletic director Don DiJulia said. "People became fans because of the way they played and how they carried themselves. I've met total strangers, and when I say I'm from Saint Joseph's University, they'll say, 'Jameer.'"

Lannon said the players embodied what Saint Joseph's is all about.

"All that we have are gifts from God," he said. "I think our players and coaches really understood that. And I think the spirit of the men helped upgrade the spirit of the university. I think St. Joe's students and alums and all of us that work there just try a little harder to make it a better place. Companies would say we want to hire St. Joe's grads because there is something special about them. I think that something special is that we can hold our own against anybody as our team did."

***

The Hawks had proven they could compete with Oklahoma State, but the loss remains difficult today. It would be 10 years before Nelson watched the game. Martelli has chosen never to watch it.

Clearly, St. Joe's proved it belonged. The game could've gone either way. After a nervy start, the Hawks dominated the final 14 minutes of the first half. The Cowboys dominated the first five minutes of the second half. From there, it was an even match. Many believe the Hawks were the better team. Dick Jerardi thinks that if they met 10 times, the Hawks would have won eight. At the very least, everyone likely would agree that either team could have won and that both were worthy of reaching the Final Four.

Much of the pain for the Hawks and their supporters lies in the unknown, of what might have been, what could have been. St. Joe's would have met Georgia Tech in the national semifinals. A win over the Yellow Jackets would've set up a matchup versus eventual national champion Connecticut, which was led by future NBA standouts Emeka Okafor and Ben Gordon. Certainly, it is reasonable to believe the Hawks would have been competitive. Maybe they would have defeated Georgia Tech. Maybe they even would have beaten UConn, cut down the nets, and hung a national championship banner in the Fieldhouse.

Or maybe not.

Maybe the Hawks shooters would have struggled from long range in the cavernous Alamodome, where the Final Four was held. Maybe St. Joe's would have gotten blown out by Georgia Tech. Sadly for everyone involved with the program and the school, the reality is that St. Joe's didn't reach the Final Four. It just wasn't meant to be.

And that's OK.

"It can't take away what that team meant to me," John Bryant said. "I'd take the relationships that we had over the championship that we could have won. I'm not sure a championship would've made our bonds better, would've made the friendships stronger, would've made Coach a better coach, or would've made Jameer, Delonte, DJ, Dwayne, Chet, Pat, or Dave better professionals."

"We didn't get there, we didn't take that next step, but it doesn't take away what we were able to accomplish that year," Mallon said. "From the very first meeting that year, follow your role and we would be successful. It was absolutely right. It's tough to be hard on yourself when you put so much blood, sweat, and equity into it. We came up short. It happens."

When the Hawks got back to campus after the Oklahoma State game, Martelli gathered the players for one final time in the tiny Fieldhouse locker room.

"He said, 'You guys don't understand what you've done because you're in it right now, but you will understand how big of a deal it is and what you just accomplished,'" Mallon said. "And he was exactly right."

***

Throughout their lives since 2003–04, the coaches and players have encountered people who were struck by *that* team.

Fellow pro competitors overseas would recognize Mallon's name.

"'Yo, you were on *that* team,'" Mallon recalled of the conversations. "It was a huge pride that I was on that team and contributed. It was a really cool feeling. As I got into the professional [business] world, obviously I'm 6-foot-10 and stand out a little bit, the first question is, 'Did you play basketball?' When I say I played at St. Joe's, they say, 'Oh, were you on *that* team?' It always comes back to that

206 • A SOARING SEASON

team. It's such a cool feeling to be able to say, 'Yeah, I was on that team.' It's been really exciting throughout every stage of my life. I still run into people all over the country and can be in any city or state for a meeting and someone will say, 'Oh, *that* team?!' So, it's been exciting."

Pat Carroll has the same experience on a regular basis.

"I can be unassuming sometimes and blend into the crowd," Carroll said. "Sometimes, they'll recognize me and say, 'Oh, you're Pat Carroll.' If I'm meeting new people and I just say that I went to St. Joe's, they're like, 'Do you remember *that* team?' I say, 'Yeah, I was on that team.' They're like, 'You were on *that* team?!' It's probably the best conversation starter ever."

Martelli, along with Nelson the most recognizable member of the 2003–04 Hawks, hears from people all the time about *that* team. Ironically, on his way to a 20-year reunion to celebrate the 2003–04 Hawks, Martelli was stopped in an airport by a youth basketball coach who just wanted to say how much he appreciated watching *that* team play.

"I said, 'Thank you, that's a message from above that this weekend is going to be great,'" Martelli said.

So, what exactly is it about the 2003–04 Hawks? Why did they resonate with so many people, then and today? Why did they move people to tears?

***

In 2003–04, Saint Joseph's went 27-0 in the regular season. The Hawks rose to the unanimous No. 1 ranking in the country. They came within a three-pointer made after a broken play of reaching the Final Four. And they did it while playing in a gym tinier than those of many high schools, with a budget smaller than those of the competition to which they were compared, with players who were underrecruited, with a head coach who didn't get a chance until he was almost 41 years old, and with so many obstacles and odds against them.

But they had an unbreakable spirit, a mascot who wouldn't stop flapping, and a mantra that *The Hawk Will Never Die*.

So, maybe what moved people to tears is that they could relate. People were inspired by the Hawks. They provided hope for others then and still do today.

The 2003–04 Hawks showed that with belief in one's self, teamwork, hard work, strong leadership, and everyone pushing toward a singular goal while setting their own personal interests aside, human beings can overcome seemingly insurmountable odds, something that can be applied to all aspects of life and not just basketball. It's true that the Hawks did not reach the Final Four in the 2003–04 season. They did not win a national title, cut down the nets in San Antonio, or raise an NCAA banner to the roof of the Fieldhouse. It's also true that the 2003–04 Hawks didn't need a trophy to show everyone exactly what it means to be a champion.

Success, Disappointment, and Tragedy

On Sunday, September 3, 2023, members of the 2003–04 Saint Joseph's Hawks gathered at Llanerch Country Club in Havertown, Pennsylvania, for a 20-year reunion. Phil Martelli organized the get-together, inviting each player and coach to record a 90-second video to commemorate the anniversary. Some were poignant, some were funny, all were meaningful.

It was the first time that such a celebration occurred to honor the greatest team in Saint Joseph's history. Later, many players from the team would reunite again to be recognized prior to a Hawks home game against George Washington on February 21, 2024.

There were smiles, hugs, and tears of joy at the events but also sadness. Delonte West was not present at either gathering. Neither Martelli nor Jameer Nelson were there in February at Saint Joseph's, though Martelli sent a message to his players that was read by his longtime secretary, Clare Ariano, after a commemorative video was shown in a private event before the on-court recognition.

The Hawks had captivated the country in 2003–04, going 27-0 in the regular season, rising to the No. 1 ranking in both the Associated Press Top 25 and *USA Today*/Coaches Poll. They earned the No. 1 seed in the NCAA tournament and finished with a 30-2 record, losing a heartbreaker to second-seeded Oklahoma State on a three-pointer in the final seconds off of a broken play. They had overcome many doubters and long odds to come within a whisker of reaching the Final Four. They had inspired countless people on campus, in Philadelphia, and around the country. The season did not end with a national championship trophy, but it had been a resounding success.

In the years since, success has continued to follow many members of the team. There also has been disappointment and tragedy. Here is a glimpse at them since the magical 2003–04 season.

Phil Martelli

Martelli would lead the Hawks back to three more NCAA tournaments (2008, 2014, 2016) but was fired on March 19, 2019. It was an acrimonious parting that came one year after Don DiJulia's retirement as athletic director and has resulted in the severing of ties between Martelli and the school. Martelli is St. Joe's all-time leader in career coaching victories, leaving with a 444-328 (.575) record in 24 years at the helm. He led the Hawks to seven NCAA appearances, three Atlantic 10 tournament titles (1997, 2014, 2016), and was named the league's Coach of the Year four times (1997, 2001, 2004, 2005). Martelli was honored as the National Coach of the Year in 2004 after directing the Hawks to a school-record 30 victories. He joined Juwan Howard's staff at Michigan in 2019, serving as an assistant coach for five seasons. Martelli got back to the Elite Eight in 2021 but fell just short of his first Final Four again when UCLA defeated Michigan 51-49. He got to coach one final game at his beloved Palestra on January 7, 2024, when Howard tabbed him to take the reins in the Wolverines' 79-73 loss to Penn State. As he glanced around at the announced crowd of 6,200, many of whom sat high above the bleachers and in the corners at the storied "Cathedral of College Basketball," Martelli stopped and took a moment to reflect. "There was a point maybe early when I said, 'You know what, in my head, Dorothy in the *Wizard of Oz* is absolutely right, there's no place like home,'" he said. Martelli announced his retirement from coaching in July 2024 when he and his wife, Judy, launched P and J Make a Difference to share his knowledge and wisdom from nearly 50 years of coaching. He remains active in Coaches vs. Cancer.

Jameer Nelson

Nelson finished his historic career at Saint Joseph's as the school's all-time leader in points (2,094), assists (713), and steals (256). He was named the 2004 National Player of the Year. St. Joe's retired his No. 14 jersey on April 23, 2004, after he compiled a 98-28 mark in four years on Hawk Hill. Nelson was selected No. 20 overall in the 2004 NBA draft and went on to a 14-year NBA career, the first 10 of which were with the Orlando Magic. He averaged 11.3 points, 5.1 assists, and 3.0 rebounds as a pro, making the All-Star team in 2009. Nelson was inducted into the Saint Joseph's Hall of Fame in 2011, the Big 5 Hall of Fame in 2017, and received his bachelor's degree from St. Joe's in 2018. On November 10, 2023, he was named the general manager of the Delaware Blue Coats, the NBA G League affiliate of the Philadelphia 76ers. Before that, in March 2019, Nelson reportedly interviewed to replace Martelli as St. Joe's head coach.[59] After Nelson was bypassed for the job, his son and St. Joe's recruit, Jameer Nelson Jr., decommitted. Since, Nelson has made infrequent appearances on Hawk Hill, though he has denied animosity toward the school. "Ton of great memories," Nelson told Joe Lunardi during a halftime interview on December 29, 2023, during a Hawks home game against Loyola. "It's good to be back. I always will have a special place in my heart for St. Joe's University. People have this misconception that I'm mad at the university, or mad at this or mad at that. Until you get to know me, you can speculate but you won't know the truth." Nelson received a standing ovation that night when introduced to the crowd. He was not present two months later when the school recognized the 2003–04 Hawks.

Delonte West

West would finish the 2003–04 season by averaging 18.9 points while shooting 89.2 percent from the free throw line, still a single-season school record. He was named to the All-Atlantic 10 First Team for the second consecutive year. According to his high school coach, Glenn Farello, West's mind was made up to leave Saint Joseph's for the NBA with one year of eligibility remaining when he was in a convenience store after the season with little money for snacks and his picture plastered on the pages of a Philadelphia newspaper. After scoring 1,235 points in three seasons on Hawk Hill, West was selected No. 24 overall, just four spots behind Nelson, by the Boston Celtics in the first round of the 2004 NBA draft. On the court, West had a very good NBA career, averaging 9.7 points and 3.6 assists in 432 games for Boston, Seattle, Cleveland, and Dallas over eight seasons. Off the court, he had legal run-ins and publicly disclosed a diagnosis of bipolar disorder. After the NBA, he continued his professional playing career in China and, briefly, in the NBA G League, after which tragic, well-documented incidents have occurred. There was a disturbing video of a disoriented West being arrested, and images and videos showing West panhandling outside of gas stations and convenience stores despite having made more than $16 million in his NBA career. In 2021, Dallas Mavericks owner Mark Cuban helped check West into a rehab center in Florida. It appeared, briefly, as if he was getting the help he needed. However, West left the rehab center and, sadly, more arrests have followed. In a June 2024 arrest, police officers reportedly resuscitated West by using Narcan, a drug that reverses an opioid overdose, according to the National Institute on Drug Abuse.[60] Through family, West was informed about this book, and the author was told that West was amenable to an interview. But the interview never happened.

Pat Carroll

As a senior in 2004–05, Carroll led St. Joe's to a runner-up finish in the National Invitation Tournament (NIT) after a stellar season. He averaged 18.3 points per game while making 135 three-pointers, a school record for a single season, and totaling 640 points, which ranks sixth all-time on St. Joe's list for points in a season. Carroll was named the Atlantic 10's Co-Player of the Year and the Big 5's Player of the Year in 2005. He ended his career with 1,324 points while shooting 44.5 percent from three-point range, ranking second on the school's career list with 294 three-pointers. Carroll played professionally from 2005 to 2010, including stints in Italy, France,

Greece, and Spain. He also was a member of the Houston Rockets' NBA Summer League team in 2005 and '06. Carroll got a huge surprise when he walked into the Rockets' facility for his first season. Not knowing whom he'd be teaming up with, Carroll was stunned when he saw former Oklahoma State rival John Lucas III also there. "We started laughing and I'm like, 'You mother,'" Carroll said. "To be honest, he was one of the best teammates. He was an awesome, awesome teammate. My hate for him definitely went away. I loved playing with him. But when I walked into that training room, I'm like, 'Oh my God.'" Carroll was inducted into the Big 5 Hall of Fame in 2014 and has helped teach kids the game at basketball camps. He works today as a senior director of virtual sales for Inizio Engage, a company in the healthcare industry.

Dwayne Jones

Jones was named to the Atlantic 10 All-Defensive Team following the 2003–04 season and would win the league's Defensive Player of the Year the following year when he helped the Hawks to the NIT final as a junior. He bypassed his final season of eligibility to pursue a pro career. In three seasons, he compiled 832 rebounds and 232 blocks to rank 16th and third, respectively, on the school's all-time list. He played professionally for 12 seasons, including 82 games in the NBA and 131 games in the NBA G League. He also competed overseas in China, Qatar, Venezuela, Argentina, and the Philippines. Jones joined the Philadelphia 76ers' coaching staff in 2016 before returning to his alma mater as an assistant coach for player development in 2023.

John Bryant

After helping the Hawks to the NIT final in 2004–05 as a senior, Bryant went on to play six years professionally. In addition to 49 games in the NBA G League, he competed overseas in Australia, England, and Germany. He started his coaching career in the G League as an assistant with the Bakersfield Jam in 2011 and, after three seasons, moved to a similar position with the 76ers' G League team in Delaware in 2014. From there, Bryant joined the 76ers' staff in 2016 and left in 2021 for his current position as an assistant coach with the Chicago Bulls. It is reasonable to think that Bryant will be a head coach in the NBA someday.

Tyrone Barley

Barley earned the Atlantic 10's Sixth Man Award and was named to the league's All-Defensive Team following the 2003–04 season. Along with Nelson, his 98 career victories are the most of any four-year class in school history. He briefly signed with a professional team in New Zealand following his college career. Barley's life took a tragic turn on February 20, 2013, in West Chester, Pennsylvania, when he robbed three women at gunpoint. In September 2013, Barley pled guilty and was sentenced to 10 to 20 years in prison; he was released in 2023.[61] Barley said that leading up to that horrible night he was under enormous stress and depressed after incurring gambling debts with illegal bookmakers. "The pressure of the downward spiral that my life was taking at that time, I was just lost. Is life even worth living? Those are the thoughts I was having. At the same time, it's like people are coming after you. It was a very stressful time. … It was a bad stretch, a really bad stretch, an all-time bad stretch." On February 19, 2013, after his shift working at Glen Mills, a former school for adjudicated youth where he was a counselor, Barley went to a bar and then to a hotel party, where alcohol and drugs were being consumed. Barley left the hotel and thought only about getting money. Questions have been raised as to whether some type of drug was put into Barley's drink at the hotel party. Barley doesn't place blame on anything or anyone other than himself. "I made the decision. I feel like I'm in control of myself no matter what, or I should have been," he said. In prison, Barley reflected on the path of his life. "Even though it can be the worst experience in your life and being away from your family and your name is tarnished, really having time to reflect and work on myself was something that I took advantage of. It was beneficial to me because what came from that was a completely different person in the sense that I was more focused on other people than myself and just seeing the beauty in life and not taking it for granted, which I always did. Even though I've grown from a terrible experience, I would never do it again because you would never want to wish harm on anyone or do harm or bring harm into this world," he said. "I was fortunate that I had the help and support to improve myself." After his release, Barley rejoined his wife and children in their Delaware County home, found steady work, and today continues to focus on trying to be a better person.

Chet Stachitas

After being a valuable reserve in 2003–04, Stachitas would start all 69 games in which he played as a junior and senior the following two seasons. He would end his career with 1,122 points in 130 career games. After coming to St. Joe's with an old-fashioned, ineffective set shot from long range, Stachitas became a jump-shooting, three-point threat and finished his four years with 171 career three-pointers. After playing two seasons overseas in Poland, Stachitas returned to the Philadelphia area and today works as the vice president of training and development for Worldwide Express, a third-party shipping company.

Dave Mallon

Mallon continued to do the little things needed for winning following 2003–04, helping the Hawks to consecutive NIT appearances and 43 combined victories in his final two seasons in 2004–05 and 2005–06. Statistically, Mallon's best season came as a senior when he averaged 4.1 points and 3.3 rebounds in 22.1 minutes per contest. He played professionally in Portugal and England. Today, he lives in South Jersey and works as an insurance broker for Apex.

Dwayne Lee

After limited playing time as Nelson's backup as a sophomore in 2003–04, Lee excelled as the Hawks' starting point guard in 2004–05. He dished 188 assists, second only to Nelson's 213 in 2000–01 on the school's all-time, single-season record list, to help St. Joe's reach the NIT final. Lee would start all 69 games in his junior and senior seasons, ending with 371 career assists. He played professionally in Germany and Cyprus and with the Vermont Frost Heaves of the ABA. Today, Lee is an assistant coach at George Washington University after previous stops at Quinnipiac, St. Bonaventure, and Fairleigh Dickinson.

Monté Ross

Ross left St. Joe's after the 2006 season to become head coach at Delaware. He led the Blue Hens to 132 victories in 10 seasons, highlighted by a berth in the NCAA tournament in 2014 after a 25-10 overall mark and 14-2 league record. He then was an assistant coach at Temple for three seasons before being hired as North Carolina A&T's head coach on April 10, 2023. In Ross's first season in 2023–24, the rebuilding Aggies won five games in the highly competitive Coastal Athletic Association.

Matt Brady

Brady departed St. Joe's right after the 2003–04 season to become the head coach at Marist. After 73 victories in four seasons at Marist, Brady took over at James Madison. He led the Dukes to 139 wins in eight seasons, including a conference title and berth in the NCAA tournament in 2013. He followed that with assistant coaching jobs at La Salle, Maryland, and DePaul, where he was promoted to interim head coach on January 22, 2024. In August 2024, Brady was hired as an assistant coach at High Point University.

Mark Bass

Bass remained on Martelli's staff until the head coach's exit from St. Joe's, ending a 20-year tenure as assistant coach. In 2021, he was hired at his alma mater, which had changed its name from McCorristin High School to Trenton Catholic Prep. Bass had success immediately as a high school head coach, leading Trenton Catholic to the Mercer County title and a runner-up finish to Roselle Catholic in the New Jersey State Interscholastic Athletic Association (NJSIAA) Non-Public B state final in 2022. However, a disagreement with the school's athletic director, reportedly over funds from a car wash, led to his parting with the school.[62] Bass continued his coaching career with an AAU program, WeR1, in the Philadelphia area and was hired as an assistant coach at South Kent School in Connecticut in the fall of 2024.

The Hawk

The tradition of The Hawk continues. Michael Sorochen, an accounting and business intelligence and analytics major from West Chester, Pennsylvania, was selected to be inside the costume in 2024–25 for the 69th season of the school's beloved mascot. Just like Chris Bertolino, Bobby Gallagher, Chuck Sack, and all others who have been The Hawk, Sorochen would be running figure eights across the court during timeouts and wouldn't stop flapping his arms from the moment the beaked head of the costume went on until he took it off, continuing to represent and embody the school's mantra that *The Hawk Will Never Die.*

Acknowledgements

Ever since reading Bill Lyon's columns in the *Philadelphia Inquirer* with my morning bowl of cereal, I always wanted to be a sportswriter. I figured to be good at writing I needed to read a lot. So, I printed out *Sports Illustrated*'s top 100 sports books of all time and began going through them, one by one. My reading interests also include history, and I have enjoyed great books by the likes of Ron Chernow, Walter Isaacson, and Doris Kearns Goodwin, just to name a few. In addition to sportswriting, I have worked for the last 15 years in education and have read many award-winning novels and nonfiction works targeted to middle school and high school students. The more books that I read, the more I wanted to write one, something that I dreamed about doing. But finding just the right topic proved challenging. It seemed like every idea that I had was taken. And, really, with three children and multiple jobs, how was I ever going to find the time anyway?

But a few things happened that led me to the point where I am, joyously and tearfully, writing these acknowledgements after submitting *A Soaring Season: The Incredible, Inspiring Story of the 2003–04 Saint Joseph's Hawks* to the publisher. Both my father, Paul Bracy, and my stepfather, Martin Perrotta, died within nine months of each other in 2022 and '23. It got me thinking more about how precious life is and going after things that I've always wanted to do while I can. Also, in August 2023, I was moved from social studies to English language arts in my role as an academic designer at McGraw Hill. My new assignment was to read middle school books that were being considered for the company's curriculum. A colleague, Howard Gutner, would send lists of many wonderful books, and I would devour one after another. The combination of Gutner telling me he was a published author and reading all of those books really got me thinking again about writing one. But what would be my topic?

Well, soon after having the thought, I was watching on television as Villanova played Penn at the Palestra in an early-season Big 5 game in November 2023. At that game, longtime *Philadelphia Inquirer* college basketball writer Mike Jensen was courtside covering his final game before his retirement. I previously had covered the Big 5 but had to retire the website because it just became too much work despite my love for it. Now, though, I was in a different place with more time to try again. With Jensen retiring, I knew there were precious few covering the Big 5 and thought

I could be filling a need while following a passion, so I launched Big5Hoops.com. Not long after, I started thinking about writing a long-form feature story for the site to commemorate the 20th anniversary of the 2003–04 Saint Joseph's Hawks. Oh, wait! Maybe that could be the book that I've always wanted to write, I thought. Very quietly, I started doing some research to that effect. Then, in December 2023, I hosted a Spaces show on X with my friend and former St. Joe's radio play-by-play broadcaster Ken Krsolovic. There were maybe five people listening as Krsolovic and I talked about his St. Joe's days, including his production of Phil Martelli's *Hawk Talk* television show. After hearing about this from family, Martelli surprised us by joining in, bringing many listeners to the Spaces. Much of the conversation was about *Hawk Talk*, but the former St. Joe's coach also brought up the 2003–04 Hawks without prompting.

When the Spaces ended, I thought maybe this was a Godsend and that the story of the 2003–04 Hawks was the book I was intended to write. So, I made a list of people to contact for interviews and connected first with Marie Wozniak, the former St. Joe's sports information director. As soon as I hung up from our 30-minute conversation, I just knew there was a book there. Now, I just had to pursue it. I did interviews between December 2023 and mid-May 2024 when I began writing, finishing in early August 2024. It was everything that I thought it would be and more, and I have so many people to thank.

I would like to thank God for all of my gifts and blessings and for giving me the strength and energy to see this project to the finish line. My family—especially my mom, Susan; my wife, Jeanne; and my three children, Gabe, Julia, and Evelyn—has been amazingly supportive and loving throughout this process. Jeanne has turned into quite an editor! Paul Bracy helped me believe in myself and read to me at an early age. Martin Perrotta helped to expand my interests beyond sports and taught me how to take one day at a time. My brothers, Adam and Andy, constantly texted me with support throughout this process. My late grandparents, Richard and Ceil Fakoury, always made me feel like a million bucks. Thanks to my extended family, Maria Pluta, Chris Pluta, Peg and Toby Hanna, and Rob Pluta for all of their love, support, and prayers. Our good friends, Brett Claffee and Mary Jane Guy, Reno and JoAnn Bianco, Jim and Angela George, Rob and Michelle Tartamosa, Jen Taylor, Howard Taylor, and Tim and Lisa Melroy have been supportive and encouraging throughout. Thanks to all of my soccer friends, especially John Barna, Marc Block, and Geoff Filinuk. Jason Grattini and Matthew Osborne are friends who live far away but stay close through texts that always bring me a smile.

There would be no book without Martelli and Jameer Nelson's cooperation. A special thanks to Martelli for giving up three hours on a weekend morning to meet with me. And every person that I interviewed—more than 100 interviews with 90 people—was so gracious and informative. Thank you to all of the following for agreeing to be interviewed: Clare Ariano, Bill Avington, Tyrone Barley, Mark

Bass, Chris Bertolino, Mark Blaudschun, Dean Bozman, Matt Brady, Linda Bruno, John Bryant, Ryan Butt, Joe Cabrey, Steve Campbell, Jerry Carino, Pat Carroll, John Cox, Jim Crowley, Ryan Darrenkamp, Steve Del Fra, Phil Denne, Don DiJulia, Larry Dougherty, Fran Dunphy, Randy Dunton, Howard Eskin, Glenn Farello, Bruiser Flint, Bobby Gallagher, John Gallagher, Frank Garafalo, Lynn Greer, Matt Guokas, Neil Hartman, Rob Hartshorn, Mike Jensen, Dick Jerardi, Brian Jesiolowski, Dwayne Jones, Andy Katz, Andrew Koefer, Dan Kropp, Ken Krsolovic, Alicia Lange, Father Timothy Lannon, Steve Lappas, David Leach, Dwayne Lee, Dan Leibovitz, Alex Loughton, Bill Lukasiewicz, Joe Lunardi, Glen Macnow, Dave Mallon, Ralph Maresco, Judy Martelli, Phil Martelli, Phil Martelli Jr., Tom McCarthy, Trip McClatchy, Michael McCormick, Greg McDermott, Jim Nantz, Jameer Nelson, Tyler Newton, Brian O'Connell, Jonathan Okanes, Ray Parrillo, Owen Patterson, Chris Paul, Brendan Prunty, Dawan Robinson, Monté Ross, Matt Ryan, Chuck Sack, Jeff Schiffner, Andy Schwartz, Frank Sciolla, Mike Skrocki, Mike Slattery, Chet Stachitas, Joe Sullivan, Rob Sullivan, Artur Surov, Blaine Taylor, Bob Thomason, Cory Violette, Keith Waleskowski, Dick "Hoops" Weiss, Marie Wozniak, and Jay Wright.

So many people helped to coordinate the interviews or provide contacts. Don DiJulia was particularly helpful with connecting with several people, including Matt Guokas and Linda Bruno. Rob King from the 76ers and Raymond Ridder and Brett Winkler from the Golden State Warriors helped set me up with Chris Paul. Alex Yoh and Genna Koskinen from the Delaware Blue Coats arranged my interview with Jameer Nelson. Melissa Miller and LeslieAnne Wade put me in contact with Jim Nantz. Jason Vida at Richmond got me in touch with Mike Skrocki. Joe Lunardi and Sarah Quinn at St. Joe's connected me with Father Timothy Lannon. Robbie Kleinmutz at Pacific provided a contact for Bob Thomason. Deb Moore at Kentucky set me up with Bruiser Flint. Dan Lobacz at La Salle assisted with John Cox. Jack Jumper at St. Joe's was helpful on multiple fronts, including coordinating my interview with Dwayne Jones. Mike Sheridan at Villanova arranged for me to talk to Jay Wright. Brian Holloway from North Carolina A&T did the same for Monté Ross. Marie Wozniak provided my contact information to members of the 2003–04 Hawks. Also helpful were Brendan Prunty with Andy Katz, Tom McCarthy with Steve Lappas, Kevin Cooney with Frank Sciolla, Joe Sullivan with Mark Blaudschun, Phil Martelli with Clare Ariano, Steve Campbell with Jim Crowley, and Steve Curry with Ryan Darrenkamp. Mike Mahoney at Penn, Mike Tuberosa at Drexel, Jordan Viener at La Salle, and Chad Cooper at Temple always help with my requests.

Greg McDermott not only provided interesting stories about his online Hawks merchandise store but also mailed his original copy of *The Perfect Season* postseason DVD after the copied version that he mailed the first time did not play. This proved especially helpful to seeing what I was researching. Ralph Maresco not only told me a great story about having the Hawks over to his house for dinner before the Xavier game, but he drove from Philadelphia to South Jersey to meet me at my daughter's softball game to share pictures from that memorable night. So many other people offered to share stories and show me memorabilia, and I am sorry that I was not able to talk to everyone or see all of their memories.

As a first-time author, I had a lot to learn. Google provided much help, but I couldn't have done this without leaning on the advice of many people. Todd Zolecki of MLB.com explained his process for his phenomenal book on Roy Halladay. Mike Sielski of the *Philadelphia Inquirer*, the author of several books, including his latest on the evolution of the slam dunk, spent a half-hour over dinner before a Villanova game at Seton Hall detailing how to do a book proposal, something that proved to be invaluable. Mike Jensen was a sounding board for advice throughout, and Craig Haley, my former colleague at the *Trenton Times* and a top-notch editor who taught me so much, was gracious enough to give my prologue a review before I submitted it for consideration to publishers. Mark Mazza provided helpful legal advice, and I look forward to working with him more on this project and future projects. Thanks to Alan Wandalowski for putting us in touch. My brother Adam Bracy also helped, through a colleague, with ideas on navigating the contract process. My brother Andy Bracy has given me great ideas for book signings. Ike Richman and Larry Dougherty have provided great ideas for public relations, and I am looking forward to working with Dougherty more on this project.

In nearly 30 years of covering sports in Philadelphia, I have learned from so many. The late Bill Lyon was my idol growing up. Thank you, Bill. One of the cool things about this project was reading Lyon's columns about the 2003–04 Hawks during my research. Dick Jerardi and Ray Parrillo not only were amazing interviews for the book, but their stories of the season in the *Philadelphia Daily News* and *Philadelphia Inquirer*, respectively, provided helpful research. Thank you to the Cherry Hill Public Library for its online resources for research. The Mercer County Library also was helpful for research, including reading many of my own stories from the *Trenton Times*. And both the Cherry Hill and Pennsauken libraries provided places to work when I needed a change of scenery from my home office. Also, St. Joe's basketball media guide and archived press releases from 2003–04 were extremely helpful, as were the website RealGM.com for box scores from the season and Sports-Reference.com for facts and history about the Hawks and other teams. Brian Ferrie's feature stories on St. Joe's website from nearly 20 years ago provided helpful background information.

I am grateful to Dan Gelston for assigning me to cover Philadelphia sports for the Associated Press. The same for Rob Maaddi, Ken Berger, and Jay Bonfatti before that. Thanks to Bill Avington for recommending me to the AP in 1997 when the organization was looking for a freelancer to cover the Philadelphia Rage. It was through the AP that I met the late Jack Scheuer, who became a mentor and a great friend. Scheuer has had a strong, lasting impact on my career and my life. I'm also grateful for all of my colleagues in Philadelphia press boxes who are so kind to me, especially Adam Aaronson, Josh Abrams, Michael Barkann, Colin Beazley, Kale Beers, Matt Breen, Rob Brooks, Jerry Carino, Ky Carlin, Kevin Cooney, Jake Copestick, Jaden Daly, Ty Daubert, Matthew DeGeorge, Bill Evans, Ryan Fannon, Kyle Fisher, Riley Frain, Martin Frank, Scott Franzke, Matt Gelb, Dan Gelston, Mel Greenberg, Bob Grotz, Jordan Hall, Giana Han, Marcus Hayes, Donald Hunt, Andy Jasner, Mike Jensen, Dick Jerardi, Gordie Jones, Tim Kelly, Mike Kern, Jeff Kerr, Adam Kimelman, Destiny Lugardo, Mike Luongo, Rob Maaddi, David Malandra, Lochlan March, Jon Marks, Matt Martucci, Tom McCarthy, Mike McGarry, Bill Meltzer, Tom Moore, Kyle Morello, Gregg Murphy, Chris Murray, Jeff Neiburg, Michael Notaro, Glenn Papazian, Rob Parent, Keith Pompey, Olivia Reiner, Matt Ryan, Jim Salisbury, Anthony SanFilippo, Jack Scheuer, Corey Seidman, Mike Shute, Mike Sielski, Jackie Spiegel, Jonathan Tannenwald, Jerome Taylor, Terry Toohey, Kevin Tresolini, Dave Uram, Josh Verlin, Delgreco Wilson, and Todd Zolecki.

And a big shout-out to my friend Joe Fedorowicz, who designed Big5Hoops.com and always is there for technical advice and ideas for the site, including helping to set up a system to take orders for this book. At the Phillies, the PR staff of Kevin Gregg, Chris Ware, Dillon Siddiqi, and Elyssa Kaplan are always helpful. Thanks to Rob King, Dave Sholler, and Erik Chambliss at the 76ers, and Joe Siville and Allie Samuelsson at the Flyers for making my job easy. Greg Carroccio from Sideline Photos shared images that not only enhanced the book but also helped me to see the words that I was writing.

Thank you to Casemate Publishers and Brookline Books for taking a chance on a first-time author. Jennifer Green at Brookline was enthusiastic about the project from the moment I emailed her the proposal, and she has been wonderful to deal with ever since. Lauren Stead and Daniel Yesilonis in the publisher's marketing department impressed me immediately with their ideas and enthusiasm for the book, and I am looking forward to working with both of them.

Lastly and importantly, thanks to every single person who read this book or has ever read any of my work. I really appreciate it.

Aaron Bracy
August 7, 2024

Endnotes

Chapter 1

1   In a *Philadelphia Inquirer* feature story on Nelson on January 4, 1999, Chris Morkides wrote that Fareed Burton was injured and Jameer Rasheed went out for football, thus opening a spot for Nelson as the Chester High School starting point guard.

2   Chester's 1997–98 record of 23 wins and seven losses was recounted in Morkides's story in the *Philadelphia Inquirer* on January 4, 1999. "If he works real hard, if he keeps his head on his shoulders, on the floor and in the classroom, the sky's the limit," Chester coach Fred Pickett told Morkides about Nelson for the story.

3   Morkides detailed Nelson's improvement between his sophomore and junior seasons playing for the Gym-Rats in his *Philadelphia Inquirer* story on January 4, 1999. "Even though he'd only be a junior, we wanted him to take a role as coach on the floor," Pickett told Morkides.

4   A *Trenton Times* story by Mike Olshin on March 6, 1999, provided helpful background information on the game, including the crowd size, Nelson's scoring, and game details. Olshin previously wrote, on March 3, 1999, that Chester had advanced to the District 1 title game for the fifth time in the decade and the 22nd time in school history.

5   Nelson told Gordie Jones in the Lancaster (PA) *Intelligencer Journal* that Martelli's presence had no effect on him. "That really doesn't bother me," Nelson said. "I'm not worried about college. I still have another year." Jones also provided details of Nelson's performance that night.

Chapter 2

6   On page 4 of his book, *Don't Call Me Coach* (Camino, 2007), Martelli recounted the story of wanting to coach Saint Joseph's: "I recall exactly where I was standing, even which way we were facing, when in the eighth grade I said to a friend of mine, Stevie Stefano, 'You know, Stevie, some day I'm going to coach the St. Joe's Hawks.'"

7   In the March 7, 1990, *Philadelphia Inquirer* article, written by Mike Missanelli, St. Joe's athletic director Don DiJulia said, "It's a very sensitive time right now to talk about specific names because people are still playing. But we have a pretty good idea of the direction in which we're going." Missanelli reported that DiJulia said his original wish list included 32 current Division I head coaches. Then, the writer mentioned five leading candidates: John Griffin, Paul Cormier, Paul Westhead, Bruce Parkhill, and Bob Staak.

8   In his *Philadelphia Daily News* article covering Griffin's introductory news conference, published on April 5, 1990, Dick Jerardi quoted Griffin as follows: "We're here to play Division I basketball at the highest level. We'll make no excuses for anything less than that."

9   In a *Philadelphia Inquirer* story, written by Stephen A. Smith, on July 13, 1995, Flint openly expressed his interest in the Saint Joseph's job. "I usually don't pay attention to rumors," Flint

told Smith. "But this is different. This is where I played ball and where I graduated from. And it's in Philly, my home. I haven't been contacted by them, but it's simple: I want to be the next coach at St. Joseph."

10 On page 61 of his book, *Don't Call Me Coach* (Camino, 2007), Martelli recounted the following story: "'How did your first season go?' Cathy Rush asked me that summer. 'Not very well,' I was honest enough to reply. She asked to see my game plans. I hadn't any to show her. That would be the last time I didn't have any plans for my teams."

Chapter 3

11 West recounted his childhood experiences to Jerardi in a January 27, 2004, article in the *Philadelphia Daily News*. "We've been bouncing around all over the metropolitan area," he told Jerardi. Later he said, "The people in my community were going through the same type of thing. It was normal." On developing his love for basketball, West said, "There was just something about basketball, making the ball go in the hoop. ... You didn't have to say any words, no trash talk, just the ball going through the hoop says it all." He told Jerardi that there also was an alley where he played football and basketball, using a crate attached to a telephone pole for a basket. West also stated in the article the various towns in which he lived growing up. From the article: "I definitely have a lot of friends over in Maryland," says West, who then starts rattling off the Maryland towns. "I lived in Largo, I lived in Suitland, I lived in Clinton, I lived in Oxon Hill, oh man, I lived in Hyattsville for a while. That's a lot of places." He also lived in several places in Washington. Sometimes, he lived in different spots during a single school year. "We stayed in cousins' basements," he says. "At one point, we lived with my aunt in her two-bedroom apartment. All four of us, three kids plus my mom, stayed in one room. We had the back room and they stayed in the front."

12 In the January 27, 2004, article in the *Philadelphia Daily News*, West told Jerardi: "It was a great community and all that good stuff. I looked down the back of the media guide and they had the most TV games on there. It was the biggest school [recruiting him] at the time. I said, 'That's where I'm going.'"

Chapter 5

13 In a *Philadelphia Daily News* story on November 14, 2000, Martelli told Jerardi of Nelson, "He's everything I thought he would be. He's probably even a little better."

14 In a *Philadelphia Daily News* article on June 5, 2003, Jerardi detailed the play in which Green inadvertently elbowed Nelson in the jaw, cracking a tooth and requiring two stitches.

15 In a *Philadelphia Inquirer* article on June 19, 2003, Parrillo listed Nelson's stats from three games at the NBA predraft camp as 10.3 points and 6.3 assists.

16 In a *Philadelphia Inquirer* article on June 12, 2003, Martelli told Parrillo that he received positive feedback from NBA scouts on Nelson's performance at the predraft camp. "Everyone agrees that he did nothing but help himself with a phenomenal performance and proved himself a first-round talent," Martelli said.

17 In the June 5, 2003, *Philadelphia Daily News* article, Nelson told Jerardi that he measured 5-foot-11 with his shoes off and joked that there wasn't anything he could do about it. "I wanted to stand on my tippy-toes, but they were kind of looking," Nelson said.

18 In the *Philadelphia Daily News* on January 27, 2004, West recalled his preseason prediction to Jerardi. "At the beginning of this preseason, I threw something out there just to see how the

teammates would react." He continued: "I mentioned something about a national championship. I felt compelled to say it."

Chapter 6

19   In the *Philadelphia Inquirer* on November 14, 2003, Parrillo reported that St. Joe's sold 4,100 tickets.

20   In the *Philadelphia Daily News* on November 15, 2003, Jerardi wrote the following: "An estimated 6,000 Saint Joseph's fans were at MSG last night for the marquee game of the Coaches vs. Cancer Classic. They had waited for months to see their team. And they were not going to miss the opening act in what promises to be a season to remember."

Chapter 7

21   In Jerardi's game story in the *Philadelphia Daily News* on November 26, 2003, Martelli said of West's practices leading up to the game, "He went offensively ballistic (in practice). He was basically unstoppable."

22   In Jerardi's game story in the *Philadelphia Daily News* on November 26, 2003, he wrote of Case Gym, which is nicknamed "The Roof": "The Roof was not exactly jam-packed on the night the Boston University students began their holiday exodus out of town. The atmosphere was not exactly frenzied. Located between the south shore of the Charles River and Commonwealth Avenue, Case Gym was just a place to play some hoops last night. "You had to bring your own energy," Jameer Nelson said.

Chapter 8

23   In Parrillo's game story in the *Philadelphia Inquirer* on November 30, 2003, Nelson said he was practicing shooting three-pointers from near half-court the day before the game.

24   Saint Joseph's press release said there were nine seconds remaining, but Parrillo's account indicated that there was even less time, with 8.2 seconds showing on the clock.

25   Both the Saint Joseph's press release on November 29, 2003, with details about the game, and Parrillo's game story in the *Philadelphia Inquirer* on November 30, 2003, say that Nelson's shot was from 38 feet, likely deemed as such by the official play-by-play in the box score. However, a freeze frame analysis of the replay appears to indicate that the shot was closer to half-court and likely from 40 feet or more.

26   Parrillo reported on Martelli's postgame reaction in his game story in the *Philadelphia Inquirer* on November 30, 2003: "Some of our Achilles' heels were evident," Martelli said, his face red with anger. Swatting at the box score in disgust, he added: 'We're not a great rebounding team, but 23 offensive rebounds? That's embarrassing. Allowing 43 points in the second half is unfathomable to me. ... We're not good enough to just throw our jerseys on the court and expect to win. Who would be scared of us? We've got to bring our fire, our fight. The better team didn't win tonight.'"

Chapter 10

27   In Parrillo's game story in the *Philadelphia Inquirer* on December 7, 2003, Dunphy was quoted as saying this about Nelson: "Jameer imposes his will on the game, and he did that today."

Chapter 11

28 In Parrillo's game story in the *Philadelphia Inquirer* on December 10, 2003, Martelli said, "Credit this one to John Bryant. That kid (Smith) is a beast. John Bryant changed the game because of the way he guarded him."

29 In Michael Vega's game story in the *Boston Globe* on December 10, 2003, Smith said, "Whenever they play against a good role-player, they seem to have a tendency to know how to stop 'em. They did a very good job on me. I tip my hat to them."

30 In Parrillo's story, West said, "I've been settling for jump shots and I hadn't been finishing like I used to, but I felt good today." And in Jerardi's story in the *Philadelphia Daily News* on December 10, 2003, West said, "My legs felt a little bit normal."

Chapter 12

31 In Parrillo's game story in the *Philadelphia Inquirer* on December 15, 2003, Flint said, "I hate to say it, but they're not as good as the team we were on that went 26-6." (Author's note: Drexel assistant coach Geoff Arnold also was on the 1985–86 Hawks team with Flint, thus the reference to "we.")

Chapter 15

32 In the Associated Press game story on December 30, 2003, the following was written: "Martelli talked with Jones earlier this week about his role on the team and the uneven transition from reserve to starter. 'He had almost become satisfied with being a starter and we needed attitude,' Martelli said. 'He certainly had attitude tonight.'"

Chapter 17

33 In Mike Jensen's article in the *Philadelphia Inquirer* on January 7, 2004, Nelson and Martelli explained what happened prior to the George Washington game. "Coach took me aside and said it was time to get going," Nelson said. "I had to agree with him. I was stinking the gym up." "Really, what I said to him was, 'You know, for a long time, Jameer, we've got a lot of notoriety because you've played great,'" Martelli said. "'And I think now you're getting a lot of notoriety because we're playing great.' ... I thought that there was another level."

Chapter 18

34 On May 7, 2002, in a press conference that was broadcast live by Comcast SportsNet and is now readily available on YouTube, Iverson, when questioned about his practice habits, repeatedly said, "We're talkin' about practice." Iverson later added in the viral press conference, "How the hell can I make my teammates better by practicing?"

Chapter 19

35 In Parrillo's game story in the *Philadelphia Inquirer* on January 14, 2004, Martelli said, "The way we played in the second half is significant. When we come with that much energy, it's kind of hard to deal with. I'm pleased with the amount of energy we showed."

36 In Jerardi's game story in the *Philadelphia Daily News* on January 14, 2004, West said, "We could see in their eyes they were a little overwhelmed. It was just one of those games where you just try to better your team instead of adding on to your stats."

Chapter 22

37 On March 10, 2003, John Wawrow of the Associated Press reported that the Bonnies had used a transfer player that season who was ruled ineligible because he did not have an associate's degree but had earned a certificate in welding at his former school.

38 An Associated Press story on January 26, 2004, reported that Martelli said, "Shut up, you nitwit. You should be embarrassed by your own team, you moron."

39 On January 27, 2004, Brian Moritz of the *Olean Times-Herald* wrote that Martelli said he had written Palmer a letter of apology and planned on calling her and called St. Bonaventure head coach Anthony Solomon to apologize. "I've known all year that this would be a challenge for my team to conduct themselves in a manner befitting our standing and the attention that we're getting," Martelli said in the story. "And as the head coach, I need to set that example."

Chapter 24

40 In the *Allentown Morning Call* on February 3, 2004, Jones detailed the switch in date and location of the game.

41 In her preview story on February 1, 2004, in the *Philadelphia Daily News*, Dana Pennett O'Neil quoted Wright saying the following about Nelson: "That's what makes Jameer so great. He can score like Allen Iverson but he chooses to do all the other things."

Chapter 25

42 Larry Eichel reported this in the *Philadelphia Inquirer* on February 8, 2004.

Chapter 29

43 In the *Philadelphia Daily News* recap on February 23, 2004, Jerardi wrote the following: "Mark Macon, who happens to be the school's all-time leading scorer, had said on Comcast SportsNet that Nelson was no better than former Temple point guard Howard Evans (a very good player, but not a lock player of the year) and that he, Macon, was far better than West—so much better that, if he had two weeks to get in shape, he would be better than West now."

44 In the *Allentown Morning Call* on February 22, 2004, Andre D. Williams wrote the following: "Macon said on a Comcast Sportsnet interview that Temple's dream team in 1987–88 was better than Saint Joe's at every position, especially guard."

Chapter 33

45 In the *Philadelphia Inquirer* on March 3, 2004, Parrillo quoted Martelli as saying, "What you have seen may never be repeated in college basketball. And by the way, they are far from finished. We've got nine games left."

46 In the Saint Joseph's press release on March 8, 2004, Martelli said, "If you are expecting us to celebrate now, we're not. We're very happy with this but we know we still have work to do. We have one job right now and that's to bring home a trophy from Dayton on Saturday night."

Chapter 34

47 In the *Philadelphia Inquirer* on March 15, 2004, Pat Carroll would tell Parrillo the following: "I think we went into the Xavier game without the same hunger we had in the other games. We're looking at this as a fresh start, feeling we have to prove ourselves again."

48 In an Associated Press story on January 27, 2023, Steve Reed wrote: "Packer was viewed as a controversial figure during his broadcasting days, often drawing the ire of college basketball fans, particularly on North Carolina's 'Tobacco Road.'" Packer's son, Mark, was quoted in the story saying, "He would cover a North Carolina game and Tar Heels fans would be like, 'you hate North Carolina.' Wake (Forest) fans would be like, 'you hate us.' And Billy just sort of got a kick out of that." The AP story also indicated that Packer played three seasons at Wake Forest, leading the Demon Deacons to the Final Four in 1962, before broadcasting 34 Final Fours.

49 In Parrillo's Selection Sunday follow-up story in the *Philadelphia Inquirer* on March 16, 2004, Martelli said the following: "I think that if you listen to the body of what he said, it's even more bizarre than what I initially thought he said." The story also includes the following Martelli quote: "I initially thought he said that Oklahoma State and/or Texas were much better than St. Joe's—not a litany of nine schools that were better than us."

Chapter 35

50 In a school press release on March 17, 2004, previewing the game against Liberty, Martelli said, "The only thing that is of any value to us is this opportunity. We're going to try to play the best 40 minutes of the year tomorrow, and then we'll deal with the next things."

Chapter 36

51 In St. Joe's press release on March 19, 2004, previewing the contest, Knight is quoted as saying the following: "They did it against good teams, and they beat teams on the road. The Atlantic 10 is a pretty damn good basketball conference. For a team to do what it has done is a remarkable achievement."

52 In the *Philadelphia Inquirer* on March 21, 2004, Parrillo quoted Knight afterward as saying, "I told Phil that their team, from watching the film, I really liked and enjoyed watching them play. It's good for kids to see a really good team play the way those kids do."

Chapter 37

53 NBA.com says Paul was selected as the national freshman of the year by College Insider, *Sporting News, Basketball Times,* and Dick Vitale.

54 Comcast SportsNet broadcast Martelli telling the Hawks the following in the pregame locker room: "Yeah, there are big stakes. But this is just about what's inside of you. Taking what you want. Taking what you've earned. When this night ends, we know that it's going to be down to eight. And one of those eight is going to be you because you've earned it. You're that good."

Chapter 38

55 On *Hangin' with the Hawks*, Martelli said this to his players at 2:30 a.m. on Friday, March 26, 2004: "Everything that you've ever dreamt about in basketball is now in front of you. Forty minutes away. But it's the game that's important, not the result. And this is going to be a mother. This is the toughest, most physical team that we've played in two years. We'll get a plan together. I'll have a plan for you."

56 On *Hangin' with the Hawks*, Martelli told the players the following at the 11:30 a.m. film session: "If we don't go quickly on offense, it's going to be hand-to-hand combat. And these are not little boys. These dudes are men across the board."

57 In his pregame speech, Martelli told the Hawks how they had overcome their doubters and would do so again. As shown on *Hangin' with the Hawks*, he said the following: "We couldn't beat Gonzaga, and we did. We couldn't beat Cal, and we did. We wouldn't go 16-0 in the Atlantic 10, and we did. We couldn't sweep the city again, and we did. We weren't going to beat Texas Tech, and we did. We weren't beating Wake the other night, and we did. So, your dreams are alive. And they will come true."

58 As shown on *Hangin' with the Hawks*, Martelli said the following at halftime: "It's a small play. It's a blockout. It's a loose ball. It's somebody stepping up and making a free throw. Everyone in the first half made a small play. Make one more and your dreams will come true."

Epilogue

59 On March 30, 2019, Nelson discussed interviewing for the St. Joe's job with Jensen in the *Philadelphia Inquirer*. He said that interviewing after Martelli was fired was difficult. "I was emotional about it, even when the conversations started with me entertaining the idea of being the next coach. I was sensitive about my relationship with Phil." And Nelson expressed his disappointment about not getting the job. "I'm not bitter or anything like that. But because I wanted it, I am disappointed."

60 In an ESPN.com story on June 6, 2024, Baxter Holmes detailed the incident that led to West's arrest and subsequent resuscitation.

61 The interview with Barley was done by this book's author. Information about the night of February 20, 2013, came from the author's interview and reports from ESPN.com on November 22, 2013, and the *Delaware County Times* on November 23, 2013, that was updated on August 19, 2021.

62 On November 9, 2022, Delgreco Wilson detailed events that led to Bass's parting with his high school alma mater on his website, The Black Cager.

Index